THE WAR'S LONG SHADOW

*The Second World War
and Its Aftermath
China, Russia, Britain, America*

Bradley F. Smith

SIMON AND SCHUSTER
New York

Copyright © 1986 by Bradley F. Smith
All rights reserved
including the right of reproduction
in whole or in part in any form
Published by Simon and Schuster
A Division of Simon & Schuster, Inc.
Simon & Schuster Building
Rockefeller Center
1230 Avenue of the Americas
New York, New York 10020
SIMON AND SCHUSTER and colophon are registered
trademarks of Simon & Schuster, Inc.
Designed by Irving Perkins Associates
Manufactured in the United States of America
1 2 3 4 5 6 7 8 9 10

Library of Congress Cataloging in Publication Data
Smith, Bradley F.
The war's long shadow.

Bibliography: p.
Includes index.
1. World War, 1939–1945—Diplomatic history.
2. World War, 1939–1945—Influence.   3. World
politics—1933–1945.   4. World politics—1945–1955.
I. Title.
D749.S65   1986   940.5   86–1870
ISBN: 0-671-52434-8

Manuscript quotations are acknowledged as follows: Transcripts of Crown-copyright records in the Public Record Office appear by permission of the Controller of Her Majesty's Stationery Office; Extracts from the William Sewell Papers, now in the Library of the School of Oriental and African Studies, appear by permission of R. Baker; quotations from the papers of Sir Horace Seymour appear by permission of Lady Seymour.

Quotations from books are acknowledged as requested by the following authors and publishers: Robert L. Messer, *The End of the Alliance: James F. Byrnes, Roosevelt, Truman and the Origins of the Cold War*, University of North Carolina Press; Saburo Ienaga, *Japan's Last War*, Basil Blackwell, Oxford; Jerome Ch'ên, *Mao and the Chinese Revolution*, Oxford University Press; Lincoln Li, *The Japanese Army in North China*, Oxford University Press;
(*continued at the back of the book*)

Acknowledgments

In addition to the individuals and publishers who granted permission for quoted material to be used in this volume, I would like to thank the people who cleared the way for me to research and write it. Rosemary Seaton of the School of Oriental and African Studies, London, and Marion Stewart of Churchill College, Cambridge, guided me through research materials, and Leslie Smith assisted me in the documentary research. At one time or another Sue Adler, Mr. and Mrs. Richard Hart, and the Institute of Historical Research, University of London, provided places where I could write, and the Library of the University of California, Santa Cruz, extended substantial assistance regarding published works. Throughout, my friend and agent, Toby Eady, provided valuable counsel and moral support, and Rosemary Brogan and Gary and Thomas Caballero have kept me upright at the western end of my transatlantic shuttle. Near the project's end, I was greatly aided by the editorial skills of Alice Mayhew and Piers Burnett.

For Jenny

Contents

INTRODUCTION

The Second World War produced such monumental instances of human bravery, endurance, horror, and suffering that our awareness of the dramatic events of the war easily overshadows our appreciation of its long-range effects. A conflict which gave the world phenomena such as the defense of Stalingrad, Auschwitz, the Battle of Britain, and Hiroshima seems to so transcend the customary, that it is difficult to fit it into normal explanations of social, political and economic change. Intense memories remain to those who lived through the conflict, while film, television, and literature keep many less vivid wartime images alive in the rest of the population. But aside from an awareness that in some vague and indirect way the war cleared the map for a postwar era of East-West confrontation, there is little understanding of how the great midcentury cataclysm released forces—in addition to atomic energy—which have come to shape the vital context of our times.

The basic dynamic that made World War II the fulcrum of change was the system of popular mobilization of resources and population that operated within each of the belligerent countries. The general mobilizing of production, manpower, and popular will provided the powers with the means to increase the ferocity of war, and simultaneously made the Second World War a truly global conflict. Inevitably this broad and deep mobilization also changed the distribution of international power, for some states were destroyed by the total-war system while others expanded in both power and influence. Within each state, the recourse to total mobilization also produced profound and long-lasting changes. Not the least important of these was that hence-

13

forth a government's power in foreign affairs would be much more dependent on the willingness of its public to pay enormous costs in an era of high-tech international competition. Traditional divisions between domestic and foreign policy thus came to be permanently blurred, and the world was thereby made ready for an era of militant confrontations.

Of course the Second World War cannot be given all the credit, or blame, for developing the system of mobilizing societies broadly and deeply. The general populace was first called to arms during the wars of the French Revolution, and World War I made a further long leap down the road to "total war." One might even contend that in the interwar period such regimes as Communist Russia and Nazi Germany made halting attempts to institutionalize the system of popular mobilization, and even in democratic countries, post–World War I domestic emergencies could produce a centrally directed marshalling of resources and public opinion such as the New Deal's assault on the Great Depression.

But until the mid-1930s, the tone of the world's international life was dominated by a desire to mute and contain the mass mobilization pressures that had threatened to get out of control during the years 1914–1918. Between the wars, Great Britain and France, although overextended by their imperial commitments, losses in the First World War, and depression troubles following 1929, still seemed to be the dominant powers in Europe. The Soviet Union, which was forced to stand apart because of capitalist-Communist suspicions and hostility, appeared in the 1920s and 1930s to be some strange, ominous, but possibly impotent aberration, harassed by despotism, bloody purges, and a feverish effort to industrialize rapidly through the five-year plans. Across the Eurasian landmass, despite its huge size and nominal independence, China was torn by bitter factional and ideological strife, while Western economic domination remained more or less intact. No one in the developed countries seriously believed that the China of the mid-1930s was a modern state which could be considered the equal of any great power, and there were also widely held doubts about the last of the future Allied "Big Four," the United States of America. The U.S.A. spent the whole of the 1930s lamed by the debilitating effects of the Great Depression; isolated, disarmed, and tormented by the misgivings which had resulted from economic failure.

The rearmament of Japan, Germany, and Italy during the early 1930s and the subsequent expansionist moves of these three states gradually forced the countries that would become the Allied Big Four (China, Britain, the USSR and the U.S.A.) to take diplomatic countermeasures, and then to emulate the Axis powers by stoking the fires of general mobilization. Between 1937 and 1941, as the Axis powers advanced, China, Britain, the USSR, and the U.S.A. were drawn into the war one by one. Faced by the extreme Darwinian challenge posed by the clash of the Axis and Allied giants, the populations and governments of all warring nations were compelled to abandon all caution, embark on limitless mobilization, and radically change themselves in order to survive and triumph.

While trying to gain as much support as possible from its allies, each belligerent, whether Allied or Axis, sought to wring the maximum war-making capability out of its own society. Every country attempted to put as many of its citizens into uniform as possible, while striving to increase its production of commodities essential to the war effort, especially arms, ammunition, and high-tech weaponry. To extract the necessary human and financial resources from their populations, the governments made generous use of the draft, heavy taxation, and war bond sales. To make certain that the assets so acquired were effectively utilized, the authorities resorted to extensive central planning, compulsory allocation of resources, and rationing.

The crucial element in achieving, and sustaining, optimum war mobilization lay in raising the support which the public was willing to give to the war effort. Far more important than police repression and censorship in this regard were the propaganda activities of the governments, and in the Western countries, of the private media. Appeals to national pride, hate-filled denunciations of the enemy, and cries that the other side had to be defeated in order to establish one's own national security were the foundation stones of prowar propaganda everywhere. But as the conflict went on, and even as the system of mass mobilization actually reduced the operative systems of all governments to a similar authoritarian pattern, governmental propaganda in each country increasingly portrayed the war as an ideological crusade in which the complete defeat of nations that represented a hostile ideology, whether they be Nazi, Fascist, Communist, or "plutocratic," was universally called for.

Wherever a belligerent nation made serious efforts to mobilize its resources and population, its armed strength and productivity dramatically increased. All nations were open to nationalistic cries for sacrifice to protect the nation's security, and no country showed itself immune to the call that every allegedly threatening state and ideology should be ruthlessly crushed. At the high point of the war, every single major belligerent—except perhaps Fascist Italy and Kuomintang China—had become much more powerful by means of a popular total-war mobilization.

Much of the impetus for this great increase of public commitment and expansion of governmental power quite naturally had arisen from deeply held feelings of nationalistic rights and the alleged political and moral wrongs of others. The Allied peoples and their governments quite rightly believed that the Axis states bore most of the responsibility for aggression, and that the Nazis had a clear lead in the realm of dreadful atrocities. On the other hand, many Asians, in addition to the Japanese, believed that an anticolonial war in Asia was fully justified, and throughout the Axis countries the general feelings of thwarted nationalism were reinforced in the latter stages of the war by a belief that the ferocity of the advancing Red Army, when coupled with the slaughter caused by Anglo-American air raids, had seriously tarnished much of the Allied claim to moral superiority.

Whatever conclusions may ultimately be drawn from these tangled wartime feelings of right and wrong, the ironical long-term effect of mobilizing through moral and nationalistic passion was that most of the wartime changes that took place in the relative power of nations actually had little or nothing to do with morality. Those belligerents, such as China, which were underdeveloped and politically unstable, lost relative position during the war, as did countries with too many international commitments and traditional, sluggish economies such as Great Britain. Large modern nations, with vast industrial and agricultural resources and huge populations, preeminently the United States and the Soviet Union, inevitably increased their actual, and relative, power in the course of the conflict. Since the righteous passions that fueled the mobilization also decreed that the use of virtually any weapon was justified which could help to win the war, whoever lost the conflict—ultimately Germany, Japan, Italy, and their small associates—would experience enormous destruction, great loss of life, and the elimination of their governments from the ranks of the great powers.

Therefore at the point where the Allies won their ultimate victories—V-E Day in Europe in May, and V-J Day in the Pacific in August 1945—three obvious and inevitable facts about the immediate postwar era had already been clearly established. The world which had survived the war was in many of its parts a wasteland; tens of millions were dead, swaths of destruction had been cut across whole continents, and the political and economic systems of dozens of nations were either destroyed or badly contorted by their wartime exertions. Consequently, somehow, someone would have to set about putting the pieces together again.

Secondly, due to the nationalistic and moral frenzies that had shaped the war efforts of all the powers, the victors were unanimous in their determination that their major enemies should have no part in establishing the new postwar political and economic system. Italy would receive a touch of mercy, but Hitler's Reich and Imperial Japan would not even receive the modest concessions which had been made to Weimar Germany after the First World War. Their fate would be a protracted period of military occupation by the Allied powers. Thirdly, within the Allied camp, not only had the wartime mobilization permitted the Big

Four to overshadow all the other states that were opposed to the
Axis (with France just crawling back to a position of some influence at war's end), the Soviet Union and the United States
had amassed such enormous military and economic might that
they dwarfed their Chinese colleagues, and though many people
were not yet ready to recognize it, had outstripped the British
Commonwealth as well. A portion of the awe which began to
surround the Soviet and American superpowers in 1945 arose
from the fact that both of them had made much of their leap to
the top rank within the shockingly short span of four years. But
despite much subsequent ideological boasting, communism and
capitalism had had precious little to do with the amount of power
which the United States and the Soviet Union held at the end of
the war, or the speed with which they had acquired it. Together
with the fortunes of war, their size, level of economic development, and the gusto with which they had embraced the system of
mass mobilization, were the primary factors which had brought
them to the pinnacle of power. Once they were placed in that
position, no limitations prescribed by their ideology, morality,
caution, or greed could alter the simple reality that many of the
crucial questions about the future of the postwar world would
have to be answered by the Soviet Union and the United States.

Yet one must be very careful about concluding from this that
the governments of the Allied powers, especially those of the
U.S.A. and the USSR, were free to pursue any postwar foreign policies which struck their fancy. During few periods in the history
of the modern world have the people of the world been as little
inclined as those of the immediate post–World War II era to let
governments make international decisions solely on the basis of
the cold calculations of cabinet diplomacy. In the broadest sense,
the war had aroused in all the peoples of the world, but especially in those of the Allied countries, a greater awareness of
international relations than had existed before, and the public's
moods, aspirations, and the lessons they had drawn from their
wartime experiences were therefore much more important influences on big-power foreign policy. Populations everywhere had

learned to focus at least some of their future aspirations and hopes on foreign affairs, and within a wartime environment saturated with ideological and national security incantations, they had come to accept as necessary at least some of the obligations of international power.

But the inevitable consequence of this symbiotic relationship between those in authority and their more consciously assertive populations was that governments following the war had to have public support in order to secure the money and armed might that would permit them to act in foreign affairs with the authority which the troubled times and wretched state of the world actually called for. Public attitudes made themselves felt in different countries in different ways, ranging from elections and lobbying pressure in the West, to the shrewd assessments of a superpower dictator, and protracted civil wars, elsewhere in the world. Postwar governments tried, and frequently succeeded, in adjusting and redirecting public opinion so that it ultimately came around to support the policies which the national political leaders thought were necessary. But even then, postwar public attitudes had to be given serious regard. Any government which tried simply to ignore the public's views, and the lessons it had learned from the war, did so at great peril, as Chiang Kai-shek learned to his sorrow.

The wartime experience of each country set the boundaries within which its government was forced to operate after 1945. But the war had dealt such sharply different fates to each of the belligerents that the population of every country had been compelled to go its own way, allowing the wartime social, political, and economic changes simply to work their will. By the end of the war, most of the prewar contrasts in the conditions and public attitudes of the warring countries had been magnified. In many vital ways they were "more different" from each other than ever before, and none of the governments had made much headway in gaining control over the alterations that had been produced at home by the war.

Seen in this context, the great changes and vital experiences which each of the Allied Big Four had just passed through appear much more significant in determining the nature and form the world would assume after the war than the supposed iron laws set forth by any ideology. In fact, only if the ideological explanations which have subsequently been laid on top of postwar developments by East and West are held at bay, and a detached historical analysis is made of the basic changes which shaped each of the Big Four during the second great world conflict, is there any prospect of grasping the dynamics that shaped the beginnings of our own era.

This volume will therefore simply attempt to move the big cold war ideological explanations to the sidelines, and begin at the war's beginning, looking first at what the conflict did to China from the time of the Japanese attack until V-J Day in August 1945; then moving on to survey in the chronological order in which the others entered the war, the tone-setting wartime experiences of Britain, the Soviet Union, and the United States. It should then be easier to appreciate that these wartime developments had such immense impact on the Big Four that during the immediate postwar period the primary focus of each of them was directed toward working out the domestic implications of their wartime heritage. After the war's long-term reverberations at home have been sketched out for each of the Big Four during the years 1945–1950, most of the diplomatic phenomena of the postwar era, which led step by step into the cold war, may be seen to fall into place as the rather natural foreign policy consequences of the great changes which had been unleashed by World War II.

The war and the early cold war will then appear quite properly as aspects of a phase in history, which can be explained without invoking moralistic scenarios or demonology. By restoring this era to its proper place within normal historical processes, we may be able to undercut rigid determinism and secure a more meaningful perspective on the widespread claims of the cold war's inevitability, which have prevailed for so long.

1

China's War

Although Westerners tend to think of the start of World War II in terms of 1939 or 1941, China and the world had their first brush with the Second Great War in 1931, when Japanese military forces "peacefully" occupied the north Chinese border province of Manchuria. Six years later, in the late summer of 1937, following a clash between Chinese and Japanese military units at the Marco Polo Bridge near Peking, general armed conflict expanded to cover the whole of eastern China. This struggle, intensified and amplified by other conflicts, gradually enveloped the greater portion of the globe between 1937 and 1945, and in the course of this expansion received the title of the Second World War.

China was highly vulnerable to attack from Japan due to a sequence of developments which had begun in the early part of the nineteenth century. Taking advantage of the military weakness of the Manchu dynasty which ruled the country through a unitary but archaic administration, the great powers, led by Britain, had forced the Manchus to grant extensive economic and political privileges to the West. Western naval vessels soon patrolled Chinese rivers, international settlements—independent of Chinese law and guarded by Western soldiers—were established in Chinese cities, and Western businessmen were given a free hand to trade throughout China and bend the economic activity of the country to their purposes.

During the late nineteenth century, with all the developed powers, including the United States and Japan, occupying seats at this great exploitive banquet in China, the old-fashioned Manchu administrative system was gradually undermined, central government broke down, and in 1911 a revolutionary republic was proclaimed by Sun Yat-sen. But Sun and his republican associates were unable to discover any way to hold the country together, modernize it, and at the same time satisfy the great powers that still maintained their privileges and demanded their pounds of flesh.

Therefore, at the time the Japanese military operations occurred in 1931 and 1937, though nominally an independent republic, China was less a modern country than a vast political-economic cauldron. Warlords and independent military bands boiled and bubbled up to the surface in every part of the country, spreading out over a province or two, and then attempting to flow into the territory of their neighbors. In the great cities, and along the major rivers, Europeans, Japanese, and Americans, all powerful in their international settlements and protected by their navies, loomed up from the political landscape like volcanic outcroppings of power, occasionally erupting into diplomatic and military activity to demonstrate their supremacy. Farther out into the countryside, Christian missionaries formed other small points of Western influence; tiny spots of foreign effervescence that showed that China was neither united nor powerful. So many Western missionaries were active in China in the 1920s that one thousand of them were on home leave each year in the United States alone. A decade later, this vast network of tiny rivulets carrying a foreign and divisive message through an already mortally divided China was joined by yet another current producing fragmentation and fracturing. In the 1930s a crowd of Japanese businessmen, propagandists, and political agents surged forth, spreading their influence across the land, long before the Japanese armies actually came to most of China in 1937.

Having been forced into modernization by Western pressure during the mid-nineteenth century, Japan began to industrialize, and as she became stronger, emulated the European great powers by modernizing her army, constructing a navy, and launching off down the road of imperial expansion. Victorious in the Sino-Japanese War of 1895, Tokyo acquired the area of Korea, as well as Formosa. Japan was thus well placed in the early twentieth century to expand into north China and challenge tsarist Russian power in northern Asia. The Japanese triumph over Russia in 1904–1905, which marked the first defeat of a European state by a Third World country in modern times, also gave Japan control of the railroads of Manchuria and made possible further economic expansion in north China.

When the doddering Chinese imperial government finally disintegrated in 1911, and "the Manchus left the feast," Japanese opportunities for applying pressure increased. They increased again in consequence of the First World War, which weakened the relative power of Britain and lessened the influence of Russia for long periods due to defeat, civil war, and the inward-looking struggles of the young USSR.

The great international economic paralysis that followed the Wall Street crash of 1929 brought tempting opportunities, as well as grave economic difficulties, to Japan. The depression produced a catastrophic drop in Japanese exports, threatening the whole economic and political system which had been erected by Tokyo during the previous seventy years. But the slump also tended to paralyze the Western powers, especially Britain and America, whose strength had long acted as a barrier to Japanese expansionist ambitions in China. Many Japanese military and business leaders therefore concluded that the answer for their country was not to try to give up industrialization and retreat into the past, but to become more aggressively imperialistic and seize by force the necessary raw materials and markets of north China, which would make possible the creation of a largely self-sufficient Japanese-controlled zone on the mainland of Asia.

The attempts at centralization which the Chinese had made during the 1920s seemed to offer few serious obstacles to Japanese ambitions. In the first half of the twenties, Sun Yat-sen, unable to secure an administrative or military power base, had been forced to limit his activity as the president of the Republic of China to spreading the message of popular government and Chinese national unity through the Kuomintang, which was less a political party than a political and military popular fellowship. When Sun died in 1925, the military side of the Kuomintang, in the person of Chiang Kai-shek, tried his hand at unifying China by force. Chiang, like Sun before him, received a modicum of military assistance in the form of weapons and advisers from the Soviet Union (which was passing through its apprenticeship in trying to weaken Western capitalism by providing limited support to national liberation movements in Asia), and he also formed a tentative and nervous political alliance with the young Communist party of China.

Chiang's plan of action was unusual both for its literalness and its simplicity. He gathered the strongest military force he could in the Cantonese region of southeast China, and marched due north, trying to conquer all the independent warlords in his path. Every conquest was seen by Chiang as another step in the unification of China, and the fall of Hangchow to his forces in 1926 seemed a hopeful sign that this peculiar policy of securing national unity by military patchwork quilting might actually succeed.

But in 1927 Chiang's singlemindedness was deflected into a series of confusing highways and byways. He became deeply embroiled in the labyrinthian, and frequently sordid, politics of the great city of Shanghai, married into the powerful Soong family, and converted to Christianity. In the course of that year he also had a sharp falling out with his Communist allies. Not only were the Soviet military advisers sent home, Chiang caught and executed many of the prominent Chinese Communists in the great cities of the coastal area. The surviving Communists fled into the interior, and one major grouping under Mao Zedong managed to build up a strong military position in a remote region far to the west of Canton.

Chiang responded to the Communist escape and southern regrouping by elevating the "Communist threat" to the number-one target of his campaign to achieve national unity. Henceforth he only pursued the old advance against the northern warlords in a halfhearted fashion, and committed his main effort to the military defeat of the Communists. In 1934 he succeeded in putting the south China Communists under such pressure that Mao had to give way, and the Communist remnants marched across the interior until they could build up a new defensive sanctuary in the remote northern region of Yanan.

Throughout the years 1928–1936, while carrying on this struggle with the Communists, Chiang tried to modernize his military forces (this time with German advisers) and to increase public morale and efficiency by means of quasi-Fascist and paramilitary pep squads called "Blue Shirts." In so doing he became not so much a sovereign as a kind of "national warlord" who sought, through the manners and reality of militarism, to give China the means to become a modern, unified, country.

The relative peace and security provided to coastal China by Chiang's efforts helped to make a more favorable climate for business, and a currency reform produced a modest industrial spurt in 1935–1937. But there was no real national economy, and no general economic statistics through which one could judge the scale of economic activity. China had no gross national product or national income; her economic reality lay in the hundreds of thousands of largely self-sufficient villages inhabited by hundreds of millions of peasants, the majority of whom were illiterate. Politicians and warlords bled the villages for taxes and soldiers, and Chinese labor everywhere suffered unspeakable horrors of exploitation.

Between 1927 and 1937 Chiang only had firm control of two provinces, partial control of eight, and little or none in eighteen. The provinces on the fringes of Kuomintang authority received no beneficial reforms, and they were often caught on the edge of Chiang's campaigns against the Communists and the independent warlords. In the Kuomintang fringe province of Sichuan, for example, the local military commander was for all intents and purposes an independent warlord in the early 1930s. As one visitor noted, the result was that Sichuan was the "worst for opium, worst for squeeze, and worst for lazy officials, and for military adventurers who do nothing but bleed the peasants." A missionary in the Sichuan city of Chengdu observed in 1935 that when he went to the post office to collect a parcel, he was routinely presented with a bill for six legal and two illegal taxes.

On occasion, when things got too far out of hand, or just by the chance of military operations, a fairly well-disciplined body of Kuomintang troops and officials would arrive in such a province. This occurred in the spring of 1935 when Chiang himself led a force into Sichuan to harass the right flank of Mao's Long March. Then the Kuomintang's crack units marched about, administrative reforms were made, and the trade in opium was sharply curtailed. University students found themselves dressed in army uniforms with their heads shaved, and the citizens were ordered by Kuomintang Blue Shirts to change their personal habits and stop spitting in the streets.

But then a more serious crisis always arose elsewhere. First Chiang and his personal aides would leave, then the crack army units, and finally the Kuomintang officials. Soon the local authorities went back to their old ways, and the local military commander began again to feather out in the plumage of a local warlord. Within weeks of the departure of the visitors in late 1935, "squeeze" was back in full force in Sichuan, and within a year opium was not only sold openly, it was once again taxed by the local government.

What jolted Chiang, the Kuomintang, and other Chinese political factions out of this inefficient merry-go-round was a gradual shift in public hatred and hostility. The Western exploiters were still despised and resented in the mid-1930s, but they had assumed a certain quietude, and therefore sank to a lower strata in the deep exploitative geology of China. The Japanese, however, were more aggressive, more demanding, and more dangerous, and they were also very close to the surface. Whether the ageless peasant masses of China actually felt greater hostility to the Japanese than to the Europeans or the landlords or the tax collectors is highly debatable, but the bulk of the urban population, especially the businessmen and the students, surely did, and they were Chiang's main constituents.

The tales which later circulated during the war alleging that Japan had a master timetable for the conquest of China were certainly myths. There was actually little Japanese agreement on means or clarity on ends. The Tokyo government did not effectively control its military chiefs in Japan, and even less so its garrison officers in Manchuria and in the international settlements of China. The Japanese Kwantung army in Manchuria was a nearly independent force which more often made policy decisions than implemented those of the Tokyo government. The smaller Japanese army units scattered about the cities of China, such as the one at Tianjin which set off "the Marco Polo Bridge incident" of 1937, were also independently minded and anxious to emulate the ambitious activities of their northern neighbor, the Kwantung army. It is also true, as the Japanese historian Saburo Ienaga has observed, that despite its bravery and high combat morale, the Japanese army was hardly a modern military force. "Charging around Manchuria in the dark, shouting 'banzai' " did little to make up for the fact that Western armies were gradually becoming highly mechanized, and that of Japan was not.

Nonetheless the Japanese army in the 1930s was far superior militarily to anything in China, and partly encouraged by the appearance of right-wing expansionist governments in Germany and Italy, there was a rising inclination among a broad spectrum of Japanese military and political leaders to establish their country's future on the basis of expanded influence in China, rooted in armed control of a sizable portion of its territory. A precise timetable there was not, but there was intense aggressive pressure by Japan, and repeated incidents in which Japanese officials, businessmen, and military officers tried to walk like masters, to humiliate the Chinese, and to prepare them for submission and a servile condition. Nothing could have better stimulated rising

Chinese national consciousness, and that in turn was guaranteed to make the Japanese move more quickly and more arrogantly in an effort to achieve some degree of supremacy before Chinese nationalism beat them to the goal.

Surely Chiang was aware of these developments, and it may be, as his defenders have asserted, that he merely ignored Japanese advances in Manchuria and elsewhere because he realized his own military weakness and wanted to gain time to unify China before the showdown came. Even if Chiang was a closet opponent of Japan in the 1930s, however, his decision to try to ignore Japanese expansion, and continue to woo hostile warlords and fight Communists while the popular cry for resistance to Japan rose to a fever pitch, was untenable. Even some of Chiang's northern warlord associates understood that the path he was on would lead to nothing but disaster, and in December 1936 they acted to force him onto the main road of national leadership against the Japanese. During an inspection trip to Xian, Chiang was seized and held hostage by his warlord hosts. The warlords insisted that he reverse course, make a truce with all his political opponents, including the Communists, and give top priority to resistance against Japan. How the deal was cut, and the necessary face saved in this incident, is not clear, but when Chiang left Xian and returned to the coast in early 1937, a national front had been formed, the campaigns against the Communists ceased, and the Kuomintang assumed a more overtly anti-Japanese stance.

In the first months of 1937 the Japanese did not need reports from their host of confidential agents to realize that there had been a turn, and the tide of government and popular resistance in China was running against them. The great upsurge of Chinese national consciousness, which embraced the whole political spectrum from the Communists to the right wing of the Kuomintang, had come to focus on opposition to further Japanese expansion. Anti-Japanese propaganda was being taught openly in the schools, even in the interior, and the pace of economic modernization had quickened. Most "friends of China" rejoiced as they saw her "beginning to find her feet in the modern world." A sympathetic Quaker missionary in Sichuan, while acknowledging that the "present national movements are not very far removed from Fascism and are not free from the conception of the totalitarian state," managed to add that "one cannot help but admire the government that can conceive and arrange such things (however much one may tremble)."

Chiang's increased militancy hardly caused the Japanese to tremble, but it certainly made Japan's army officers more eager to "teach the Chinese a lesson" that would make them submissive. The Japanese army's brutal attack on Chinese soldiers and civilians at the Marco Polo Bridge in July 1937 therefore had a certain element of inevitability about it. So did Chiang's decision to stand and fight, and the consequent Japanese response in accepting the challenge, pouring in more troops, and striking at Chiang's armies in the Shanghai area as well as in the north.

Thus July 1937 marked the start of real war. The Kuomintang leader recognized that there would be "very heavy defeats," and from the beginning realized that his best chance lay in some kind of war of attrition. On 30 August he confided to the British ambassador that if his armies could "stand the first big shock" then time would be "entirely on their side." The army did stand, and fought valiantly, but the casualty toll was frightful. In the first sixteen months of the war Chiang lost the bulk of his modern weapons, and one million Chinese soldiers were killed or wounded. In ten days during December 1937, the Japanese killed upward of three hundred thousand Chinese civilians in Nanjing alone.

Yet even these losses failed to teach the Chinese the lesson which Japan wanted them to learn. They did not surrender, and Chiang did not become a Japanese puppet. So the Japanese military leadership fell back on the oldest (and also the most recent) fallacy regarding how to win such a conflict on the mainland of Asia—it extended the war both to the south and farther into the interior. The Chinese then replied with the equally old (and new) device of a measured retreat, which lengthened the invader's lines of supply and stretched his manpower across the immense distances, and primitive communication system, of rural China. A Kuomintang wartime poster proclaimed that "good strategy is better than good arms," but Chiang's course of action was due less to a choice of strategy than to a lack of alternative. Since he would not, or could not, make a deal with the Japanese, he had to retreat into the interior because he simply did not have the means to continue the fight against Japan in the coastal areas.

It was to be a very crude war of attrition, based on the belief, set forth by a university student newspaper in the early months of 1938, that even though "China does not expect to win this war, . . . if she resists long enough and has perseverance she can make the Japanese lose the war." Such a position not only went contrary to the basic tenets of modern technological warfare, it also challenged the fundamental principles of economic survival. China had a primitive economy with its few industrial assets hugging the coast. It was not the USSR, and there was no industrial complex, such as the Soviets had built in the Urals, awaiting Chiang on the upper reaches of the Yangtse River. On the eve of the war in 1937 the Kuomintang was only aware of 3,935 industrial plants in the whole country (compared with 167,000 in the U.S.A. in the same year). Ninety percent of the Chinese factories were located in the coastal areas that were to fall to the Japanese armies, including the 56 percent which were in the immediate vicinity of Shanghai.

By a prodigious use of labor and miracles of improvisation, 450 industrial and mining establishments containing two hundred thousand tons of equipment were moved into the back country ahead of the Japanese advance. Most of this was accomplished by the use of ancient riverboats and on the backs of millions of coolies, because China had very few railroads. In 1936 the total rail freight for all of China had only been 6.5 billion kilometer tons, one-fifth the figure for India, which was a geographically smaller area, and a full British possession.

With a sense of great national sacrifice and achievement, the

Kuomintang fought a long rearguard battle, moving ever westward until in early 1938 it settled into a simple defensive position in the Sichuan highlands, which surrounded its wartime capital of Chongqing. During the long retreat, Chiang's warlord rivals, as well as the Communists, cooperated with the Kuomintang and generally acknowledged Chiang's leadership. The warlords' tattered armies failed miserably in their clashes with the Japanese, but the Communist units, though not properly equipped, fought bravely, and the Communist commanders worked effectively with those of the Kuomintang.

Against this background, Chiang's decision to plant himself in Chongqing and outlast, and outimprovise, the Japanese had a measure of plausibility. This was especially true because from the earliest stages of the campaign Japan's army and administration had shown signs of being overstretched. The Japanese army had 1.5 million men in active service, the largest relatively modern army in the world in 1937–1938, but this was still too small a force to seize successfully and hold the immense area of China in the face of prolonged resistance. By mid-1938 Japan was obviously unable to find the necessary forces and logistical support to pursue the offensive any further. Even in the areas she had nominally conquered, Japan could not establish a comprehensive occupation system. The cities, railroad, and telegraph lines, and even the major towns were all taken firmly in hand. But Tokyo soon turned miserly in providing both men and supplies, and overextended Japanese units were forced as much as possible to live off what could be obtained from the occupied areas. The military authorities in consequence tended not to try to hold in depth the vast marginally productive territory, but concentrated their attention on regions of strategic importance that could help fill the army's enormous supply requirements. This increased demand for goods in areas devastated by battle and occupation immediately began to push up prices. By November 1938, commodity prices in the Japanese region of north China had risen by 200 percent, and would go up a total of 430 percent by June 1941.

The conqueror was showing signs of being conquered, and Kuomintang officials therefore had a right to feel pride in their achievement, and in the national resolve, during the first years of "exile" in Chongqing. Foreign observers noted that the "spirit of nationalism" had grown quickly and the national ego appeared to have taken warmly to a stance of angry defiance. To some it was "as if overnight" China had finally put her centuries of humiliation behind her, and had "entered full manhood."

But even in the first moments during which the Kuomintang was in Chongqing there were definite indications that Chiang had his eye fixed less on the immediate struggle with Japan than on the postwar position of his regime and the Kuomintang cause in China. From the time of the initial clashes with the Japanese, strenuous efforts were made to move the universities into the interior, and when the exile began, the colleges of Sichuan and Guizhou were also rapidly expanded. By the fall of 1939, forty thousand students were in Kuomintang-controlled universities, compared with thirty-two thousand registered university students in all of China before the war. This transfer, and the shielding, of the educated elite, was a high-priority government project, because as a foreign university teacher observed, "it *is* important in Chinese eyes" that they be saved so that "afterwards they may lead."

In addition, because the government was uneasy about student loyalty to the Kuomintang, and because it hoped that the students might be turned into a steadying factor, there was "little call upon them." The fact that only three of the five hundred male students at the University of Chengdu had volunteered for officer training by February 1938 shocked some of their foreign teachers. Even when allowance had been made for the wisdom of not throwing away the cream of the nation's youth as the Europeans had done in 1914, one professor was taken aback by the "readiness of the best brains to be saved and their lack of desire for personal participation."

Initially such observations might be written off as the carping of pretentious foreigners who did not have to fight, or to pay

China's price. But as the war of attrition wore on, the lack of resources became more obvious, and the social-economic fissures began to widen more ominously. By 1941, Chongqing had been battered by Japanese bombing and there were few vehicles left on its pedestrian-jammed streets except for charcoal-burning buses with hopelessly worn-out tires. In 1937 the Kuomintang had proclaimed a war to the last man, but within a year Mme. Chiang had adroitly altered the phrasing to declare that the fight would go on "until equipment is exhausted."

Inflation was a bigger threat to the war effort and the viability of the regime than was the rundown of equipment, however. War production and maintenance of the army and the refugees greatly increased costs, while the loss of the coastal productive and financial resources eliminated much of the Kuomintang's income. The small quantities of foreign equipment and credit which Chongqing received during the first four years of the conflict could not begin to cover the deficit, although it is true that the Soviet Union sent Chiang five times as much aid during that period as the United States did. Under these circumstances, only the harshest price and luxury controls could have kept inflation within reasonable limits, but such measures were beyond the means, and probably beyond the desire, of the Kuomintang.

Official Kuomintang figures acknowledge at least a 35 percent inflation by the end of 1938, and a foreign observer with long experience in China thought the general price level rose tenfold between December 1938 and December 1940. Some specific indicators suggest a soaring inflation pressure from the earliest phase of the Chongqing period, for a student's board at Chengdu University, which had cost twenty Chinese dollars for one term in 1937, had risen to six hundred by November 1941.

The rapidly rising inflation carried with it all the negative social-economic effects usually associated with such phenomena, including pressure on fixed incomes and a move out of money into physical assets and barter. There was also a large measure of insecurity and dread. By 1941, even foreigners in the Kuomintang area were expressing the standard feelings associated with high inflation: "It is almost impossible to live," "Nobody knows where it will stop," "I don't know what will happen." To make matters worse, there was a special intensification factor to this inflation. Since capitalists could find few profitable investments in the interior, and had great difficulty moving their capital outside to invest, by 1941 a large block of investment had been built up in hoarded rice. This commodity, both durable and the single most vital commercial product in China, thereby became one of the lead factors in the inflationary pressure. Between 1939 and February 1941 the price of a bushel of rice had gone up from 2.3 to 32 Chinese dollars. Along with the speculators, landowners in rice-producing areas therefore made substantial gains. Fifty acres of rice fields constituted a marginal farm in 1939, but by 1941 it could make a man wealthy. In 1939, the rice from twenty-five acres was required to send a child to a university for a year, but by February 1941 all it took was the rice from five.

For every landowner and speculator who benefited from this process, there were dozens, if not hundreds, of people on fixed incomes and among the city poor and rural landless, who suffered greatly. The poor coolies had gained some benefits from the initial campaigns of 1937, because the movement of the Chinese armies, and especially the long retreat, had required backbreaking labor, which meant employment for millions. But it must be emphasized that in addition to the inflation burden, the Kuomintang's decision to try to win the war through the "sheer force of numbers" generally meant that the weight of the conflict had to be borne by the peasants, since the "actual fighting" would be left to the "soldier class." Even in 1938 a knowledgeable foreigner was shocked "by the readiness of the elite to allow unlimited numbers of peasants to be mown down so that they themselves may be left to lead China when the war is over." The peasants and city poor were ruthlessly seized for the army, where they were treated so unspeakably and supplied so inadequately, that "not one of them comes back."

Such oppression was as old as China, but the Kuomintang's attempt to fight a popular war of attrition by such methods was

e. American consular reports from the early 1930s, some of
m written even before the Manchurian incident, make this
nt very clearly. Even some pro-Kuomintang missionaries who
e in the interior during the battles of the mid-1930s could see
t along with their harshness, the Communists had a popular
se, "a principle at stake," and that they possessed generals
o "were doubtless some of the most able men in China."

Therefore, although it is fair to say that the Communists
ned additional popular sympathy through their participation
he common military effort against the Japanese in 1937, and
t many of the circumstances which the war imposed on China
rked to their advantage, the core of their success was their
icalism and their commitment to a peasant revolutionary
vement. When the battle lines stalemated in late 1937, it was
ir ideological position which put them in the best position to
it a grass roots war with a minimum of supply and equipment.
the interior of China there were far more poor people than
litary resources, rich people, or modern arms. Activating the
isant masses was Mao's trade, and through that approach he
ild create forces capable of carrying on aggressive tactical options against the Japanese, because irregular warfare works
it against an overstretched conventional army of occupation.

In consequence, the Communists quite naturally appeared
re militarily assertive than the Kuomintang, and this allowed
m to appeal to idealists in Kuomintang areas to throw off the
e of a "preserved elite" and go north to help lead the peasants
an aggressive "people's war." As early as 1938, a missionary
cher noted that "the Communists see the potentialities of
uth and realize the desire for service which is filling many
ung people." A newly opened Communist university's "special
rt courses" and its "training school for the direction of guer-
a warfare" acted like magnets drawing young people to Yanan.
February 1938, at least a thousand students from the mis-
nary university of Chengdu had left for Yanan, to seize the
portunity "to undertake immediate service."

Such recruiting, as well as the Communists' energetic prosecu-

inevitably to ask for trouble. This was especially
cause, by the 1930s and 1940s, there was a signifi
alternative in China whose rise had been fueled by
pression. Even in the earliest days of the war or
could see this clearly. China has "plenty of soldier.
ant class," he wrote in his diary, "but the burden be
exclusively on them meant that the hammer an
brought closer."

This was true because the Kuomintang's war e
the inequitable features of the traditional Chinese
social order that invited revolution. In addition, th
erally brought the Kuomintang and the Commu
tions nearer to each other. The truce that follov
incident in late 1936 gave way to a tacit military
fighting with the Japanese actually began. Furthern
mintang's retreat up the Yangtse River to Chongq
much closer to the Communist center at Yanan. Al
ground the two "capitals" were still separated by d
travel on primitive roads and trails, they were in
hundred air miles apart.

The similar situation in which the two regim
themselves from 1937 until the end of the war too
of Chiang's urban luster, and inevitably invited c
to how well the two groups were coping with the
life in remote western China. The intensification (
tionalism, and the need for change which accompa
also opened up new avenues of appeal for the Co
were the more revolutionary of the two movements.

But it should not be ignored that there had alw
of support for Communist radicalism and that th
ously been stirred into motion by crises such as th
incident and the economic troubles of the early
more basically, the Communists had selected a h
means of achieving basic social-economic change.
pressed masses of rural China, if awakened and o
the real stuff out of which change could come with

tion of the war, undoubtedly made the Kuomintang nervous and further worsened the always tense relations between Chongqing and Yanan. The difficulties came to a head in a murky clash between the Communist New Fourth Route Army and Kuomintang forces in January 1941. Who started the incident is still a matter of dispute, but there is no question that it was the Communists who suffered the main casualties. The staff of the New Fourth Route Army was wiped out in what looked like a massacre, and from that point on it was impossible to speak of serious collaboration between the Communists and the Kuomintang. An occasional conciliatory phrase was muttered by one side or the other, and some high-ranking Communists, including Zhou Enlai, served as liaison officers and subtle propagandists in wartime Chongqing, but no foundation of real trust was ever established. Throughout the rest of the war, each side kept a suspicious eye on the other, and large forces that outsiders thought were being used against the Japanese were actually kept on guard along the operational border between the Communist and Kuomintang armies.

Two largely separate Chinas therefore waged their wars against Japan, but it is important that this picture not be seen as a still life. Not only were strong trends, especially inflation, working to erode the Kuomintang's strength; a new dynamism was being pumped into Mao's regime by the symbiotic guerrilla war which developed between the Japanese and Communist forces in north China.

From the beginning, the Japanese army had tried to use brutality coupled with relatively modern military technology to intimidate the Chinese and make them docile. In 1931, and again in 1937, this approach had produced incidents of appalling savagery, which, though the logic was certainly difficult for the victims to appreciate, basically arose from a Japanese need to disguise their deficiencies of manpower and supply by an appearance of ferocity and determination. From 1937 on, Japanese occupation policies revealed the same pattern of attempts to make up for shortages by means of massive intimidation.

Shocked outside witnesses were only able to view parts of this process clearly in the area surrounding the great international settlements such as Shanghai. By 1940, experienced observers believed that Shanghai itself had greatly deteriorated due to Japanese operations, with notable growth only visible among its major vices—"more beggars and more prostitutes." The statistics available show an even grimmer picture, for in 1938 alone, 101,047 "exposed corpses" were removed from the streets of that city.

In the less developed, and more thinly populated, regions of north China, Japan concentrated her limited forces in the urban areas and initially did not make use of Chinese puppet troops in the countryside. Extensive rural areas, up to twenty or thirty miles across, therefore had no regular Japanese garrisons, and aside from an occasional unit sent through to show the flag and the fist, such districts were only metaphorically within Japanese-occupied China.

These conditions offered excellent opportunities for guerrilla warfare, and from the time the tide of battle moved westward in the fall of 1937, Kuomintang stragglers began to form guerrilla bands within the rural havens inside the Japanese lines. Sporadic clashes between such bands and Japan's army of occupation took place throughout the years 1937–1940. But a more significant development in the course of that period was the movement of Communist organizers into these haven areas of north China. The Communists gradually sorted out the scattered guerrilla bands and gave them a base of local power by developing political and organizational links between the guerrillas and the peasant villages. By August 1940 the Communists had achieved sufficient centralized direction over the north China guerrilla groups to launch a regional attack, the "One Hundred Regiments" offensive, which gave Japan's army a bad shock.

The Japanese made a number of organizational changes following August 1940 in an effort to widen their areas of effective occupational control. Village leaders were held accountable for the good behavior of the population, blacklists and Japanese military tribunals were extensively used, and the occupation authorities withheld essential goods, especially salt and matches, from villages suspected of guerrilla activity. Chinese puppet troops were also employed, and the Japanese expanded the number of farm cooperatives so the army could draw the maximum volume of supplies from the areas where its troops were concentrated.

Even these measures failed to break the guerrillas or give the Japanese physical control of more than a slice of rural north China. Although kaleidoscopic changes in operational zones occurred from early 1941 on, the Communist-led guerrillas always held at least a quarter of the territory of the northern region, while another quarter or more was made up of "neutral" zones into which both Japanese and guerrilla forces penetrated. To hold back the guerrillas, and in an attempt to sever their connections with the peasant villages, the Japanese resorted to punitive expeditions through the neutral zones and into the areas of the guerrilla base camps. Repressive terror was the sole function of these operations, which a later age would refer to as harsh measures of "rural pacification." In the 1940s, the Japanese were more succinct. They named this the policy of the "Three Alls"— "Take all, burn all, kill all."

At best such operations could only provide limited security to Japanese vital centers, while keeping the guerrillas temporarily at bay. Every expedition had to withdraw eventually, and each one left behind an increased desire for revenge among the surviving victims. A steady diet of such expeditions guaranteed that the peasants' longing for national dignity, freedom, and a decent life would inevitably come to identify with the cause of the Communist guerrillas. The Communist movement in the north thus had the means and an increasingly popular cause with which to fight an offensive war against the Japanese. Like Chiang's forces, those of Mao were involved in a costly war of attrition. But the Communist war, unlike that of the Kuomintang, was expanding and aggressive, with the Japanese, not the Chinese, cast in the role of defenders. Mao's guerrilla armies had found a way of waging war against Japan that worked, and by late 1941 these armies seemed to have time and circumstances on their side in regard to both the Japanese and the Kuomintang.

Then on 7 December 1941 the Chongqing government was dealt what appeared to be a wild card of near-magical power.

The Japanese, long frustrated in China, had been given unexpected opportunities for expansion in Southeast Asia during 1940–1941 due to Hitler's triumphs in Europe. With France and the Netherlands defeated in May–June 1940, and the British sorely pressed, the West's imperial possessions in the South Pacific and the Indian Ocean could not be adequately protected. Tokyo jumped at this chance to gather up economic and strategic prizes on the cheap and sent units of its army into Indochina in the spring and early summer of 1941.

Japan's occupation of Hanoi and Saigon was the decisive step which persuaded Washington to force a showdown with Tokyo over its aggressive expansion in Asia. Just as it would do a quarter of a century later in another conflict in the same area, the United States government issued an ultimatum to cease what it saw as aggression, and ended up getting more than it bargained for. Washington cut off all trade with Japan in July 1941, and in cooperation with the Dutch and the British, stopped petroleum shipments to the Japanese. The Americans hoped that the trade cutoff, and especially the oil embargo, would force Japan to back away and make a general settlement that would not only remove Tokyo's forces from Indochina, but would also terminate the "China Incident" and compel the Japanese to disgorge what most Americans saw as the ill-gotten gains that Japan had acquired since 1931. Given the nationalistic and expansionist mood of the Japanese people, and the enormous political power of the militarists both in Tokyo and the occupied territories on the mainland, however, there was no possibility that Japan would do as the Americans wished. Too much blood had been spilled and too many hopes had been raised by the expansion of the years 1931–1941 for Japan to throw in her hand, but since her military power was ultimately dependent on petroleum imports, if she

could not quickly get a favorable political settlement—and negotiations with Washington between July and December persuaded
her that she could not—there seemed no other choice but to hit
the Americans, as well as the Dutch and the British, with everything she had.

The Japanese attack on Pearl Harbor, which brought forth an
outpouring of shocked outrage in the United States, actually unleashed an emotional outburst in Chongqing appropriate to a victory celebration. "Kuomintang Government officials went around
congratulating each other" as if a great triumph had been won.
The military council was "jubilant," and as one eyewitness reported, Chiang was so happy that "he sang an old opera aria and
played Ave Maria all day." Overnight, Kuomintang China had
become a senior member of an Allied coalition against Japan in
which United States military forces, backed up by enormous production and copious amounts of money, seemed guaranteed to
carry the day. Chiang's policy of holding high the standard of
"Free China," while hoping that a stalemate would ultimately
bring him massive outside aid, seemed to have been completely
vindicated.

However, the initial course of military operations following
Pearl Harbor was hardly encouraging to Chiang or to the Allied
cause. As Sir Horace Seymour, soon to be appointed British ambassador to Chongqing, wrote to his wife on 9 December in the
scurrilous language common at the time, "the Japs seem to have
started very well and the little beasts are going to be a serious
menace."

In December 1941, Tokyo had eighteen capital ships together
with a strong modern air force in the Pacific, and her active-
service army had been raised to over two million men at a time
when Britain had only modest forces remaining in Asia. The size
of the United States Army still fell three hundred thousand men
short of that of the Japanese, and American forces were mainly
spread out over the Western Hemisphere, and were divided between those being prepared for deployment in the European and
Pacific theaters of operations. Therefore, when fighting in the

relatively narrow and lightly defended territories of Southeast Asia, with concentrated ground forces backed up by strong naval and air units, the Japanese were able to move much more decisively than had been possible in China.

Sweeping through Hong Kong, the Dutch East Indies, and Malaya with blinding speed, they had seized Singapore by February 1942, and though the Americans held them off longer in the Philippines, on 6 May 1942 Japan conquered the last bastion of Corregidor. A week earlier, Chiang's initial dreams of a torrent of American supplies had turned to dust, for on 30 April Japanese columns in Burma took Lashio, and thereby closed the Burma Road.

Instead of affluence and the prospect of immediate victory, the first four months of the Allied war against Japan had brought a string of humiliating defeats and had severed the Kuomintang's last land route to the outside world. For two and a half years the only link between Chongqing and the Allies would be "hump" flights from India. But no matter how many supplies were hauled halfway around the world to India from Britain and the United States, there was no way that two-engined propeller-driven aircraft flying over the Himalayas could actually deliver sufficient matériel and men to wage large-scale modern military operations in China. So through 1942, 1943, and most of 1944, Chiang and the unfortunate American commander in the China-Burma-India Theater, General "Vinegar Joe" Stilwell, were left to quarrel in angry frustration as one failed to receive the supplies of which he dreamed, and the other was denied the means and authority to fight the offensive war which he craved.

Despite his disappointments, and his endless pleas for more material assistance, Chiang did secure some political benefits from Allied, especially American, participation in the anti-Japanese war. Many foreign observers were initially impressed by Chiang's aura of calm self-confidence and the many varied talents that Mme. Chiang's "very-remarkable family" brought to the Kuomintang. American propaganda's portrayal of the Kuomintang as the legitimate government of the whole country certainly helped Chiang's image in China, even if listing the Kuomintang among the "democracies" was purely gratuitous, and its inclusion among the Big Four Allied powers a pure pipedream. American good offices helped net Chiang a major diplomatic triumph in January 1943 when the Allied powers formally relinquished the extraterritorial rights that had tormented China for generations. But this was counterbalanced two years later at Yalta when the Americans used what appeared to nearly all Chinese to be their bad offices to grant the Soviet Union the cities of Lüshun and Dalian along with special privileges in Manchuria.

Chiang was very aware that his position was critically dependent on the goodwill of the Allies, and large sums were spent on courting foreign visitors and press representatives in Chongqing as well as on propaganda in the United States. By the summer of 1943, however, Chiang's public relations magic began to run into some trouble with the American press. A number of critical dispatches were filed by "liberal" reporters such as Theodore White, and even such staunch advocates of "Free China" as Henry Luce's *Life* magazine and the *Reader's Digest* printed articles showing some of the darker sides of the Chiang regime. In consequence, the Kuomintang propagandists in America redoubled their efforts. Ambassador to Washington T. V. Soong was thrown into the breach to wax eloquent on the glowing future which awaited the postwar Kuomintang, and his sister, Mme. Chiang, spent months touring the United States, beguiling politicians and opinion makers, while lining up support for Chiang's organization within the large Chinese-American communities.

Certainly not every American was convinced by this propaganda blitz. The president himself seems to have been somewhat put off by Mme. Chiang's efforts, and in 1944 Vice-President Wallace reported to Mr. Roosevelt that in his view Chiang was at best "a short-term investment" who lacked "the intelligence or political strength to run post-war China." Yet even Wallace agreed that as long as the war lasted, the United States should continue to support Chiang and send him all possible assistance.

Since recognition and aid were the bottom-line goals of the Kuomintang propaganda campaigns in America, even liberals like Wallace ended up helping Chongqing.

The United States government sent over the hump all the technical support it could beginning in 1942. Most of the aid consisted of weapons and assorted military supplies, but some of it assisted basic production with beneficial effects for the economy. Between 1937 and 1944, for example, electrical output in Free China reportedly increased 250 percent, which represented a distinct achievement in technical assistance. Other technical aid projects were not so salutory, however. For three years, the United States Navy and the Office of Strategic Services provided the Kuomintang secret police units led by Tai Li with weapons and "FBI type" training, purportedly to increase their effectiveness in guerrilla operations. The primary effect of this project, however, was to make the secret police more efficient in suppressing political dissent and eliminating Chiang's rivals.

This seems to have been the first of a long series of American training operations for the secret police of repressive regimes, and at the time, United States officials in China apparently had enough foreboding at least to try to distance themselves from its most unsavory aspects. In January 1945, Tai Li even had to assure General Wedemeyer that Americans "would not be asked" actually to assassinate Communists; "their job was to train the Chinese to do it." But such sops to American sensitivities did not alter the fact that United States aid, to the degree that it was effective at all, merely increased the efficiency of a military dictatorship. Outside assistance had virtually no effect on the basic deficiencies and suffering which dominated the lives of nearly everyone in China. In 1942, for example, a horrendous famine struck the province of Henan, and two to three million peasants died, while corrupt Kuomintang officials went right on collecting confiscatory taxes from the dying peasants as if nothing unusual were happening. Indeed, nothing of fundamental importance had changed, for famine had been eternal in China, and all the press releases proclaiming that the Kuomintang was a great power and that vast assistance was arriving from the United States had no significant effect on that. In 1943 wheat and barley acreage was still only half that of ten years earlier, and the rice output was but 70 percent of the 1934 figure. Rail freight had actually declined further after American aid began to arrive, dropping from a minuscule 605 million ton kilometers in 1939 to 546 million ton kilometers in 1943.

The arrival of American military and support personnel actually increased the pressure on Chiang's threadbare resources. In Chinese terms all Americans were voracious consumers, and every use of local supplies and labor to support the newcomers and to prepare for waging a more aggressive war meant that there was less for the Chinese. The Americans also represented a vast increase in inflationary money—money to buy what they needed, money to provide financial aid to Chiang and the Kuomintang, money exchanged at an artificially high rate for the Chinese yuan, which allowed corrupt Chongqing officials to rake off enormous fortunes.

The overall effect was an inflationary disaster. In 1938 there had been 2.3 billion Chinese yuan in circulation. By 1943 there was an eightyfold increase to 189.5 billion, and by 1945 the total of circulating Chinese dollars had gone up an additional five hundredfold, standing at over one trillion. Faced with this currency explosion, the people responded in the only ways they could. They bought everything in sight before their cash lost value, and they withdrew all possible money from the bank to buy additional commodities. With wholesale prices up 900 percent by 1943 and an additional 10,000 percent by 1945, it would have been ridiculous for anyone to leave money in the bank. Loanable funds dried up, as money ceased to function as an effective economic instrument, and the efficiency of the whole society sank to the level of a near-barter economy.

On the individual level, even the most privileged among foreigners were devastated by the inflation. As early as October 1942 the British ambassador was complaining "in a year or so I don't see how I shall exist at all." A month later, while out for a stroll he encountered a fisherman carrying a five-pound fish. The ambassador attempted to buy it for three pounds sterling (then the handsome sum of twelve to fifteen American dollars), only to learn to his sorrow that the fisherman had already sold his catch for three pounds and ten shillings. By 1943, the ambassador's wife had so adapted herself to the all pervasive inflation that she made use of an abbreviation "h.c. of 1." for "high cost of living" in her letters to England. Nor were diplomatic ethics totally immune from the inflation's corrosive effects. In December 1942 the ambassador was offered the sum of thirty pounds sterling for four tins of powdered milk, and a week later in a letter to England, he quietly admitted that he had indeed sold the four tins for thirty-one pounds and five shillings.

An economic catastrophe so calamitous that it led the British ambassador to the black market inevitably brought forth calls for change. American authorities in Washington and Chongqing periodically screamed at Chiang, demanding that he institute financial reforms and threatening that if he did not, they would buy Chinese yuan on the black market rather than pay the artificially high exchange rate established by the Kuomintang. But the United States government was unwilling to face up to the fact that Kuomintang graft was less the basic cause of the runaway inflation than was the American demand that this ramshackle regime should attempt to form a modern army that could combine with that of the United States to fight a major offensive campaign in China. From Stilwell to Wedemeyer and from Marshall to Roosevelt, the Americans never let go of the fantasy that Chiang could be inveigled or bribed into waging an active war against Japan.

This vain hope gave Chiang all the political leverage on the Americans that was required. He habitually threatened that any proposed change, from fiscal reform to improved relations with the Communists, would endanger the prospects for the mythical great offensive. This was always enough to make Washington back down and allow the flow of supplies and money to continue. Therefore, by 1945, no modern Chinese army had been created, inflation was out of control, the Kuomintang had disintegrated as a governing force, and neither Chongqing nor Washington had made a serious high-level overture to Mao. The United States was reduced to clutching after the ultimate fanciful straw. If only Stalin could be persuaded to restrain the Chinese Communist party, the State Department reasoned in the last year of the war, then perhaps the Kuomintang would be able to assert itself and actually rule China when Japan surrendered.

That such daydreams were taken seriously in Washington proved that Chiang had won his private battle against the American military reformers. It also meant that so few options were left open to him that he too was forced to chase after phantoms. When offensive operations reopened the Burma Road in mid-1944, the Kuomintang leader once again convinced himself that a multitude of supplies would soon be pouring into Chongqing and that these would equip his ragtag forces with enough weapons to intimidate both the Japanese and the Communists. However, the Burma Road was just an interminable dirt track, and it soon became apparent even to Chiang that no miracles would be coming down that road. He therefore fell in easily with Claire Chennault's obsessive belief that modern ground forces were not necessary to defeat the Japanese, and that victory could be won by air power alone. In the summer of 1944 the Fourteenth Air Force was given top claim on supplies coming in from Burma, and hundreds of thousands of coolies were employed to hack huge airfields out of the soil of south China. In the fall of 1944, B-29 bombers from these bases began to strike at Japanese offshore shipping, and then at the home islands of Japan. In October–November 1944, the Japanese hit back hard with the first major offensive in China since 1938. They quickly conquered a huge zone of southern China, overran the new airfields, and put Chiang and Chennault out of the strategic bombing business.

With all the miraculous options used up, Chiang was forced to cooperate with the more humble plans of the new United States theater commander, General Wedemeyer, who wanted to create limited ground forces and make a modest drive toward the coast.

In the summer of 1945, after war ended in Europe, vast quantities of men and equipment were released for service in Asia, and with the Burma Road and hump flights working efficiently, the China Theater received far more military hardware and battle-hardened United States units than ever before. Mixed Chinese and American forces launched their assault in July, making good headway against the overextended and undersupplied Japanese occupation army of south China. The campaign suggested that under ideal circumstances, elements of the Kuomintang army could have been turned into real fighting units, but this possibility appeared much too late. Before Wedemeyer's forces even reached the coast, Japan had surrendered in August 1945. The war had been won in the Pacific, not in China; decided by American naval, air, and atomic power, not by Kuomintang soldiers.

V-J Day was therefore celebrated in Chongqing more in a spirit of deliverance than of triumph, for the Kuomintang had not really won its war, and most of its officials immediately made hurried preparations to leave their rustic exile and return to the coast. The war had cost China 2 million military dead and 1.7 million wounded. Fifteen million Chinese civilians perished as a result of the war of 1937–1945, 85 percent of them peasants, and virtually all were victims of deprivation rather than direct military action. Yet the Chinese military death toll was no larger than that of Japan, which had less than a fifth of China's population. Furthermore, despite the large number of Chinese civilian deaths, and the horrid conditions under which much of the population had lived between 1937 and 1945, China's population of approximately 422 million at the beginning of the war seems to have increased at regular, roughly equal, annual increments to 590 million by 1953. War conditions and battle deaths did not even produce significant changes in the distribution of the population. The census statistics gathered in 1953 show that there were fewer women than men in every age group in the population below the age of sixty, and that the 3.7 million battle casualties between 1937 and 1945 had not noticeably affected the rate of population growth or altered the ratio of males to females.

The social values which favored men, and dictated female infanticide, continued to exert a stronger influence on the composition of the Chinese population than had the war.

What romantics were wont to call "eternal China" had thus not been destroyed by the conflict; it was the Kuomintang regime which had been the main victim. Corruption and inflation had virtually ruined its infrastructure because the policy of inactive endurance had not coincided with its economic situation or the aggressive anti-Japanese nationalism which had swept over China; and, even more fundamentally, by basing its system on the old class structure the Kuomintang had built on shifting sand, for the war created conditions which turned the broad mass of the peasantry into a revolutionary class. The low morale and generally dispirited state of the Kuomintang leaders in the final stage of the war suggests that even they felt that their time was passing. In November 1944, when the British ambassador in Chongqing was informed that London believed the Asian war might last two more years, he noted, "It is going to be hard for the Chinese to stand it, I fear, and I wonder what will be left of poor free China by that time . . . a depressing prospect for them, poor lambs." Indeed the war had transformed the Kuomintang lions into sacrificial lambs by 1944–1945. Translated into Chinese and back into English, that meant that they had lost the mandate of heaven.

But that was merely the problem facing Chiang and the Kuomintang, because the war ended on a far different note in north China. The period following the attack on Pearl Harbor had seen the position of the Japanese army pass from bad to worse. Once the Tokyo government locked itself into mortal combat with the largest industrial power in the world, the economic strain of the conflict had to affect adversely the undermanned and underequipped Japanese military forces spread out across the impoverished regions above Shanghai. The Japanese home government tried to rise to the new war's technical challenge, but the gap was just too great. As Saburo Ienago has observed, "While America was putting enormous scientific resources into the atomic bomb project, Japan was developing a technique of attaching [small] bombs to [paper] balloons . . . and launching them against the American west coast." Even to keep going against a country which could produce fifty thousand combat aircraft in a single year, Tokyo had to make enormous sacrifices. Much of her economy was shifted from light to heavy industry, and in defiance of all traditional social norms, Japanese women moved into the factories to serve as an industrial labor force. Even farm rents were reduced in an effort to increase output. All these emergency measures struck at the dominant social and economic position of the very landlord-warrior-business class that had promoted Japan's expansionist policies and was determined to fight the war most aggressively.

With the population and the ruling groups at home shouldering such burdens, it was self-evident that the Japanese would try to wring everything they could out of north China at the lowest cost. This was especially true because this region was one of the few from which shipping was not highly vulnerable to attack by American submarines. The army of north China was compelled to increase its shipments of food to Japan, and since the attack on Pearl Harbor cut off the Japanese textile industry's major source of raw cotton, an ambitious campaign of cotton cultivation was also begun. Yet the Japanese army was not given additional men and matériel to carry through these expanded responsibilities. On the contrary, both in the 1942 period of Japanese advances into the South Pacific, and later in the 1944–1945 era of bitter defensive stands to protect the Home Islands from the advancing Americans, the army of north China was required to reduce its garrisons and send units to the Pacific war.

The Japanese forces in north China therefore had little choice except to concentrate their strength further to protect the most vital urban, transport, and cultivation centers, while employing the "Three Alls" policy with ever-greater ferocity. Since Communist guerrilla operations were "essentially a Chinese response to the internal security measures adopted by the Japanese army," as the latter became more ferocious, the former reacted by increased aggressiveness and more offensive activity. Guerrilla units grew in size, received improved leadership, and were also better equipped, because every victorious action netted the Chinese additional caches of Japanese weapons. From 1943 on, the areas directly controlled by the Japanese army gradually shrank, and by 1945 it had lost all initiative in north China. At war's end virtually all the northern countryside was in the hands of the guerrillas, and the Japanese garrisons were desperately clinging to their last entrenched positions in the cities and along the railroad lines.

What a world of difference between this and the situation that prevailed among the Kuomintang five hundred miles to the south! After years of gradually closing in on the zones of Japanese control, by August 1945 the Communists saw themselves on the edge of victory, under the direction of seasoned battle commanders, and possessed of a set of tactics and a strategic plan that had torn the initiative away from Asia's most modern and aggressive army. Even the general international situation seemed favorable, for in the last months of the war Mao had established cautious contacts with various low-level American military missions, and in the final weeks before V-J Day the Soviet army had poured into Manchuria.

The war had so accelerated the tempo and altered the form and direction of political change in China that by August 1945 Mao had taken charge of a large part of the country and had successfully identified himself with the interests and aspirations of the peasant class. V-J Day was therefore a supreme moment of military triumph and political promise for the dynamic Communist leadership and for the countless ordinary people of the north who had suffered untold misery in order to strike back at the Japanese invader. Surely millions in north China must have come to share the feelings of another victorious partisan soldier halfway around the world who rightly felt at war's end that the dawn had come for his "divided and desperate land," and that the future belonged to Communist activists like himself who hoped "to leap over centuries of slavery and backwardness" and if necessary "to by-pass reality itself."

2

Great Britain at War

All the aid we have been able to give has
been small compared with the tremendous
efforts of the Soviet people. Our children's
children will look back, through their history books, with admiration and thanks for
the heroism of the great Russian people.

Ernest Bevin, 21 June 1942

The war of 1939–1945 was a long era of endurance, of grit, and
of self-denial for the people of Britain. It was the penultimate
stage in the United Kingdom's long reluctant retreat from the
glories of imperial dominance. World War I had been a major
step down that road, with great losses of men and treasure, and
a serious slump in London's standing among the powers. In the
interwar period, the United Kingdom remained unreformed at
home while clinging to overextended commitments in Europe
and the rest of the world. The depression brought another drop
in morale, and a sharp rise in the already high rate of unemployment. Poorly armed, hesitant in dealing with Nazi Germany,
Fascist Italy, Japan, and the Soviet Union throughout the 1930s,
Britain stumbled unwillingly into war in 1939 with little bellicos-
ity and a small, generally outmoded military machine.

The quick fall of Poland brought a tremble, and the rapid
German seizure of Norway and Denmark a shock, but the Cham-

berlain government was as dilatory in organizing for total war as it had been in erecting diplomatic barriers to Nazi expansion. As late as January 1940, four months after Britain had gone to war against what was then the most powerful army in the world, there were still 1.6 million unemployed in the United Kingdom, 7 percent of the *total* male population!

The fall of France and the evacuation from Dunkirk in May–June 1940 finally turned the trick and made Britain become a serious belligerent in what had rapidly revealed itself to be a mortally dangerous war. The new war cabinet led by Churchill chose to fight on, confront Hitler with defiance, and mobilize every possible resource in the British Isles and throughout the Commonwealth in order to "stand alone" and successfully meet the Nazi challenge.

The British people rose to meet the test, and the Commonwealth countries—Canada, New Zealand, South Africa, and Australia—provided large numbers of men and vast quantities of matériel. But from the first moments in which British leaders assumed the stance of bulldog defiance, they knew that the United Kingdom could never match German ground power. The Chiefs of Staff Committee concluded as early as the late summer of 1940 that whatever Britain did, her army's size would never be more than half that of Hitler's. Her population of 48 million was only two-thirds that of Germany, not to speak of German-occupied Europe, and British leaders were convinced that the nation could not take another bloodletting comparable to that of 1914–1918. It had required thirteen volumes of close print for the government merely to list the names of Britain's 750,000 dead after the Great War, and every village square and city district had its long stone roster of those "who gave their lives that we might live."

The only hope of holding Germany at bay, and ultimately defeating her, seemed to lie in the old weapons of blockade and propaganda, reinforced by the new weapons of strategic bombing and subversive warfare. Yet some clear-eyed observers in London quickly recognized that the most Britain could hope to achieve even by these methods was a shaky survival. Blockade, propaganda, strategic bombing, and aid to the European resistance were not enough to destroy Hitler's power. The initial bombing raids were extremely costly to Bomber Command, and had no serious effect on the Germans. The Third Reich rapidly showed itself nearly impervious to psychological warfare, and the early attempt to rouse popular resistance on the Continent met with no significant response. Britain's financial weakness, coupled with the vulnerability of her supply lines to air and U-boat attack, even suggested that this time, she, rather than Germany, might be the fatal victim of economic warfare.

Gradually there penetrated into the hidden recesses of the British mind the realization that the United Kingdom was in fact too weak to win the war by herself. She could hold out on her own, possibly for an extended period, but without the full intervention of the United States, or perhaps the Soviet Union, there was no real hope of ultimate victory. By the end of 1940 most people in Britain knew in their heart of hearts that this was true, and if pressed, most would have also conceded that for succor Britain would have to pay in the form of a further loss of economic position, international status, and political power. Most Britons sensed this in the winter of 1940–1941, but they instinctively closed ranks to hide it. In part this was done to deceive the Germans, in part to fool the Yanks and the Russians, but most importantly it was done so that the British people could keep their eyes focused on the immediate task rather than long-term consequences. Once the United Kingdom had assumed the responsibility to fight on to the end, Hitler had to be beaten whatever the short- or long-term costs. For the sake of this war effort it was best not to dwell on the fact that all the wartime suffering and sacrifice would actually result in a long-term weakening of Britain's economic and political power. Inevitably this meant that the leaders and people of the United Kingdom muted so much of their awareness of their relative weakness between 1940 and 1945 that they were nearly as ill prepared to face their precipitous decline in the immediate postwar period as the Americans were to assume the international responsibilities which inevitably accompanied their meteoric wartime rise to the status of a superpower.

The British government simply marched on during the last five years of the Second World War, putting war needs first, and only here and there attempting to lessen the harmful aftereffects which this great national exertion would have on the position of Britain during the postwar period. This had to be done first of all because Britain stood alone "for one whole year of mortal peril" facing a deadly foe. British shipping lost 1,715,000 tons between May and December 1940, and throughout the years 1940 and 1941, the United Kingdom's unfavorable balance of trade hovered around three pounds sterling worth of imports for every pound's worth of exports.

An unprecedented mobilization of domestic resources was therefore required, and it began with high enrollment in the armed forces. Of its 24 million males, the United Kingdom had 4,693,000 in uniform by 1945, 19 percent of the whole male population, a percentage substantially higher than that attained by the United States in the same year (14 percent). In addition, the British Women's Auxiliary Services had a half million members in 1945, roughly 2 percent of the female population. Britain's combat death figure of 264,443, although sharply lower than that for the First World War, was proportionally much higher than that for America. In fact, United States battle deaths only exceeded those of the United Kingdom by thirty-six thousand, while the American armed forces were two and a half times larger. One in every thirty-five British males was a war casualty, including over a quarter million wounded and 177,000 prisoners of war.

Although 20 percent of British military personnel captured during the war were held by Japan, less than 10 percent of British dead and wounded resulted from the Pacific war. Therefore, in the highly sensitive matter of casualties, Britain mainly fought a European war with the mortal enemies Nazi Germany, and to a lesser degree, Fascist Italy. Furthermore, over 50 percent of

Britain's total battle dead fell in the final twelve months of the European conflict. It was from the beginning, up until the last year of heavy losses, essentially a war of endurance between Britain and the Nazi colossus.

The intensity of the mobilization effort showed up graphically in the area of labor mobilization. Under the National Service Acts, all males up to the age of sixty-four could be ordered into any work the government considered essential for the war effort. By September 1941, an unemployed woman without dependents requiring her to remain at home could be sent to prison if she refused war work, and three months later a statute authorized the government to conscript into the forces single women between the ages of nineteen and thirty. There were individual slackers, of course, just as there were in every other country, and the minister of labor, Ernest Bevin, made certain that the general call-up did not trample on the rights of unions or of labor in general. But Britain had nonetheless mobilized its population for war service much more thoroughly than Nazi Germany did, and with infinitely greater rigor than the United States did.

By stringent measures of labor allocation and the concomitant control of raw material and manufacturing plant, Great Britain also ground out a 25 percent increase in gross national product, and upped munitions production 300 percent between 1940 and 1944. She produced 259 destroyers, 66,000 aircraft, 2.5 million rifles, .5 million wheeled vehicles, and a host of other war-related products ranging from small arms to 146 Mulberry harbors for D Day. During the war her gross production compared favorably with that of the USSR, although the larger Soviet economy suffered much more serious damage from enemy attack.

At the same time, Britain waged a highly successful "battle of the land" to increase farm production. This lessened the amount of food which had to be shipped past the U-boats and also reduced the money outflow which would have been necessary to pay for more massive food imports. Although British meat production fell 30 percent between 1936 and 1945, milk output rose 20 percent, grain 65 percent, and potatoes 90 percent. To help secure the production increases, Britain raised the number of her farm tractors 80 percent, but the main factor in the output rise was a 25 percent expansion in the farm labor force between 1939 and 1945. Many of these new farm workers came from the ranks of the Women's Land Army, plus children and prisoners of war. But it is noteworthy that Britain clawed her way to a higher farm output by increasing the size of her labor force, while the United States raised its high agricultural output still higher through mechanization and also managed to *reduce* the number of its farm workers by 25 percent. Clearly, due to wartime supply and monetary pressures, Britain was compelled to put its labor and production emphasis on economic sectors, such as grain production, in which she could not hope to be competitive after the war. No matter what happened following the conflict, the United Kingdom would never become a competitive exporter of grains and cereals, and this aspect of her wartime exertion therefore had to prove detrimental to her long-range economic position.

There were other ominous signs for Britain's economic future hidden away within the statistics of her wartime productive achievement. Much of her increased industrial production came less from modernized techniques than from pouring in large numbers of extra unskilled workers. Alongside the total of 2.7 million prewar employees in the engineering, metals, explosive, chemical, and shipbuilding industries, 2.1 million additional workers had been added by 1943, nearly 1.5 million of them women. Although it was an impressive testimonial to the willingness of the British population to make sacrifices and get on with the job, this massive inflow of temporary workers probably impeded, rather than encouraged, new mechanization.

Britain was in such a desperate corner that there was little time to think of long-term economic effects, and despite the prodigious efforts of the government and the population, the country was often fortunate just to break even. For example, the war greatly increased the demand for merchant ships, due to the multitude of vital military shipments which had to be added to Brit-

ain's essential import-export trade. Indeed, by straining every
productive nerve, and adding hundreds of thousands to the labor
force, 4,200 new merchant vessels were built in British yards.
But 2,637 British-flag merchant vessels were also lost during the
war, and even the vast increase in the production of British ships
was therefore unable both to make up for these losses and meet
all the services' demand for additional shipping.

Even the arrangements made by the various allies to specialize
and divide up essential production often worked to the disadvantage of Great Britain. Under the terms of the lend-lease, Commonwealth, and subsequent agreements, the bulk of overall Anglo-American production of specific military items was left to
one country or another in order to standardize equipment and
avoid wasteful duplication. In consequence, the United States
tended to concentrate on bulky, expensive, high-tech items, while
leaving a greater proportion of conventional small-scale military
production to the British. This was primarily due to a desire to
conserve essential shipping and make best use of existing plant
rather than an American effort to secure postwar economic benefits. But the effect of the arrangement was to concentrate British
productive efforts in the old rather than in the new. The atomic
bomb project is the best-known example of this trend, but it
should be noted that while 250,000 trucks in the one- to five-ton
category were manufactured in Britain during the war, only
12,500 heavy trucks of six to ten tons were produced there.
Similarly, although she did build 27,000 tanks between 1939
and mid-1945, 31,000 tanks were supplied to the United Kingdom from overseas during the same period.

There were exceptions to this picture, of course—the United
Kingdom was far ahead of the United States in jet aircraft development at war's end—but in general, the wartime specializations
worked more to the advantage of American industry. The wartime heavy truck and tank production figures alone explain a
great deal about the relative success of Birmingham and Detroit
in the postwar period, for the U.S.A. had gained the inside track

in meeting the rising worldwide demand for heavy motor vehicles, construction, and farm equipment.

Additional postwar troubles for two of Britain's vital industries were created by the government's decision early in the war to secure all possible manpower for the armed forces. The initial loss of skilled labor from the steel industry meant that the output of crude steel actually fell steadily throughout the war, a trend which was not reversed until the very end of the 1940s. Military conscription of skilled miners at the beginning of the war dealt an even deadlier long-term blow to the coal industry. Once these miners left the pits, nothing could lure many of them back, not even government offers to release such individuals from the army. The low productivity of the unskilled labor drawn into the mines, coupled with strikes over poor conditions and low pay, therefore caused a sharp fall in output. Although the production of coke remained high throughout the war, British coal output was lower in 1944 than in any year before or since, and until this day, coal production in the United Kingdom has never again reached the level of 1939!

However, the most important wartime development that later adversely affected Britain's industrial export position was not any one of these specific factors, such as coal output or the division of war production between the United Kingdom and the United States. The war forced every country to go all out in expanding its productive capacity, and since Britain had the smallest industrial base, the universal expansion of productivity widened the gap between the United Kingdom and the bigger producers. It was all very well for the British governmental statisticians to stress that if American wartime output was calculated proportionally on a basis of population, then the United States would have only manufactured 56,000 armored vehicles while Britain produced 77,000, and the United States would only have turned out 62,000 aircraft and the United Kingdom 66,000. Such statistical adjustments were good for Britain's ego and showed the scale of her productive achievement. But the United

States actually had two and a half times the population of Britain, and her real wartime production was 154,000 armored vehicles and 171,000 aircraft. Therefore she ran away with the lead in the world's production of these, and virtually every other heavy industrial item, while Britain, with all her effort and grim sacrifice, was left in the dust.

The United Kingdom's wartime financial trials and tribulations also produced serious postwar troubles. Government expenditure rose 6.5-fold during the war, peaking at over 6 billion pounds sterling in 1945. In the same period the national debt went up 350 percent. Though the new debt burden (21 billion pounds sterling in 1945) was serious, it had been held at a lower rate of growth than government expenditure by draconian increases in taxation. Treasury receipts from the income tax rose 350 percent between 1939 and 1945, peaking at 1.4 billion pounds sterling in the latter year. This stringent taxing policy, when combined with price and wage controls, rationing, and encouragements to savers, held inflation for the war period to about 17 percent. This was a remarkable fiscal achievement considering the inflation danger posed by the shortage of consumer goods and the drastic increase in the level of employment.

But there were flashes of deep popular resentment about the heavy taxation. Beginning in 1940, the minimum income level at which individuals were required to pay tax was sharply lowered, which meant that 70 percent of the 12.5 million Britons who paid such taxes in 1945 had not paid income tax before the war. The complexity of the tax system, the sharply progressive rates at which individuals were liable for tax, and the slowness with which the government introduced the "pay as you go" system compounded popular confusion and discontent. The Ministry of Information's confidential surveys of public opinion made between 1941 and late 1943 are dotted with tax worries and complaints.

The public did gradually resign itself to the fact that full employment did not provide a great increase in net income to most people. In any event, the scarcity of consumer goods was always a greater cause of lamentation than high taxes. A May 1942 Ministry of Information survey declared that for a significant number of workers, the shortages of beer and tobacco, as well as the high excise taxes on these goods, was a far heavier cross to bear than the income tax.

The only bright spot the war seemed to bring to most people, in addition to survival and employment, was the chance to put a little money aside. Deposits in British banks had risen nearly 90 percent by war's end, and when National Savings certificates, Postal Savings deposits, building society accounts, and the like are added in, the gross savings increase was nearly 250 percent. It seemed that both the nation, and countless hard-working Britons, were building up a substantial nest egg for the future.

But it was not to be. Sharp rationing of consumer goods continued long after the war as the United Kingdom struggled to increase her exports, but by the time her trading position improved sufficiently to make a reasonable supply of consumer goods available again, a large portion of the savings which people had accumulated during wartime and postwar austerity had been eaten up by inflation.

That much of this saving, which had been made through such sacrifice, turned out to be worthless certainly contributed to a gray mood of disappointment and bewilderment in postwar Britain and was indeed another instance of the British people's wartime effort and idealistic self-denial falling victim to the hard fact of decline. The main villain in the piece was not a vague and mysterious new force, however, but a product of the trade and international payments deficit that has plagued the United Kingdom during the whole of the twentieth century.

Throughout the 1920s and 1930s, Britain had an unfavorable balance of trade. In 1935, for example, she exported goods worth 426 million pounds sterling and imported .75 billion pounds' worth of foreign products. Even in the 1930s her unfavorable balance of trade with the United States was serious. In 1937, Britain exported goods valued at 31 million pounds to America and imported 114 million pounds' worth in return.

Much of the latter consisted of processed raw materials rather than manufactures, with tobacco, cotton, and refined copper near the top of the list. In the pre–World War II period much of this trade deficit was covered by British "hidden exports" or "invisibles" such as income from banking and insurance services, merchant shipping charges, and the return on overseas investments. But throughout the interwar period the United Kingdom was compelled to resort to a most serious measure to keep the international payments deficit under control. A large block of the nation's investment abroad was sold off in those years, including 80 million pounds' worth in 1938 alone.

The start of the war against Hitler exacerbated all these economic troubles. Exports fell, imports rose, and to help cover the deficit, sales of foreign securities rapidly increased, leaping 300 percent to 250 million pounds sterling in 1939. Still the deficit continued to rise, reaching 700 million pounds in 1940, and at that point, Franklin Roosevelt acted to help reduce the financial pressures on the United Kingdom. The Lend-Lease Act, passed by the American Congress in the spring of 1941, authorized the president "to Lend or Lease" material to a friendly state whose defense helped to protect the security of the United States. This convoluted language was intended to get around the necessity of making the kind of loans which had created such difficulties after World War I, and to avoid use of the dangerous word *gift,* which would have unleashed a clamor among the isolationists. By employing the phrase *lend-lease,* Roosevelt hoped to aid Britain by funneling war supplies to her without making it obvious to the American people that the material was in fact being given away. He succeeded brilliantly, and thereby unintentionally contributed to the creation of a measure of bitterness on two sides of the Atlantic. During the war, the population in both countries thought that this was a commercial transaction with goods being bought and sold. Public opinion polls in the United States repeatedly revealed that the majority of the population believed that Britain and other recipients of lend-lease were really paying for what they received, and a February 1942 British public opinion survey showed that 54 percent of those questioned thought their country actually paid for lend-lease goods. In fact, except for the extension of a limited number of goods and services to American forces in the form of "reverse lend-lease," this assistance was a free gift of substantial importance. In the course of the war the United States government gave the United Kingdom lend-lease material valued at $30 billion, which equalled the total value of British munitions production for the years 1940–1943. Nor was this assistance a mere trifle in terms of American output, for in the years 1943–1944, lend-lease to Britain took 11 percent of United States munitions production and 5 percent of its yield of food.

But lend-lease could not, and did not, cure Britain's wartime balance-of-payments troubles. It obviously failed to cover imported goods from countries other than the U.S.A., such as meat from Argentina, nor did it write off the cost of regular commercial imports from the United States. A vast array of products the British government believed were essential imports were not so regarded by the American lend-lease authorities, and for these the British were charged. Given the dearth of British exports to help cover these imports, even with lend-lease the United Kingdom's balance-of-payments deficit continued to rise sharply during the remainder of the war. The deficit for 1943 stood at 1.5 billion pounds sterling, and even in 1945, the year of peace, the deficit was still 700 million pounds.

The government tried to strike back against the unfavorable balance of payments by accelerating the sell-off of British overseas investments. The annual sale of foreign securities rose from 250 million pounds in 1939 to 875 million in 1945. Over the six years of war, nearly 4.8 billion pounds' worth of foreign securities were sold, which amounted to approximately half of Britain's total prewar overseas investment. Although absolutely essential to the United Kingdom's credit position during the conflict, this enormous loss of foreign investment would be a major cause of the painful slowness of Britain's postwar economic recovery.

Beyond the liquidation of securities there was little the government could do in the international sphere during the war to improve the financial situation. Along with the loss of a quarter of her merchant fleet between 1939 and 1945, there was a sharp decline in her international banking and insurance business. Therefore no alternative existed but to minimize the fiscal damage by making the British public take up as much of the slack as possible. The most important single factor which the United Kingdom used to limit the balance-of-payments deficit was the reduction of the standard of living of the British people. Ultimately they were the ones who paid in underconsumption, self-denial, and a gradual loss in most of the amenities of daily life. Britain not only withstood Hitler, but also paid for most of the costs of her war effort by turning the life of the population into a grim round of toil, which made it especially difficult for the British people to reconcile themselves easily to postwar national decline.

In the long list of ways that Britain's people bore the cost of the nation's war, civilian deaths from enemy action was not among the most significant. The Blitz of 1940–1941 and the V-1 and V-2 attacks of 1944 accounted for most of the sixty thousand British civilians killed, a figure which, when compared with Polish or even Dutch losses, was very low. But of the 13 million private houses in Britain in 1939, a quarter million were totally destroyed and a million damaged by enemy attacks during the six years of war. Since only eleven thousand new houses were constructed even in 1944–1945, a large number of Britons were badly housed through much of the war and early postwar period. So little preparation had been made for the protection and welfare of the poor at the time of the Blitz that many East Enders took matters into their own hands every night and went "up west" to find shelter in the affluent and relatively safe basements of the fashionable West End shops.

The ability of the poor to take it, their need to work, and their desire to work no matter how poorly the government provided them with protection and amenities during the Blitz, was in all likelihood the major reason why Britain hung on so well during the early phase of the war. Later, during the middle stage of the conflict when the danger of air attack and invasion receded, and governmental social welfare protection increased, the working class still had to bear the bulk of the burden in the form of normal work weeks of sixty hours for men and fifty-five hours for women. No matter how threadbare and colorless life became, they stuck to it with their traditional understatement and humor, even as queuing became the national vocation and "not to worry" everyone's daily slogan.

The British wartime public did not quite attain sainthood. There were slackers and flourishing black markets. Complaints about governmental inefficiency and waste were never-ending, as were bitter criticisms of the privileges, and alleged self-indulgence, of the upper classes. There was also some scapegoating directed at the traditional outsiders in British life. Many expressions of animosity toward the British Communist party occurred during the first two and a half years of the war, presumably because the BCP did not support the war effort prior to the Nazi attack on the Soviet Union in June 1941. Under the heading of what the Ministry of Information called "subversive activities," there were also reports in 1942 of bitter opposition to the rigid pacifism of the Jehovah's Witnesses. But it was the Jewish population of Great Britain which remained the chief target of public animosity throughout the war. Although physical attacks on Jews were extremely rare, and the frequency of anti-Semitic grumbling waxed and waned, the Ministry of Information concluded that it was always at least "latent." Perhaps the paradoxical low point was attained in the last weeks of 1942 and the first part of 1943. In that period the Ministry of Information's home intelligence teams indicated that press reports of German extermination of Jews in Poland had produced strong expressions of public outrage, but at the same time there was an increase in the number of anti-Semitic remarks about Jews in Britain!

Yet it would be misguided to conclude from this anti-Semitic

puzzle that the stresses and strains of the war produced dangerous new fissures in Britain's social order, for anti-Semitism had
been strong in the prewar period as well. Most indicators suggested great social stability in wartime Britain. Although the
number of people convicted of crimes rose slightly during the
war era, as the government took a tougher stand during a period
of national emergency, the number of people charged with
crimes actually decreased between 1939 and 1945. Even the
family structure showed remarkable stability in face of all the
tensions and temptations of wartime. The number of divorces in
the United Kingdom only rose from ninety-five hundred to
twenty-seven thousand per year in the course of the war, while
the divorce figure for the United States soared to nearly half a
million in 1945.

One of the major reasons why British society remained so
stable was that even though the stringent wartime controls imposed great inconvenience, and demanded much self-sacrifice,
they also actually improved the health of the population. On the
face of it, the rationing system should not have done wonders for
the people's health, for even with six million tons of lend-lease
food added to commercial imports and home production, meat
and dairy consumption declined while that for cereals and sugar
rose. Even the amount of tea available to the British people actually fell, which must have produced some of the great silent
agonies of the war. But a few basics, especially bread, were never
rationed during wartime, and the government's concern about
the nation's health and the numerous campaigns to improve diet
and food preparation surely helped many people make better use
of their rations. Workers' canteens and national restaurants produced well-balanced, inexpensive meals, although there was endless lamentation about the shortage of chips and deep-fried
foods, and when American soldiers were polled in March 1943
regarding what they liked least about Britain, the "terrible food"
came out near the top of the list.

The war threw people from differing classes into closer contact, and many of those in the upper social order were deeply

shocked by their encounters with the wretched life of the poor. The horrified reaction produced in stately country houses during 1940 by the arrival of evacuated East End children, some of whom had been sewn into their shabby clothing, is still proverbial in the United Kingdom. Because of this cultural encounter, as well as the need to raise morale and increase production, the government had to intervene more directly in matters of public health. Ration supplements for pregnant women were introduced, for example, and these quickly helped to halve the mortality rate during childbirth. The death rate from contagious disease, especially respiratory illnesses, was still shockingly high. While a third of a million Britons died from enemy action between 1939 and 1945, nearly twice as many (six hundred thousand) perished from tuberculosis, pneumonia, and bronchitis. The latter statistic was not age-adjusted, and since doctors then frequently attributed the deaths of elderly people to such conditions rather than follow the current practice of citing heart failure, the respiratory illness totals may be inflated. What is not exaggerated is that the figure of nearly two-thirds of a million respiratory illness deaths in Britain during the war was actually a *decrease* from that of the prewar period. While an average of 85,000 a year died of such illnesses in the seven years of the conflict, 96,000 succumbed in 1936 and 102,000 in 1937. World War II was in fact the period in which Britain took the first major step toward controlling respiratory illness.

Overall, the death rate did not rise during the war, and due to much more energetic public and military health programs, the incidence of many diseases actually fell, including, suprisingly, venereal disease. With contagious disease under better control, the ration providing a relatively healthy diet, and the general death rate constant, there was a rise in the number of live births after 1941 (the year with the lowest birthrate in modern British history). The ultimate result of all these trends was that austere wartime Britain actually experienced a significant increase in population of 1.4 million, at an annual growth rate a bit under half of one percent, for the years 1939–1945.

That the general health and nourishment of the British people improved during the period of wartime shortages was as puzzling a development to most Britons as the broader paradox that the more they sacrificed to win the war after 1941 the weaker their country became when compared with her major allies. These two overarching peculiarities in the wartime experience of the United Kingdom clinched the fact that British public opinion, like that in most other countries, turned its eye inward during the war and tended to view the earthshaking events of 1939–1945, as well as their likely postwar consequences, from an especially British perspective.

Although Britain was content to fight a cleaner war than some of the powers, the Ministry of Information Home Intelligence reports reveal that there was substantial satisfaction among the British people over the first massive "reprisal" bombings of German cities, such as that on Cologne in June 1942. British equanimity about the ways of war definitely did not extend to mistreatment of British troops by the enemy, and there was a great outburst of rage in October 1942 when the Germans chained British prisoners following the unsuccessful raid on Dieppe. Even so, aside from the families who had relatives engaged in the Pacific war or in Japanese prison camps, most people took virtually no interest in the Asian conflict. As a Ministry of Information official concluded in April 1943, the British public "knows little and cares less" about the fight against Japan. This attitude carried through right to the end, for V-J Day hardly produced a ripple in London during August 1945, when even as sensitive an observer as Harold Nicholson noted in his diary, "I have no feeling of elation at all."

The near-absence of interest in the Asian war had a significant effect on the way the British people viewed their allies. Aside from occasional expressions of regret at the enormous suffering borne by the Chinese people, the war in China and the fate of the Kuomintang and Communist regimes produced hardly a ripple in wartime Britain. Similarly, the bitter American and Anzac offensive campaigns fought against the Japanese between 1942 and 1945, as well as such important triumphs as that of Midway and Leyte Gulf, evoked little enthusiasm among Britons. The British view of America and Americans tended to focus on their bravado, their behavior in the United Kingdom, and the rather embarrassing fact that they were once again cast in the role of the rich, but slow-moving savior, stumbling forward to save Brittania. As is well known, extravagance and sexual enthusiasm ranked high on the British list of American vices. Complaints about the way white Americans mistreated black Americans and the enthusiasm with which black Americans courted young English girls went on eternally from the time the first United States troops landed in the United Kingdom. But it is significant that when the Ministry of Information made a special poll of British opinion about Americans in February 1942, the most frequently mentioned criticism was that they were too given to boasting and bragging. Later on in the war whenever American troops fought well, or seemed to do better than their British counterparts, as the Corregidor garrison did when compared with that of Singapore, respect for Americans rose sharply. In 1944 there was a quite general misty-eyed British respect for the jaunty way that American air crews went off to die over Germany. In the end, on the personal level what was most important was that though they were rather peculiar cousins, they were still part of the family, for the single measure which most successfully improved British opinion of the average American soldier was the billeting of United States troops in British homes.

Beyond these questions of personality and style, British worries about America were more serious and long-lasting. As early as August 1942 the public opinion polls were marked by some nervousness concerning the enormous power of the United States and the postwar intentions of its government. Side by side with apprehension about a possible American return to isolation, there was great hostility to the idea that Britain should play the role of "junior partner" to America after the war. Overall, the prospect "that we shall be dominated by the U.S.A." in the postwar period was most disturbing to Britons.

Since the primary wartime weakness that Britain was doing its best to disguise was in fact economic, the public was quite right in seeing the United States as a most serious potential threat to the United Kingdom. It was not merely that it was galling to have the loudmouth cousins coming on another crusade, but that they arrived with such an overwhelming display of wealth and prosperity that Britain's poverty and vulnerability were made obvious. That the greatest days of imperial domination were coming to an end was accepted with equanimity by the bulk of the British public. The polls showed that most people viewed the empire as an asset in wartime, but they held guilty feelings about it, and a full 72 percent of those responding to a BBC poll in March 1943 favored self-government for India either during or after the war. However, no one was prepared cheerfully to face further economic decline in addition to all the depression and wartime sacrifices, and that was the blatant forecast of postwar prospects which the rich and flashy American presence announced in every corner of the United Kingdom from 1942 on. British reaction to United States aid, and the overwhelming nature of American power, therefore had to be cautious and rather troubled.

But although it is largely forgotten today, no such doubts or reservations applied to the British people's initial response to the wartime achievements of the other great Allied power. The Ministry of Information Home Intelligence surveys, as well as every other barometer of public opinion, show that without exception, the most impassioned and long-lasting outpouring of British enthusiasm during the whole war was occasioned by the bravery and endurance of the Red Army and the Russian people. In the summer and fall of 1941, and again between the spring and winter of 1942, the most important item in nearly every Home Intelligence report was the public's intense worry about the fate of the Soviet army and the suffering of the Russian populace. Outpourings of public gratitude to the USSR were legion, as were expressions of remorse that Britain was not providing more aid to Russia, or taking enough of the load off the Red Army. The great outcry in favor of a second front, which racked Britain all through the middle period of the war, may have been orchestrated in part by the political Left, but it rested on a nearly universal British feeling that the United Kingdom was being saved by Russia and her army, and that every possible effort should be made to help them. This sentiment had nothing to do with sympathy for communism, because the same reports which contain the most effusive expressions of concern and gratitude to Soviet Russia are also replete with bitter condemnations of the British Communist party.

In the first line, the enthusiasm was an expression of gratitude, pure and simple. It also owed much to the fact that the Soviets were standing up to Hitler, and ultimately besting the Wehrmacht, despite a paucity of equipment and a need for great courage and sacrifice. Russia had no bottomless larder because, like the United Kingdom, she was fighting a battle of scarcity and endurance, and as the Ministry of Information was quick to note, the British people were "prepared to make any sacrifice to help Russia," while even after Pearl Harbor they had "no such disposition towards America." In fact, the Soviets repeatedly bested the Americans in the British public opinion polls. In 1942, a poll asked people to choose the "greatest living man," and as might have been expected, Churchill won in a walk. But it is noteworthy that Franklin Roosevelt, who Churchill himself was later to call "the greatest American friend that Britain ever found," lost second place by four percentage points to none other than Joseph Stalin. By the fall of 1943 when those polled were asked to rank which country had done the most to win the war, the USSR came first with 50 percent, and Britain was second with 42 percent. The United States received a trifling 3 percent, with even China securing 5 percent, and thus America was placed dead last among the Big Four Allied powers.

The British public's sympathetic identification with the Soviet Union carried with it a concomitant concern that the American and British governments should not try to deprive Russia of her fair share of the fruits of victory. Such sentiments were especially

strong in 1942 and 1943, and were paralleled by doubts about
the wisdom of exclusively Anglo-American wartime meetings.
The Home Intelligence reports indicate that there was a significant current of opinion that felt that the Soviets should have
been represented at such Churchill-Roosevelt summit conferences as Casablanca and Quebec.

Only very slowly and reluctantly did the original curiosity
about life in the Soviet Union, and the passion for all things
Russian, come to be colored by a trace of nervousness about
Soviet intentions and behavior. In May 1943, the Home Intelligence reports revealed general relief at the Soviet abolition of
the Comintern, and there were also signs of suspicion that the
Soviets had indeed had a hand in the Katyn massacre of Polish
officers, just as the Nazis had alleged. But even then, there was
nothing approaching a wholesale reversal of sympathies. In fact,
the Ministry of Information found that the dominant public
reaction toward the Katyn affair was the feeling that Poland
"should subordinate her interests to those of her Allies," and as
late as November 1943, it was the conduct of Polish troops
training in Britain which occasioned some of the public's most
hostile remarks. In part this was because the "voicing of strong
anti-Russian sentiments" by the Poles had been very "ill-
received" by Scottish civilians living near their training camps.

Perhaps the most compelling indication of the state of popular
concern in the last stage of the war is a section of the Home
Intelligence report for the first week of September 1944 headed,
"What interests the British people most?" In reply to that question, 59 percent of the respondents chose the Anglo-American
advance in France and Belgium, while 30 percent selected other
military and British domestic matters, and 6 percent picked the
capitulation of Rumania. The Far Eastern war, as usual, garnered less than 1 percent, as did "Russo Polish relations with
Warsaw," i.e., the failure of the Red Army to advance and aid
the Polish resistance fighters who were being butchered by the
Nazis in the Polish capital. In face of such hard evidence regarding the public's relative lack of interest even in the Warsaw inci-

dent, which in the cold war era would be viewed as a *cause célèbre* of cynical Soviet repression, one may safely conclude that at least up to the fall of 1944, at a time when the Soviet advance into Eastern Europe was making Churchill so nervous that he had begun to lecture President Roosevelt about its dangers, the British people had not replaced their admiration and gratitude toward the Red Army with anything remotely resembling cold war fears and suspicions.

The deep and long-lingering impact of the Soviet Union's wartime achievements may also be seen intertwined within the extended discussions of postwar domestic reform that swept over the United Kingdom during the war. It was obvious throughout the conflict that Winston Churchill was extremely popular as a war leader, but equally clear that his popularity did not provide a reliable clue to what the public wanted Britain to be like once the fighting stopped. As Tom Harrison has observed, the prime minister was "a sort of intellectual deep shelter," to be used "for emergency protection only." The war experience had definitely not pushed the government sharply in the direction of Tory policies. On the contrary, the appearance of the Beveridge Report in December 1942 calling for significant social changes, high levels of employment, and the creation of some form of welfare state showed that the war cabinet's main domestic thrust was moving in the direction of reforms long favored by Labour, and away from the laissez-faire policies of the 1930s.

Polls taken during the year prior to the issuance of the Beveridge Report also revealed currents of public opinion flowing in the same direction. Seventy-one percent of those questioned in a June 1942 survey favored significant nationalization of industries and (or) public utilities, and even 60 percent of the respondents who described themselves as upper class countenanced some such government ownership. Similarly, a November 1942 Home Intelligence summary of opinion in the southwest region of the country indicated that the public's three main postwar concerns were a desire to punish Germany, the prevention of another war, and maintenance of high levels of employment.

But the most intriguing expression of the public's desire for reform at home had appeared in very early 1942. In February, the Home Intelligence reports found that sympathy for "a kind of home-made socialism" was sweeping the country. So strong was this trend that the Ministry of Information prepared a special secret summary of the phenomenon in March. In region after region, the Home Intelligence Division found, there was widespread " 'revulsion' against 'vested interests,' 'privilege' and what is referred to as 'the old gang.' " Coupled with this was "a general agreement that 'things are going to be different after the war.' " The major spur for this sentiment came only in part from Britain's wartime troubles and prewar inequalities. "Admiration for Russia," "the success of Russia," and the "ruthless speed of Russia's dictatorship" were cited repeatedly as the catalysts which had brought forth this public cry for reform. A large block of the British population, which "until recently regarded the Russians as blood-thirsty Bolsheviks," had come around to the position "that it would be a good thing if something along the same lines were introduced in this country." "The apparent unity, strength and purposefulness of the Soviets" seemed to show up what many Britons saw as "our own inefficiency" and "constant failures." Even though the willingness of some people to use "methods approximating dictatorship" if necessary to implement "home grown socialism" did not mean that large numbers of Britons had given up on democracy in 1942, a great many did want "drastic changes" that would secure "greater social security after the war" and permanently improve postwar Britain.

Surely by the time of V-E Day in 1945, the part that admiration for Russia and gratitude for her wartime sacrifices had played in awakening a British desire for basic change tended to slip a notch in the public's consciousness. The honor roll of British military victories from Egypt to the beaches of Normandy also did much to gild over with a sense of triumph the feelings of failure and inadequacy which had clung to Britain throughout so much of the conflict. At war's end, when Montgomery of Alamein strode forth in all his glory, it was possible to repress for a moment the realization that during most of the struggle, the experience of the whole nation had been akin to that of the eight-year-old Sheffield girl who, in December 1945, merely asked Father Christmas "for anything you can spare."

However, the election of 1945 showed that the British people had grasped the basic lessons which the war had been teaching them. It was not the efficacy of the system which had pulled the country through, but the people's endurance and self-denial. The United Kingdom had not been reduced to total dependence on the United States merely because the nation's belt had been tightened to the final notch, the government had used central planning to allocate the meager goods available, and the Soviet Union had shouldered so much of the burden of destroying Nazism. But it had been a very close thing. At home and in the empire, the country had taken on the appearance of a jumble sale without any buyers, and the postwar economic prospects looked dim indeed.

After six years of this kind of war, the people of Britain believed that they had little left to lose and much to gain from "drastic changes" at home. At the same time—consciously or subconsciously—the majority seem to have sensed that Britain had slipped in relative political and economic power in relation to both the United States and the Soviet Union. Though some leaders in Whitehall advocated an immediate postwar policy of standing tall vis-à-vis both the Americans and the Russians, most of the public realized that peace and stability definitely were in the interest of a weakening Britain and that Allied great power cooperation would constitute the best of all possible postwar worlds for the United Kingdom.

In July 1945 they therefore gave the Labour party a vast electoral mandate to create a new Britain which through fundamental reforms would, they hoped, make good the promises of "the people's war" and bring the country back to a front rank position in prosperity, social justice and international influence.

3

The USSR in World War II

Some day soon there will be a parade on our street.

Soviet Order of the Day
November 1942

THE Second World War did not come to the Soviet Union through a series of "incidents," followed by expanding military operations, as had happened in China. Nor did Hitler's legions move on the USSR by stepping-stone campaigns in an expanding war, such as those which had taken the Nazis through Poland, Scandinavia, the Low Countries, and France before ultimately bringing them to Britain's Channel frontier.

During the first twenty-one months of the European war, the Soviet Union had actually been able to fiddle rather pleasantly while others burned. Eastern Poland had been occupied with little Soviet loss in September 1939, and after sharp fighting, and not a little humiliation, Finland was also overcome in a border war by early 1940. There were some rather rough diplomatic scrapes within the sordid Nazi-Soviet pact in 1940–1941, and in late summer 1939, sharp frontier clashes occurred with the Japanese. But viewed in the context of the diplomatic difficulties which had prevailed during the 1930s, and the increased pressures for change which inevitably followed the outbreak of war, Russia seemed to have done very well for herself. So well, in fact, that the supreme Soviet leader managed to persuade himself in June 1941 that the huge force of Wehrmacht troops stacked along Russia's western border was merely another ploy in Hitler's eternal diplomatic poker game.

The three large German army groups that exploded into the Soviet Union in the early hours of 22 June 1941 fell upon a country of 190 million people, a country sufficiently developed to have 60 percent of its population in urban centers, and dynamic enough to have leapt into the ranks of the world's greatest industrial producers in the two decades following the Revolution. But the USSR had not established itself as a great power of worldwide influence prior to Hitler's attack. The Soviet Union's revolutionary creed, when combined with Western fears and suspicions, had been enough to make the USSR a thing apart, and despite a periodic desire in many quarters to form united fronts with the USSR against fascism, the caution of the West and the repressiveness of Stalin's rule had still left a wide gap between Moscow and the rest of the world's governments.

In June 1941 the USSR did possess a large military force, including a substantial combat air service, and an army numbering approximately 4.2 million men. But the Soviet armed forces were hobbled by much outmoded equipment, obsolete transport, and poor deployment, while their morale and efficiency were further impaired by the savage officer purges that had occurred in the late 1930s. Overall, as Churchill observed on the eve of the German attack, the USSR and its army were seen by the outside world as bodies composed in equal parts of mystery, riddle, and enigma.

But Hitler was not a man to patiently tolerate puzzling questions, and on 22 June 1941 he insisted on kicking in the front door of what he himself had characterized as "a dark room." Having achieved complete surprise, the Wehrmacht had little difficulty inflicting extremely heavy losses on the Soviet border

formations, and thereby clearing the way for the panzers to make
the deep penetrations that had brought decisive German triumphs in every previous campaign. Stalin was apparently as
staggered by the surprise attack and the speed of the German
advance as were his armies, and for a moment seems to have
given up hope. Foreign observers tended to believe that having
gotten the jump, Hitler would make short work of the USSR. A
British diplomatic official asked rhetorically on the day of the
invasion, "I wonder how long the bolsh can hold up. A month
or so?"

All through the summer of 1941, the German army swept forward, followed by units of the SS *Einsatzgruppen* ruthlessly carrying out their orders to massacre all Communists, Jews, gypsies,
"and other undesirables." Enormous battles of encirclement were
fought, in every one of which the Germans triumphed during the
first months of the campaign. But Red Army units were rapidly
reorganized, the high command purged of the incompetent and
the unlucky, and new units were formed to create additional defensive lines for every one that fell to the enemy. Nazi brutality,
coupled with Russian nationalism and the innovative vigor of the
Soviet authorities, stiffened the defense, and the Germans soon
discovered that they were immersed in a near-holy war, in which
even encircled Red Army units seldom gave up without a bitter
fight. Gradually, foreign observers began to hope that perhaps
Hitler's prediction of the Red regime collapsing "like a house of
cards" might not be realized. By late July, the Foreign Office
official who had been so ready to write off the Soviets in June
wondered aloud "if it is possible they could go on till the autumn,
in which case it would be a blow from which I don't believe the
Boches could rally."

The Soviets had to go on well beyond the autumn, however.
Only their great defensive victory in the bitter December battle
before Moscow made it clear that Hitler had failed in his effort
to destroy Soviet Russia with a single blow. But even then, the
Fuehrer was not ready to throw in his hand. After holding on
through the glacial Russian winter, Hitler made a second at-

tempt to secure total victory, tearing great provinces out of southern Russia in the spring and summer of 1942. The turning point came with the Soviet triumph at Stalingrad in late 1942 and early 1943, when the whole of the German Sixth Army was killed or captured, and the Wehrmacht's strategic offensive power in the East was finally broken. With the follow-up Soviet victory at Kursk in July 1943, the remainder of the Eastern campaign consisted of a series of massive Russian offensive drives which gradually pushed the Germans westward. Not until late 1944 was the Wehrmacht finally driven from Soviet soil, however, three and a half years after the surprise attack of 22 June 1941.

The USSR paid a prodigious economic price during those forty-two months of war, since it was fought with unparalleled ferocity, scorched-earth retreats, and a multitude of massacres by the Germans. At war's end, statisticians might bring forth a money figure to express the cost of the conflict to the Soviet Union—a popular one in the West was the equivalent of 93 billion United States dollars—but the wartime economic loss was much greater than that.

The Soviet Union had been very vulnerable economically in June 1941, despite her high gross output ranking among the world powers. Given her enormous size and huge population, her per capita industrial and agricultural production were still quite low, and much of her rich resource base remained undeveloped. Furthermore, the speed with which industrialization had been pushed in the five-year plan era of the late 1920s and 1930s had so emphasized first heavy industry, and then arms production, that there were serious shortages and underdeveloped sectors, especially in agriculture and light industry. When these deficiencies were combined with the country's enormous natural obstacles to efficient transportation, and the extreme cold that permanently gripped the whole northeastern region, it is easy to see how the Nazi invasion dealt a near-mortal blow to the Soviet economy. The already overstretched society was forced to give up most of its prime production areas, evacuate equipment and labor, and at the same time draw every possible man into the armed forces.

By early 1942, the Soviet national income and gross national product had fallen one-third below the prewar level. At that point, Soviet production of coal was off 57 percent, pig iron 68 percent, steel 58 percent, and aluminum 60 percent. Total industrial output was down at least 33 percent. Despite the extreme wartime exertion and aid from the West, only about one-half of this industrial output loss had been recovered by the end of the war.

The wartime blow to Soviet agriculture was at least as severe. In the first four months of the conflict, the USSR lost productive areas that had yielded 38 percent of her prewar grain and cattle, 54 percent of her potatoes, and 84 percent of her sugar. Almost two-thirds of the gross agricultural product was gone by 1942, and at war's end, agricultural production was still off 40 percent, and the area sown in the "victory year" of 1945 was 10 percent less than that for 1940–1941. Grain production, the single most vital item in the whole Russian economy, was especially hard hit; the 1945 output being less than half that in the last year of peace. The nation's precious stock of farm equipment, one of the proudest accomplishments of the five-year plan era, was drastically reduced. By V-E Day, over 25 percent of Soviet agricultural tractors and 70 percent of farm lorries had been destroyed. To make matters worse, as had happened repeatedly in Soviet economic history, agriculture received an ever-smaller portion of the nation's capital investment as the war went on. In 1940 there had theoretically been at least one ruble invested in agriculture for every two rubles which went to industry. But by 1945, the annual investment in industry had jumped to four and a half times that for agriculture, thus leaving the Soviet economy with an even more severe economic imbalance than had existed before the war.

Soviet economic losses would have been infinitely greater if it had not been for the massive 1941 evacuation of manpower and equipment to the eastern industrial complex in the Ural Mountains and beyond. This heroic achievement, produced by the devotion and suffering of the Soviet people in the face of icy weather and a minimum of transport, was one of the decisive factors which denied success to Hitler. But to make it effective, it was necessary to pour the bulk of available investment capital into this area. In 1942–1943, nearly 75 percent of the productive investment of the Soviet Union was made in the eastern region (the Urals, Transcaucasia, and Siberia), which resulted in a 560 percent production increase there between 1940 and 1943. This struck a great blow for Allied victory, but it should be noted that to get its productive plant out of the hands of the Germans, the Soviet Union had moved it into a remote area where inclement weather and enormous distances would act as drags on the country's postwar economic efficiency.

Therefore, just as had happened to Britain and China, the war forced the Soviet productive economy into patterns which were definitely not in its long-term interest. But such parallels should not detract attention from the fact that Soviet wartime economic losses were of a magnitude beyond the experience of every other Allied country. Economic indicators which were important in the wartime experience of nations like the United States and Britain, such as the level of personal savings and the balance of payments, shrink into insignificance when applied to Soviet Russia. It is true that the Soviet balance of payments dipped sharply to the down side during the war, and that personal savings also fell in Russia while they rose sharply in Britain and America. But such matters were trivial for a country that had been compelled to pursue a scorched-earth policy with "almost suicidal sincerity." The USSR routinely demolished mighty edifices such as the great Zaporozhe Dam on the Dnieper—analogous to Hoover Dam or Grand Coulee—which had been built at such cost and proclaimed "engineering masterpieces of the proletarian revolution." Four decades after the war, there are no grounds (aside from syntax) to quarrel with the Soviet economic historian who summed up Russia's economic losses by declaring that "never in past history . . . has any capitalist country suffered losses so great and destruction so wanton at the hands of an invader as our country."

Enormous though Soviet Russia's economic losses were, the scale of her human sacrifice was even greater, and much more horrific. The Soviet military forces lost approximately ten million dead between 1941 and 1945, one-third of them perishing in what is politely referred to as German "captivity." A further ten million Soviet civilians were killed in the course of the war, bringing the USSR's total wartime fatalities to over 10 percent of the nation's population. "Privation," including the harshness of wartime conditions and the Nazi determination to reduce Russia's population by starvation and mass execution, was the biggest cause of civilian deaths. As one would expect in light of Nazi extermination policies in the occupied areas, the shortage of food in urban centers was the most important factor in "privation." Eight out of ten Soviet wartime civilian fatalities occurred in urban rather than rural areas, a distribution almost exactly the reverse of that for China.

The effects of the gigantic wartime Soviet losses lingered on long after the war, not only in the attitudes and feelings of the survivors but in hard demographic statistics. The birthrate obviously fell sharply during the war due to the heavy losses among young males, and this slump was only partially reversed in the immediate postwar period. There was no war or postwar baby boom in Soviet Russia comparable to that in the United States and Britain. In 1950, the Soviet population was still twelve million below what it had been in 1939. Nine years later there were nearly two Russian women for every man over the age of thirty-five, and even in 1970, the female population of the USSR exceeded the male by 20 million.

The human cost of the war to Soviet Russia was so immense and long-lasting, that one must struggle to find a way to express its magnitude. Perhaps the best indicator, though even it is inadequate, is to remember that of the fifty-five million people in the world who were killed by World War II, nearly 35 percent of them were Russians.

Therefore, the people of the Soviet Union had every right to mourn the war both for the devastation that it brought to their country and the murderous toll it left in its wake. But there were also strong reasons for national pride. Despite all the human and material losses, the problems and the suffering, the people of the USSR played a major part in the great increase of war production which helped seal the Allied victory. Soviet munitions production rose nearly 300 percent between 1940 and 1944, a rate of growth well below that of the United States, but equal to that of Britain or Germany. The gross munitions production of the USSR exceeded that of Britain and at least equalled that of Germany in every year of the war. In the years 1943 and 1944, her monthly production of aircraft may have approached three thousand, and that of tanks and self-propelled guns, two thousand. Again, the self-sacrifice of the Soviet people deserves the major credit for this productive achievement, for tens of thousands of people literally gave their lives to provide the Red Army with the necessary weapons of war. But the government deserves a share of the credit as well, for whatever criticisms may be made in the West about the efficiency of the postwar Soviet economic system, it remains true that once the initial problems had been overcome, the Russian wartime armaments program worked very well. Nor is it appropriate to stress the deficiencies, which undoubtedly existed, in some Soviet weapons systems without noting that by at least 1943, the Red Army had the best heavy tanks and ground rocket launchers in the world. Like the United States, and in sharp contrast to Nazi Germany, the Soviet Union made maximum use of the potentiality of assembly-line production. Every model of Soviet tank built during the war was mounted on one of only two tank chassis, the KV and the T-34. This permitted maximum output during all phases of the war, and helped make possible the production of twenty-two thousand T-34 heavy tanks in 1944 alone.

Of course, as Western commentators have tended to emphasize, the USSR was in part able to concentrate so much of its productive effort on heavy weapons because of economic assistance received from Britain and the United States. So inflated was the view of lend-lease aid to Russia held in the United States during the war that an October 1944 public opinion poll revealed that 59 percent of the respondents believed that most Soviet tanks and planes had been produced in the United States or Britain. The eighteen thousand Western combat planes which were sent to the USSR were important to the Red Air Force, and Western light and medium tanks were also helpful. But the vast majority of Russian combat aircraft were produced in the USSR, and Soviet heavy tanks were so plentiful, and of such high quality, that Western shipments of armor were never more than marginally important supplements.

The USSR received, in addition to substantial aid from Britain, a wartime total of eleven billion dollars in lend-lease assistance. Although only a third of what went to Britain and the Commonwealth, this lend-lease aid to Russia constituted 25 percent of all such shipments and made up 3 percent of America's total disbursement for the war. The bulk of the material sent to Russia consisted of food, medical supplies, technical and transportation equipment, plus raw materials. American trucks were a vital element in giving the Red Army offensive mobility, and there is little question that without Western support the death toll in Russia would have been much higher, the war a great deal longer, and the prospects of Allied victory distinctly dimmer. The volume and importance of Western assistance was great enough to bring forth a long article of praise and thanks from the usually tight-lipped editors of *Pravda* in 1944, and it introduced a number of Americanisms into the Russian language, including "antifreeze," "pickup" (as in small truck), and "Willys" (the original manufacturer of the ubiquitous Jeep).

However, Western aid was only supplemental to the Soviet's own sacrifice and achievement. The USSR kept on its feet and won the great battle of Moscow in December 1941—arguably the most important single battle of the war—without any American aid. Furthermore, overemphasis on lend-lease assistance tends to distract attention from the basic fact that it was the Red

Army which made far and away the greatest contribution to the destruction of the German Wehrmacht. On this matter the statistical picture is crystal-clear. During the Second World War, the German armed forces lost a total of 180,000 killed and 530,000 missing in all theaters in which they were engaged against the Western powers; that is, in North Africa, Italy, and the Western front following D Day. But in the East, against the Red Army, 1,419,000 German soldiers were killed and another 907,000 went missing. Therefore at least 85 percent of all German military fatalities occurred at the hands of the Red Army, and 60 percent of the Germans who went missing were due to the Red Army as well. Westerners, then and since, have never clearly recognized who did the bulk of the real dirty work in smashing Hitler's power. But the Russians certainly have, and so did all Germans, for as a Wehrmacht veteran once observed, "The Eastern Front! There was something about the words when you told people you were going there, it was as if you admitted some fatal disease."

To have struck such terror into the hearts of so ruthless an enemy unquestionably brought great satisfaction to the citizens of the Soviet Union and gave them some compensation for their endless losses. The Soviet citizenry also benefited from the fact that the autocracy was compelled to ease controls somewhat in order to achieve maximum mobilization. Wisps of popular participation were allowed in, and the party and police stranglehold was slightly relaxed, as the power and influence of managers, engineers, and army officers rose sharply. Even the composition of the Communist executive committees showed marks of change. Until 1939, roughly three-fourths of such members had educational attainments that reflected the monopoly of office enjoyed by the intelligentsia and the proletariat. Their education was sharply divided between that of the university-trained elite on one hand (19 percent) and those having modest schooling on the other (50 percent), with very little in the middle. By the immediate postwar period however, the percentage of Central Committee members with a university education had been reduced to

7 percent and those with a secondary education or less to 13 percent, while the remaining 80 percent were graduates of various higher technical, political, or military training institutions.

Such changes might be viewed by some as the rise of something approximating a technocratic middle class, and thus a relative loss of power for "real" workers. But during the war, the overwhelming popular reaction in Russia seems to have been that this shift in favor of the technocrat was not only necessary for the war effort, but was one of a series of changes which offered prospects of greater social flexibility and openness. For paradoxical as it may seem, the dominant Russian attitude arising out of the dark days of wartime suffering and disaster was one of grim optimism. As a Soviet citizen retrospectively observed about the mood of 1941:

Even those of us who knew that our government was wicked . . . felt that we must fight. Because every Russian who had lived through the Revolution and the thirties had felt a breeze of hope, for the first time in the history of our people. We were like the bud at the tip of a root which has wound its way for centuries under rocky soil. We felt ourselves to be within inches of the open sky. We knew that we would die, of course. But our children would inherit two things: a land free of the invader, and time in which the progressive ideals of Communism might emerge.

The European war drew to a close in 1945 amid a great upsurge of Russian pride and sense of triumph. Although generous expressions of gratitude for Western assistance to the common cause were made by individual Russians, and the Soviet authorities subsequently even saw fit to name a street in Yalta for Franklin Roosevelt—a very rare honor—there was an understandable tendency for the Soviet people to see V-E Day as their victory and to be highly sensitive about any Allied failure to acknowledge their paramount role. Praise in abundance for the Soviet achievement flowed forth from the Western European resistance movement during the final years of the conflict, and as we have seen, admiration and gratitude characterized the dominant British reaction as well. But things were rather different in the United States, and here and there within the British government establishment.

Although it is too often forgotten, the Eastern and Western command structures of the Allied coalition were never integrated. The much-vaunted Combined Chiefs of Staff system was restricted to the British and the Americans, and the Soviets were never members. Many civil and military missions were exchanged between East and West, but there was no high-level integrated control organization, and in fact on only two occasions did Joseph Stalin and Franklin Roosevelt ever meet face to face.

The physical and organizational gap between East and West, along with the multitude of prewar hostilities and tensions, provided a fertile soil for distrust and apprehension. Furthermore, the Nazis, who always believed that the Allied coalition was inherently unstable, were provided with ample opportunities to try to swell doubts and mistrust. Throughout the war Joseph Goebbels poured out a torrent of propaganda to fan capitalist and Communist suspicion. By 1945 the German people, as well as those in the Nazi-occupied territories, had been provided with a steady diet of such stories for four years, and the personnel of the Allied armies had received a heavy ration of the same kind from enemy broadcasts and leaflets during the final two to three years of the war.

The residue of the Nazis' anti-Soviet propaganda effort probably produced its main fruit long after Goebbels and Hitler were dead and gone, but enough signs of anti-Soviet sentiment had manifested themselves in the Western countries even prior to 22 June 1941 to warm the heart of any Nazi propagandist. Especially in the United States, suspicion of communism and the Soviet Union was slow to recede, although the public opinion polls always revealed that large majorities favored the USSR in any hypothetical or real conflict with Nazi Germany. During the pre–Pearl Harbor period, those questioned by the major polling organizations displayed an equally strong hostility to Communists and Nazis in the United States, and neither the German attack on Russia nor the United States's entry into the war did anything to lessen significantly the American tendency to favor employing harsh repressive measures against the American Communist party.

That 99 percent of Americans polled in December 1939 favored Finland over the USSR should occasion no surprise, but that 34 percent of those questioned in August 1941 would have approved any peace in which Nazi Germany was limited to the conquests it had made at the expense of the USSR is another matter. In October 1941, one-third of the Americans questioned still felt that Nazis and Soviets were equally bad, and another third only thought the USSR was "slightly better" than Nazi Germany.

The most important factor which finally moved American opinion in a pro-Soviet direction was the Red Army's success in holding, and then hurling back, the Nazi invader in 1941 and 1942. But unlike British opinion, that of the United States shifted position in a much more leisurely manner, in part because during the first five months of the Nazi-Soviet conflict the United States was not itself a belligerent, and Americans only felt themselves to be marginally vulnerable. Since President Roosevelt cautiously delayed approving lend-lease assistance to Russia until November 1941, the very moment when it appeared that the Red Army might hold in front of Moscow, United States opinion was given an opportunity to move in the direction of sympathy for the USSR on the cheap, for until November 1941 cheering for Russia did not cost the American taxpayer one penny. By October 1941, the opinion polls revealed that two-thirds of those questioned favored at least some assistance to the USSR, but of this group two-thirds wanted to restrict the aid to just enough to "help beat Hitler," while only some 20 percent favored "a full partnership" with the USSR.

After Pearl Harbor, and the bloodying of American forces in the initial Pacific battles, United States enthusiasm for the USSR rose sharply. But the United States was never swept by the kind of pro-Russian frenzy that flowed through Britain and most of Nazi-occupied Europe. The scale of Russian suffering, and the degree to which the Allied victory over Nazi Germany was due to the Soviet Union, never penetrated deeply into the American consciousness. Furthermore, United States opinion remained doubtful about Soviet postwar intentions. Although expressions of trust in the USSR rose and fell during different phases of the conflict, there always remained a strong minority of about one-third among those questioned in the public opinion polls who harbored great suspicion of Soviet Russia. This coolness cannot be simply pinned on the old clichés about upper-class opinion or the alleged anti-Soviet fanaticism of Roman Catholics, for in some polls, members of higher-income groups showed themselves the most willing to recognize Soviet Russia as an equal partner, and in the only clear polling indication we have, a majority of the Catholic respondents in January 1943 indicated that they trusted the postwar intentions of the Soviet Union.

That the roots of American reserve toward the USSR went deeper and broader than class membership or religious affiliation is indicated by the wording of the basic Gallup Poll question on this subject that was used during the last three years of the war. The question, which was first employed in March 1942, and then was repeated at short intervals until mid-1945, read, "Can the U.S.S.R. be trusted to cooperate with us after the war?" Obviously, the egocentric form of this question indicates that the war had done little or nothing to shake American self-confidence, and that the American people would therefore always have great difficulty grasping who had done what during the conflict, or understanding what other countries might think were their legitimate claims at the peace table. Consequently it should come as no surprise that even three months after the decisive battle of Moscow, only one-half of the Americans polled thought that the Soviets could be "trusted to cooperate with us" in the postwar world.

Yet it would be silly to assert that American suspicion of the USSR was merely the result of rampant provincialism, or that the division of the Allied command structure into Eastern and Western halves was due solely to blindness or dark intentions in the West. Every Western doubt and self-centered obsession was easily matched by another in the East. The battle slogan announced by *Pravda* on 24 June 1941, "For our Country, For Stalin, Forward!" put the problem perfectly, for this was Stalin's Russia, and Stalin's war, as well as that of the Soviet people. Every foreign opinion regarding Russia during the war, whether it was warm or cool, was probably conditioned more by the Russian-Stalinist duality than by any other factor.

Joseph Vissarionovich Djugashvili was an extraordinarily complicated man, largely molded by the complex revolutionary and intra-Communist party struggles of the period 1900–1927. As a revolutionary, and especially in his successful struggle to succeed Lenin, Stalin displayed great cunning and a complete mastery of the arts of political maneuver, dissimulation, and ruthlessness. He won the great battles against Trotsky, Bukharin, etc., which were fought out within the doctrinal and organizational maze of the Communist party of the Soviet Union, because he used his own skills and organizational opportunities so adroitly, and also because he found Marxist-Leninist formulas that would help him gain dominance over the party and the state. In these struggles there were no fixed ground rules and few ideological boundary posts, for as Lenin had indicated, and Stalin followed through with enthusiasm, within broad limits, the correct Marxist-Leninist line at any moment was whatever the most successful combatant said it was. Success established orthodoxy, failure demonstrated deviation, which in turn made inevitable the loss of legitimacy. By the late 1920s, Joseph Stalin had secured absolute control over the USSR, and then while "building socialism in one country," went forward to make Soviet society as intricate and convoluted as he was himself. For, as Adam Ulam has observed, though he had secured "powers undreamed of by the rulers of any other state," Stalin was "never able to achieve security," because there was little to underpin the system except success itself.

Small wonder, then, that Stalin's Russia was characterized by obsessive controls over real, possible, or mythical enemies, and that deception and propaganda were developed into high arts. To maintain his power and to justify the system he had created, Stalin had to show concrete evidence of socioeconomic progress, as in the five-year plans, and at the same time repress or emasculate all remotely possible challenges to his own supremacy and power.

The Stalinist order lasted in varying forms for thirty years, primarily because its creator played his own game so well and usually managed to keep a grip on the distinction between those who actually were enemies of his system and those who were merely branded as enemies to secure some short- or long-term advantage. Maintenance of the distinction between what Ulam has called "real reality" and "objective reality" was the most important foundation of Stalinism. This was the difference between what someone actually did or intended to do, and what his class or factional background should "objectively" incline him to do whether he was aware of it or not. In the latter category, kulaks or former associates of Trotsky posed permanent "objective" dangers to Stalinism, for even if the individuals concerned had never had a "real" subversive thought, under certain conditions the "objective" forces of class or faction that had shaped them could turn them into dangerous enemies of the system. Stalinism was the commitment to destroy every "objective" threat in embryonic form *before* it manifested itself as a "real" danger. To this end, no charge was so absurd that it would collapse of its own weight. In the 1930s, spies and traitors were "unmasked" in the most unlikely places, and confessions of "wrecking," such as the one in the Bukharin trial when a plant manager admitted to mixing together nails and butter to sabotage his own production program, became a daily routine. Any gesture, any thought, could easily acquire enough sinister significance to attract the attention of the security services, which once prompted Osip Mandelstam to remark blackly to his wife that they should be happy to live in a country in which literature was thought to be really important, for where else were people killed for writing poetry?

The system placed an enormous burden of paranoia on all Soviet citizens, but probably most of all on Joseph Stalin himself. Therefore it is necessary to consider how Stalinism, and its concomitant psychological pressures, put a distinctive stamp on wartime Russia. The concentration of power and the "cult of personality" always threatened to place a screen of "objectivity" between Stalin and simple reality. It is likely that the Germans achieved complete surprise on 22 June 1941 because Stalin was having so much difficulty distinguishing between "objective" and "real" dangers, and was so unwilling to listen to his advisers that he did not "really" see Operation Barbarossa coming until the Germans hit him in the face.

Stalin's obsessive fascination with plot and counterplot had led him on the eve of war into a multitude of domestic atrocities such as the great purges, which seriously weakened the country's ability to resist. Furthermore, his crowning achievement in cynical international politics, the Nazi-Soviet Pact of August 1939, went a long way toward permanently alienating not only the Soviet's "natural" foreign enemies on the political Right, but also many "friendly" Socialists and a large number of Communists who quit the party when they were ordered to snuggle up with the Nazis. Unquestionably, many of the deepest suspicions of the USSR, which hung on during the war in the United States and elsewhere, owed a great deal to Stalin's prewar obsessions, cynicism, and brutality.

In the USSR as well, the legacy of past repressions did not instantly disappear in June 1941. Capitalists, peasants, bureaucrats, intellectuals, military officers, and various factions of the party had all been brutally purged at one time or another in the prewar period. Survivors had learned to keep their heads down, and even the wartime emergency was not in itself enough to make many people eager to look obvious or assertive.

That large numbers of people abroad were gradually prepared

to let bygones be bygones, and that within Russia an even larger number chose to step forward and help win the war, was occasioned by more than Soviet governmental pressure, Russian nationalism, and the monstrosities perpetrated by the Nazis. It owed a great deal to the way Stalin chose to deal with the wartime crisis. After his initial shock following the German attack of 22 June, he righted himself, and by an inordinate act of will chose to face the crisis as a battle for survival, and to keep the waging of the war predominantly within the realm of "real" reality. He continued to be "stubborn, sharp, suspicious," and certainly remained "an extraordinarily devious man," but in general he managed to shelve overt attacks on "objective" dangers and "objective" enemies for the duration. The NKVD was mainly put to work moving virtually the whole German, and much of the Muslim population to the East, and coping with "real" slackers, spies, and saboteurs, as well as carrying on foreign intelligence operations and providing support for Soviet partisan warfare. Stalin donned the mantle of a nationalist, a concerned father of his country, and of a man prepared to work hard to guarantee that everything possible was done to bring victory. Technicians and managers were granted extensive privileges, because efficiency and inventiveness actually was desired, and output did become king.

Following a shaky start, Stalin learned to accept most of the "real" realities of the military trade, and he generally kept his eye on the practical issues of modern warfare. By late 1942 he apparently came to feel some trust and confidence in his generals, and treated them with more respect. Officers' authority was increased, the power of political commissars was periodically curtailed, and tsarist-type officer shoulder boards were introduced into the Red Army. As commander in chief, Stalin gradually became more knowledgeable about modern warfare. So much so that General Alan Brooke, who studied him in action at Teheran, concluded that he had a military brain of the highest caliber, and that "in this respect he stood out compared with Roosevelt and Churchill."

But even in his wartime military activity, the manifestations of personal secrecy and remoteness never left him. For the first six months of the war his nighttime headquarters was buried deep underground in the Kirovskaia subway station, where his privacy was maintained by plywood partitions, and no trains were allowed to stop. Later, during such decisive battles as Stalingrad and Kursk, as well as the triumphal campaigns in which the Red Army swept the Nazis from Russian soil, Stalin never went near the front, and made no personal inspections. On only one occasion during the whole war did he even visit a rear-area headquarters, and that was a brief visit to a quiet sector headquarters in August 1943, where he starred in a wartime propaganda film. Thus Khrushchev's assertion that Stalin never visited a peasant village after 1928, despite the ravages of the purges and the five-year plans, was paralleled by the Soviet dictator's refusal to observe the wartime battles, or gauge the effects of his orders with his own eyes. He played within "real" military reality during the war, but his remoteness and determination to remain hidden continued unchanged. Above all, his horror at being completely alone seems never to have left him; he was always highly suspicious of unfamiliar faces and insisted on being surrounded by his cronies.

Yet in performing his diplomatic functions, as with his achievements as commander in chief, Stalin's obsession with remoteness did not seriously impede his ability to function effectively in wartime. Stepping past the "universal bias against the outside world" which characterized the Soviet leadership, he chose to act vigorously on a "real" basis in his dealings with the Western Allies. He accepted Western aid, worked out a tough give-and-take relationship with Western leaders, and in September 1941 even went so far as to ask that Western troops be stationed in the Soviet Union. At every point in East-West wartime relations, Stalin showed himself to be a very tough and perceptive negotiator. Anyone examining the texts of the summit meetings at Teheran and Yalta must be impressed by his grasp of factual detail, ability to sift wheat from chaff, and the quick decisiveness with which he could raise a protest or clinch a deal.

Professor Mastny is surely correct when he says that Stalin's mind was so subtle, and his devotion to "objective" reality so fundamental, that he often studied Western behavior too intently and found signs which were not there. But Stalin understood the social-political aspects of war, and put into practice what he knew. He once remarked to Djilas that big wars were the affairs of great powers and that "whoever occupies a territory also imposes on it his own social system." In World War II that was true, although the brutality of its implementation surely varied sharply from one great power to another. Stalin, as a Marxist-Leninist, and in part an open-eyed "realist," was no less aware of some of the political-economic implications of military operations in wartime, and he was not shy about bringing such truths to the attention of his commanders. In November 1944, while briefing Marshal Konev in preparation for the offensive into Germany, he was careful to point to the industrial zone of Silesia on the operational map and repeat the word "gold."

Overall, one must emphasize that Stalin the diplomat did not let his own psychological anomalies, or the limitations of "objectivity," put him at a disadvantage during the Second World War. He at least held his own with the Western leaders not only in his overall understanding of issues and his negotiating ability, but in the realm of personal charm upon which Roosevelt and Churchill laid such store. His ability to make a favorable impression on virtually every one of his wartime visitors from the West, to get them to trust him and convince them that he trusted them, was truly remarkable. No one in the American government ever thought of the British prime minister as "Brother Winston," nor did the image of "Cousin Franklin" rise up in the mind of any British official. But "Uncle Joe" became the companion of every high-ranking official in London and Washington, and it is still jarring to come across reminders of the degree to which Stalin's bonhomie succeeded in smoothing the jagged edges of the Soviet image, even in the minds of some devoted anti-Communists. After the war, though still gripped by the "Iron Curtain" phase, which had begun to dominate his thinking in late 1944, Churchill could still not completely cast off his acquired affection for Uncle Joe, or the myth of the "troublesome" un-Stalinist members of the Politburo who thwarted the dictator's good intentions. Even in his postwar memoirs the former prime minister was not able to see very straight about what had happened in the USSR before the war, and praised Vyshinski for having "played so masterful a part" in the great purge trials, which were, after all, the greatest purely "objective" performance of all time.

As Ulam has concluded, World War II revealed that Stalin's "greatest gift and accomplishment" lay in the field of diplomacy. Since he was able to out charm and outmaneuver the leaders of the great Western powers, the Soviet leader had little difficulty making himself the focal point of all those outside Russia who sought revolutionary change. The years 1941–1945 proved that in addition to producing great socioeconomic development, the USSR could stand up successfully to the war's greatest challenges. This was enough for most leaders of foreign resistance and revolutionary movements, and even though Stalin was as suspicious of foreign Communist parties as he was of capitalists, he managed simultaneously to accept the homage of the Western resistance, intimidate Western leaders with the threat of radical change via the Communist parties within their own countries, and hold back the revolutionaries from any rash action that might work to the disadvantage of the Soviet Union or its leader.

Seen from his version of personal and national interest, it is difficult to call Stalin's overall wartime achievement anything but masterful. By 1945 not only had his country survived and played the biggest part in defeating Hitler, the Western powers had not been totally alienated, and the Soviet Union had taken possession of a huge security zone in Eastern Europe and northern Asia. Of course new forces for change, potentially inimical in Stalin's view to his own interest, had been unleashed by the war. The Soviet Union had absorbed tremendous damage, the Russian people had been nibbled by hope and rising expectations, the worldwide revolutionary fever posed severe long-term challenges to Stalinist control, and the United States had been transformed into an active superpower.

But the war had even more dramatically enhanced Stalin's personal authority. By 1945 he was truly popular, not only among party cadres at home and Communists abroad, but among a huge sweep of the world's population, and more important, among the vast majority of his own people. As even the leading Soviet dissident historian, Roy Medvedev, was forced to admit after many pages sharply criticizing Stalin's wartime activities, "During the war years, as the Soviet people were battered by unbelievable miseries, the name of Stalin and faith in him to some degree pulled the Soviet people together giving them hope of victory." And when victory came, it was only natural that these same Soviet people would give Stalin the major credit for having saved them from an eternal Nazi hell.

What so disturbed Medvedev and other subsequent critics was the deftness with which Stalin could turn the wartime experience, and his enhanced popularity, into buttresses of his own personal power. Without permanently rejecting "objectivism," Stalin had shown that he could deal successfully with the outside world in "real" diplomatic and military terms, and this provided him with a powerful new weapon to keep everyone else in line. As Khrushchev repeatedly informs us, during his last years Stalin never tired of telling his "colleagues" that he, and he alone, could deal with the imperialist powers, and that when he was gone the West would "wring your necks like chickens."

Thus among the major winnings which the war brought to Stalinism was that it converted "real" reality as well as "objective" reality into instruments through which the leader could control the system and its people. By war's end, Stalin was not only powerful and popular both at home and abroad, he had established himself as the proven master of both realities.

This harvest of popularity and political power which Stalin had garnered from World War II inevitably transmuted and

tarnished most of the modest benefits which that conflict brought
to the socioeconomic system and the mass of the people of the
Soviet Union. The people did gain much satisfaction from having played the crucial role in whipping Nazism and having given
the lie to Hitler's claim that they were inferior *Untermenschen,*
incapable of resisting the Aryan elite of the Third Reich. As the
pivotal role which Soviet power and the endurance of the Russian people had played in the general victory brought new respect and prestige to the USSR, Soviet citizens inevitably gained
a greater sense of national pride and self-esteem. When they saw
their country take its place in the forefront of world powers and
witnessed the growing industrial might which their sacrifices and
the new technocratic class was bringing to their country, the Soviet people received some measure of psychic compensation for
their great sacrifices. That the Red Army possessed sufficient
power to pursue the Nazi Wehrmacht to the center of Europe
could not help but be gratifying to a people who had long suffered the indignity of being regarded by much of the world as
a band of bumbling semibarbarians. That this same Red Army
left other people with feelings of awe and fear, while seizing
large areas of border territory that could serve as security zones
to protect the Soviet motherland, also probably brought pride
and satisfaction to most Soviet citizens. After the horrors of
1941–1945 it would have been difficult for any of the people of
the USSR to feel that their country could possess too much
armed might or too many rings of defenses to guard against outside attack.

But all these additions to the Soviet public's pride and sense
of security would only have national and international political
significance in the form in which Stalin chose to employ them.
The Soviet leader, true to his "objective" and "real" heritage,
and strengthened by his wartime experience, would actually use
Soviet Russia's increased power and prestige in the immediate
postwar period as political weapons with which to bully his
neighbors and intimidate his former comrades in the Allied Big
Three. He also turned inside out the prestige the Soviet triumph

had given to the Communist system both at home and abroad, and used the threat of worldwide expansion of the Soviet system to scare foreign governments. Stalin even converted aspects of the terrible destruction which the war had brought to the USSR into an international political weapon by so bludgeoning the Western powers with demands for high reparations that he ultimately helped make impossible the joint four-power postwar occupation of Germany.

Therefore, however one examines the Second World War in the East and reflects on the shadows which it would cast over the postwar world, only one person out of all those millions would ultimately be decisive. After all the statistical effects of the war are added up and all the psychological factors charted, how Stalin chose to use the Soviet Union's wartime heritage would be the East's most important contribution to the beginning of the Cold War and the long period of East-West confrontation which followed.

4

The Great Arsenal of Democracy:

THE UNITED STATES AND THE WAR

For the millions of people in Asia and Europe who saw their countries tumble one after another into the maelstrom of world war between 1937 and 1941, the United States of America appeared to be utopia, a boundless paradise of peace, plenty, and prosperity. Indeed, America stayed at peace much longer than any of the other major powers, and was so endowed with natural resources and productive capacity that it could well raise the envy and jealousy of nations that found their assets mercilessly devoured by total war.

But to many Americans, the years 1939–1941 were still part of an era in which the marks of the Great Depression lay heavily upon their country. Despite seven years of strenuous effort and experimentation by the New Deal, 8.1 million people continued to be unemployed in a country of 131 million in 1940, which meant that at least one out of every seven willing and able to work (a whopping 14.6 percent) could not find employment. American exports had as yet not reached the level of 1927, and the United States would not regain the percentage of world trade that it had held in 1928 until a decade after World War II. In 1940, imports into the United States were stuck at 60 percent of the 1928 level, and American investment abroad had actually dropped 10 percent between 1935 and 1940, although United States investors had retained large holdings in the Western Hemisphere and were on the threshold of moving energetically into the oil-rich areas of the Middle East, especially Saudi Arabia.

Overall, America still felt like an isolated, largely self-sufficient, and comparatively simple country. Nearly a quarter of the total work force, 11.2 million people, was employed in agriculture in 1939, and not a few of them were compelled by necessity to take all, or a substantial portion, of their wages in produce. Many people had great difficulty in acquiring cash money, and sharecropping and subsistence agriculture were the dominant features in the lives of a substantial segment of the population. Most of the work which was performed in the country was done by people who paid few, if any, federal taxes. To be required to file a federal income tax form in 1939, a person had to have earned the princely sum of five thousand dollars (comparable to forty or fifty thousand dollars in 1980s dollars). Only 7.5 million Americans earned enough in 1939 to file for federal income tax, and after deductions and allowances, only 3.8 million—no more than a small handful of whom were blue-collar workers—ultimately paid any federal income tax. With under 3 percent of the population actually paying a personal income tax, it is not surprising that the United States government managed to collect a mere $1.1 billion from that source out of the total federal tax revenue of $5.1 billion in 1939.

The federal budget for 1939 was $9.4 billion, and at that point, two decades after World War I, and one decade beyond the onset of the great crash and depression, the total federal debt was $189 billion. Despite anguished cries from conservatives that the New Deal was turning Washington into a Leviathan, the federal government only had 960,000 employees, and the American military services were more appropriate for a Marx Brothers comedy than for the defense of a great power. The United States army had 187,000 men in 1939, just 40,000 more than the navy. Eighteen of the world's armies were larger than the American, including those of Turkey, Finland, and Spain. The United States army was bigger than that of Bulgaria, but only by 23,000 men, and it is highly doubtful whether the American forces were much ahead of their small rivals in terms of modern equipment or effective planning. The Army Air Corps possessed a mere 950 of what is optimistically—and erroneously—termed "front line" aircraft, while the total munitions production of the United States between 1935 and 1939 was lower than that of every one of the other five great powers (Germany, Britain, Japan, France, and the USSR). In fact, during those five years American munitions output was just 20 percent of the Soviet figure, and under 15 percent of that for Hitler's Germany. Isolationism and pacifism were strong forces in American life, and the United States had neither joined the League of Nations nor formed a military alliance with any foreign power.

The state of California, now one of the half-dozen greatest economic powers on earth, then had a population of only seven million, smaller than Illinois and Pennsylvania, and half the size of the state of New York. There had been virtually no increase in the urban percentage of the American population in the decade 1930–1940, and the stranglehold of mass rural poverty had not been broken. Despite the well-publicized treks of "Arkies" and "Oakies" from the dust bowl, Arkansas and Oklahoma actually gained population and even increased their representation in Congress during the depression years. Pellagra and hookworm were still the curse of the southern population, and the communicable disease rate in the country remained high, with death rates in 1940 of 42 per hundred thousand for tuberculosis and 55 per hundred thousand for pneumonia.

But the year 1940 also revealed some significant stirrings in the American economy. Exports rose slightly, the individual share of the GNP jumped $122 per person in a single year, and the overall gross national product was up 25 to 30 percent over 1935. Sales to the embattled Allies had given the United States economy some stimulus, and so had the first rearmament orders that were put in by the United States government. A factor of at least equal importance was the gradual reawakening of American economic confidence. The depression had taken the top off much of the old self-assurance, but by 1940, even as they scolded the Old World for embroiling itself in yet another of its age-old wars, and proudly pointed to the contrast between wars abroad and the tranquillity in America, the people of the United States seem to have intuitively grasped that the worldwide conflict must sooner or later put a premium on American resources, productivity, and military potential. This helped make the sap rise in the American people, stimulated the old bravado that the rest of the world found so difficult to bear, and gave great importance to the ways in which the population of the United States viewed itself, the world, and the war.

By at least the late 1930s, the vast majority of Americans had chosen sides in the spirit of sports fans, deciding that the Chinese and the European Allies were the good guys, while the Nazis, the Fascists, and the Japanese were the ones who wore black hats. But this "support" for the Allied cause was initially almost purely emotional and had nothing to do with the hard world of politics or economic aid. The public opinion polls made in late 1939 and early 1940 show that Americans overwhelmingly opposed entering the war or lending money to any of the Allies. Even Finland, a David struggling against the Soviet Goliath, and a country for which the United States public always had a soft spot because it had paid back its small debt from the First World War, could not even gain the approval of a majority of those polled for a wartime loan. And as if to emphasize to the point of caricature the near-unanimity of the American desire to stay aloof from the war, two-thirds of the Jewish respondents in a late 1939 poll expressed opposition to going to war or making a loan to help the Allies in their struggle against Hitler.

The fall of France in May–June 1940 was something of a watershed in the movement of American public opinion in the direction of active support for the Allied cause. Only then did Franklin Roosevelt have a fairly substantial base for his effort to extend assistance to Great Britain, and in the 1940 "Third Term" election campaign, both the president and his unsuccessful Republican challenger, Wendell Willkie, favored increased help to the Allies. By January 1941, opinion had swung around to support lend-lease, and interestingly enough, popular approval for this program seems to have been strongest in the West Coast and the South, two areas which were to gain comparatively most from the boom of war industries. By May 1941, just prior to the German invasion of Russia, 85 percent of the Americans surveyed in an opinion poll reluctantly conceded that the United States would probably have to enter the war eventually.

But there was still no sign of a popular stampede to become a belligerent, and the public exhibited little willingness to abandon its attitude of superior aloofness. In June 1941, a majority of those questioned indicated that they still opposed entering a postwar League of Nations, at a time when the first league lay moldering in its grave. In the same month another poll found opinion evenly split on whether it had been wise for the United States to enter the First World War!

When it came to rearmament and Western Hemisphere defense, however, both Congress and the public were ready to get moving by June 1940. The fall of France and the vulnerability of Britain effectively shrank the size of the defensive barrier that the Atlantic Ocean occupied in the American mind. Although public and congressional opinion was sharply divided on the desirability of the draft, and the polls indicated considerable public opposition to the idea of extending a small income tax to the working population to help pay for defensive rearmament, large expenditures for new weapons and increasing the size of the regular army and navy gained overwhelming support. The polls revealed strong public backing for a hard line in dealing with Japanese expansionist pressure during 1941 and great enthusiasm for the idea of trying to secure Western Hemisphere defensive bases from the Allies.

By the fall of 1941, the compound pressure of rearmament, the grave course of the war in Europe, a modest economic boom, troubles with Japan, and the promotional activities of the Roosevelt administration had produced a near-revolution in American public opinion. The polls then showed that while Congress worriedly debated the wisdom of extending the individual income tax to more of the population in order to pay for rearmament, the public had turned around so far that the majority approved higher taxes for defense than anyone in the government was asking for!

This added up to something close to a running takeoff for war, and as soon as the Japanese struck at Pearl Harbor, the country immediately went into an orbit of enthusiasm and war commitment. The string of defeats which marked the first six months of the war in the Pacific, and the catastrophic losses of American shipping to the German U-boats in the Atlantic during the same period, did nothing to dampen the popular war fever, or Washington's determination to fight the war on the basis of a long-term plan that would make maximum use of America's strongest assets. Shortly after Pearl Harbor, Winston Churchill and the British military leaders journeyed to Washington, and at the "Arcadia" conference the two countries hammered out a formal Anglo-American war strategy. The European war was to have priority over that in the Pacific, and the military command structure was to be merged in the form of a combined chiefs of staff. The latter decision necessitated, among other things, the creation of an American joint chiefs of staff organization, and put the United States on the high road to a large, permanently integrated defense establishment.

By turning much of the direction of the war effort over to the generals and admirals of the Combined Chiefs of Staff, Roosevelt and Churchill took a major step to curtail partisan political criticism of the war effort. Since the Combined Chiefs of Staff were supposed to make their strategic decisions on the basis of whatever offered the best prospects for winning the war quickly and cheaply—the principle of military necessity—there was little basis for disgruntled politicians or unhappy citizens criticizing the president or the prime minister. Few critics, no matter how keen their particular grievance, were ready to contend that they knew better how to win the war than generals of the stature of George Marshall or Sir Alan Brooke. So the Combined Chiefs of Staff system went a long way toward making the American public feel that the direction of the war was in good hands and that their efforts and sacrifices would be worthwhile.

The system was also perfectly attuned to produce economic and social changes in the United States. To win the war as quickly and as cheaply as possible, the Combined Chiefs of Staff were compelled to put maximum emphasis on firepower, high-technology weapons, and a broad and deep mobilization of Anglo-American manpower and productive capacity. Since by December 1941, Britain was already mobilized to the hilt, most of the additional demand for men and goods had to be met by the United States, and because the Axis represented a formidable enemy coalition, it was obvious that whatever was done, a long steady process of buildup would be required before the Anglo-Americans could try to bring the war to an end by means of great showdown battles, first in Europe and then in the Pacific.

The Combined Chiefs of Staff scheme for victory may be summed up as winning the war through careful planning, based on minimizing casualties, maximizing production (especially of high-tech weapons), and leaving the Soviets to carry the crushing and mortal burden of the war against Germany until the Anglo-Americans had created a large enough military machine to deliver decisive blows east and west. This system, when laid upon the economic and public opinion changes that had taken place within the United States since 1939, had to unleash a productive explosion. Since there was no danger of an Axis attack on the continental United States from 1942 to the end of the war, all resources could be devoted to the long-term mobilization plan, and with the public to all intents and purposes unanimous in its support for the war effort, the government had to do little to whip up popular opinion or control dissent. Virtually no government censorship of the media occurred in the United States during the war, and the government directly produced only a fraction of the war propaganda which poured forth between 1942 and 1945, because the press, radio, film, and advertising industries voluntarily played the propaganda role far more effectively than any government agency could have hoped to do.

With the public hungry for an economic boom and mad with war, the federal government had little to do except top up the prowar propaganda, organize a bit, and hold the ring. Boards were set up to keep wages, prices, and profits at a fairly reasonable level. The combination of rationing, price and wage controls, bond sales, heavy taxes, and some patriotic restraint on the part of the public succeeded in holding the inflation level to 5 percent per annum for the wartime period. With that accomplished, Washington was able to stand back, spend money, and let the economic explosion burst forth.

The United States government disbursed the then astonishing total of $309 billion during the war. The war disbursement figure for 1944, $95.2 billion, was ten times the federal budget for the New Deal years of 1939. The American gross national product rose 70 percent in six years while both the national income and the disposable income of the nation went up 110 percent. Between 1940 and 1945, each American's share of this rise in the GNP amounted to one thousand dollars in hard money.*

This federal expenditure, surpassing by far any Keynesian economist's depression recovery fantasy, produced a meteoric increase in American heavy industrial production. Between 1938 and 1943, United States output of iron, steel, and nonferrous metals rose 300 percent, machinery production went up 500 percent, and the production of transportation equipment climbed by 1,000 percent. Since $182 billion of the government's $309 billion wartime disbursement went to munitions production, that sector chalked up especially impressive gains. Keeping in mind that the total United States government budget in 1939 was $9.4 billion, and that the United States ranked dead last among the great powers in munitions production in the late 1930s, the

* All comparative money figures in this chapter have been weighted to eliminate the inflation factor.

American expenditure of $59 billion on munitions in the year 1944 alone is truly staggering. Even if one disregards production of marginal items such as merchant ships, in which United States output led the world, but which may not be considered pieces of pure military equipment, American munitions production in the years 1943 and 1944 nearly equalled that of Great Britain, the Soviet Union, and Nazi Germany combined (80 billion to 82.5 billion in dollar value).

The enormous scale of this production, its emphasis on heavy industry, and especially its concentration on military hardware, would inevitably have highly significant effects on the course of the war, on American society, and on the nature of the postwar world, for it put the United States in a productive league of its own, beyond the range of any other power. That $47 billion of the American government's wartime expenditure went to lend-lease (15 percent of the total) was merely one harbinger of the future worldwide economic role of the U.S.A., while the way Washington chose to finance the wartime economic outburst was also a highly significant omen for the postwar era. The supply of United States currency was increased nearly 400 percent between 1939 and 1945, and the national debt rose from $189 billion to $405 billion in the years 1940 to 1945. When allowance is made for inflation, the debt increase amounted to roughly 55 percent in 1939 dollars. Sales of government securities to banks and other large financial institutions was by far the most important factor which made possible this increase in the national debt, but the well-organized Treasury campaign to sell war bonds to individuals played a significant role in covering the federal deficit and turning nearly the whole population of the country into savers and investors. The polls indicate that the majority of the population would have been willing to go even further than the government and would have accepted mandatory purchase of war bonds. But even through the voluntary system which the government in fact employed, something in the neighborhood of 80 percent of the population purchased some federal securities during the war.

An even more significant, and much more dramatic, change took place in regard to federal income taxes. The minimum level at which individuals were liable to the tax was steadily lowered from the 1939 figure of five thousand dollars until it stood at five hundred dollars in 1944. In those years, the number of people who filed a federal income tax form leapt from 7.5 million in the former year to 49.9 million in the penultimate year of the war, and the number of people who actually paid an income tax rose even more sharply from 3.8 million at the beginning of the war crisis to 42.6 million (30 percent of the total population) in 1944. Overall, the government's income from the personal income tax rose nearly 2,000 percent during the conflict, increasing from $1.1 billion in 1940 to $21.1 billion in 1945, and providing the United States government for the first time with the means to act decisively abroad.

Nearly the whole working population of the United States had been turned into taxpayers virtually overnight, yet the people adjusted to their new taxpaying role as rapidly as Washington's civil and military officials embraced the great increase of power which this enormous inflow of money brought to them. In 1942, when an opinion poll asked respondents to pick the income tax rates that they thought would be fair, the majority selected *higher* figures than the existing tax schedules. Subsequent polls taken during the middle war years indicated that the vast majority felt the income tax was the best way to pay for the war, and they also strongly supported the "pay as you go" system. As late as 1944, 90 percent of those polled declared that they thought the income tax system was fair, and at war's end 55 percent had already reconciled themselves to the likelihood that the high tax levels would remain in force for at least a year or two after the war.

The public's willingness to pay heavy taxes and support the government's bond-selling programs was partly due to the fact that work was plentiful and wages were high. But the sense of doing one's bit for the war effort, and supporting in some way the enormous number of boys who had been drawn into the armed forces, was an important consideration too. The number of Americans in the military services rose from 308,000 in 1939 to a peak of 12.3 million in 1945. In addition, the ranks of federal civilian employees had quadrupled to a peak of 3,826,000 people by the last year of the war (which indicates the hollowness of the legend that it was the depression and the New Deal which have given the United States a swollen federal bureaucracy).

It was obvious to every American that this vast multitude had to be paid for, and that the military personnel had to be kitted out with the kind of sophisticated, and expensive, equipment that has always been dear to the American heart. The Army Air Corps, which had only had 1,760 combat aircraft on hand in the first year of rearmament (1940), accepted 74,135 from the contractors in 1944, and the United States navy, which seemed relatively formidable with 1,236 vessels in service in 1939, had 62,725 by V-J Day (compared with 512 "fleet ships" in 1985).

Beyond the costs for military equipment and the money necessary to support those in the federal military and civilian service, there was also the emotionally charged issue of battle casualties, which melted the heart of the whole population, including the handful of skeptics who harbored doubts about the costs and changes being brought about by the war. The United States military suffered 1.1 million casualties during the Second World War, one out of every sixty-five American males. Of this total, 291,557 were battle dead, less than one-half of one percent of the male population. The total casualty figure was three times larger than that for the American forces in World War I, and the number of battle dead was close to five times larger. Compared with all the other major belligerents, however, American losses were extremely low, and not in the same league with those for such mortally wounded countries as Poland, Yugoslavia, and the Soviet Union.

The American battle casualties served more as a spur to national effort than as a mournful and debilitating burden, not only because of their relatively small number, but because the vast majority of them took place in the last stage of the war in Europe. Three-quarters of America's casualties (ca. 825,000 men) fell in the European and Mediterranean theaters of operations, and 66 percent of them (ca. 540,000 men) occurred there between D Day (June 1944) and April 1945. Some units were nonetheless hit very hard. Combat infantry in Normandy, in the Italian mountain campaigns, and in the battles of attrition along the German frontier took especially heavy losses. Of the 2,897 casualties among Army Air Corps bomber crews, 2,148 were killed (75 percent). While 25 percent of the casualties among the large armies used in the European war were battle deaths, the percentage for the much smaller army forces deployed in the Pacific was closer to 33 percent. The Pacific war took an even higher toll of sailors and marines, for though the numbers involved were smaller than those for the army, nearly half of the navy and marine casualties were deaths in action.

So there were a substantial number of bereaved American families left in the war's wake, and the light casualty rate reflected no lack of bravery among American combat personnel. But the fact remains that the United States's losses were very low—the number of combat deaths had been higher in the Civil War when the country had only 30 percent of the population— and they made no significant impact on the nation's population figures. Compared with the 290,000 battle deaths, 466,000 American civilians died of pneumonia and tuberculosis during the Second World War, even though the incidence of these two communicable diseases actually fell sharply, as in Great Britain, in the course of the war. Overall, the population of the United States enjoyed a healthy increase of 8 million (6 percent), bringing the total to 140 million people by 1945.

Along with the increase of population, the massive manpower and productive mobilization also exerted other significant influences on American society. Except for Japanese-Americans, blindly locked away in internment camps, the wartime period opened up new, if frequently temporary, opportunities for minorities as well as for women. Large numbers of blacks permanently left the rural South for military service or industrial work in northern cities. Women flocked into war work in such large numbers that there was a sharp short-term 40 percent increase in the number of women employed in the United States. But even during the war, changes in the status of minorities brought sharp reactions, including violent race riots in Detroit and elsewhere, and many of the gains made by women were ephemeral. As early as January 1945, the opinion polls showed a large bloc urging the elimination of married women from the work force as one of the best ways to maintain high employment levels in the postwar period.

The tone-setting wartime social-economic change that did endure was the enormous increase in the size of the working population. Between 1940 and 1945, five million Americans joined the work force, and if those serving in the armed forces during the latter year are included, the number of employed had risen by at least ten or twelve million, or roughly 20 percent, by the end of the war. This reduced the official unemployment rate to a minuscule 1.9 percent, and if the great amount of double employment and overtime which became normal during the war years is allowed for, the country definitely had over full employment.

Among the more important sources of new industrial labor was a renewed flow of population from the countryside to the cities. The urban percentage of the population rose from 56.5 percent to 59.6 percent in just five years (1940–1944), and the size of the working farm population dropped by 3 million people, which worked out to a massive decrease of 25 percent in the agricultural work force. Much of this farm-to-city movement was not local or regional, but formed part of long-distance transfers of population. The concentrations of huge aircraft and shipbuilding enterprises along the Gulf and Pacific coasts, especially in California, attracted labor as if they were magnets. Between the census of 1940 and that of 1950, the population and congressional representation of California jumped dramatically, while states like Oklahoma and Arkansas suffered a drop in population, and even Illinois and Pennsylvania lost position relative to the western colossus.

Perceptive observers did not need to wait until the end of the war to grasp that much of the population movement was permanent, for a public opinion poll taken in the spring of 1943 indicated that 48 percent of the war workers in Detroit and 49 percent of those in California who had moved in from other areas planned to remain in their new homes after the war. But even these large, and persistent, shifts of population did not betoken a decline in American agriculture, either inside or outside California. The nation's farm output actually rose 25 percent between 1939 and 1945, due in part to such dubious programs as that which brought Mexican brocero labor to the farms of the Southwest, but mainly because of ever greater mechanization in agriculture. In the past, mechanization had always been a mixed blessing even to the farmers who had remained on the land, for the concomitant burden of debt tended to drive them over the brink into bankruptcy during lean times. In the Second World War, however, with unlimited demand for farm goods priced at a level where farmers could make a long-term profit, things went very differently. Unable to buy many luxuries or general consumer goods, and with money cheap, farmers applied their income almost exclusively to mechanization and retiring their old debts. In consequence, by the end of the war not only had the degree of agricultural mechanization increased, the farmers' debt burden had actually been reduced by 20 percent.

The war was also good to the other major categories of American debtors, even though no one else seems to have done quite as well as the farmers. The burden of debt on the nation's private noncorporate borrowers only increased 3 percent during the war, and the aggregate corporate debt went up but a total of 15 percent. In light of the enormous expansion of the industrial plant, a total wartime inflation factor of 25 percent, and a rise in the federal government debt of 110 percent, this actually meant no overall private debt increase in real terms. Due to the war, American business was able to take a productive plant seriously damaged by a decade of depression-related neglect and underutilization, and put it back on its feet and modernize it by means of subsidies and solid profits paid for by the federal government. In the final analysis, although the public remained blissfully ignorant of it, the modern American "capitalistic" productive machine that had come into being by 1943, and would dominate the world's output both during and after the war, had actually been directly financed by the American taxpayers and those investors who had purchased United States government securities.

A significant proportion of the investment money, as well as much of that which came from taxation, originated in the labors of the greatly expanded working population. With disposable personal income rising 110 percent between 1939 and 1945, and most consumer durables unavailable or rationed during the war, savings had to increase. In consequence, deposits in American commercial banks leapt from $2.8 billion in 1939 to $16.01 billion in 1945, while the total of personal savings, that is, the excess of income over consumption, taxes, etc., shot up from $2.6 billion to $29.6 billion in the same period. The American population was thereby provided with a huge pool of effective postwar demand, and the country's financial institutions also acquired an enormous fund of investment capital for use at home and abroad once the war had been won.

The great ballooning of the economy, which gave the United States nearly half of the world's industrial output backed up by vast agricultural productivity, an unprecedented supply of investment capital, and modernized productive techniques, inevitably put Washington and American business in a commanding position in world affairs. The great boom also tied the bulk of the United States population to the system body and soul, for virtually overnight nearly every American who wanted a job could have one, complete with wartime job security, high wages, and plenty of overtime at time and a half. The whole blue-collar population was soon dressed out with money in the bank and war bonds in the safety deposit box. Furthermore, as taxpayers and toilers in the nation's wartime cause, they recovered whatever confidence still suffered wounds from the Great Depression, and added to it a colossal pride in America's wartime productive achievement.

The near universalizing of employment, savings, and pride constituted a social revolution, for it gave the population three-fourths of the American dream. All that was required for the country to reach nirvana, it seemed, was the maintenance of this system into the postwar world, so that the people would have a chance to make their gains permanent and enjoy the fruits of their success in a mammoth fiesta of postwar consumption.

The wartime public opinion polls indicate that the population had a remarkably clear grasp of what had happened to them. A poll taken six months after Pearl Harbor revealed that 80 percent of those questioned thought that they were doing as well, or better, than they had a year before. Six months later, when this question was asked again, 86 percent indicated that they were at least as well off as they had been at the time the United States entered the war. When in September 1943, before the period of heaviest American military casualties occurred, a poll asked if people had "made any real sacrifices" in the war; with complete frankness, 69 percent of those questioned said no. When the question was repeated in February 1945, at the time of the heaviest American losses, 64 percent still replied no.

In this atmosphere of general satisfaction, the one issue which worried wartime Americans more than any other was the threat of postwar unemployment. In the first month after the United States went into the conflict, the polls showed that two-thirds of those questioned dreaded the possibility of a decrease in jobs after the war, and postwar unemployment was still ranked as the number-one worry (ahead of inflation and rationing) in polls of October 1943 and January 1945. A June 1943 survey indicated that 56 percent of the population believed that veterans would face dim employment prospects, and in one of the best barometers of what the war had done to the Western democracies, a comparative poll in August 1945 showed that the chief postwar worry in France was lack of food and fuel, that in Britain the shortage of housing, and in the United States the possibility of high postwar unemployment.

But the tide of American confidence and rising power was so great that even anxiety about a lack of postwar jobs gradually lost its force as V-J Day approached. In contrast to Canada, where this dread remained consistently high in the polls right up to the end of the war, the American polls revealed a gradual drop from two-thirds in December 1941 to 50 percent by the summer of 1942, and then leveled off at a third fearful, a third not, and a third undecided by April 1943. The one-third ratio of fear, confidence, and indecision about postwar unemployment then remained constant for the last two and a half years of the war, while the public's anxiety about a big postwar depression within ten years of the end of hostilities declined slightly in the last few months of the conflict.

Not all sectors of the population were equally bullish about the economic future. Workers on the West Coast, quite naturally, were much more optimistic than those in the older, traditional, industrial zones of the Northeast. As soon as it became obvious that the public was storing up a large fund of postwar purchasing power, American businessmen began to put on the most cheerful of grins about postwar prospects. As early as October 1943, 70 percent of the businessmen questioned in a *Fortune* poll predicted a boom within two years of the end of the war. If anyone had any doubts about whether this optimism was realistic, all that was necessary was to consult the immediately following polls, for these indicated in the first months of 1944 that the public had very definite ideas about what it wanted to do with its savings, and automobiles, houses, and home appliances—the lifeblood of a mass consumer boom—ranked first, second, and third in the public's postwar spending plans. Furthermore, 50 percent of those polled nationwide in March 1945 thought that their high income would be maintained in the postwar period.

The sharp improvement of the economic position of most

Americans as well as the flood of optimism about postwar prospects which accompanied it, inevitably produced a swing to social-economic conservatism within the United States. The great boom created a conservative Congress which wiped out New Deal reforms for the destitute, such as public works projects and aid to tenant farmers, and it dried up much of the public's desire for social reform. Two crucial polls taken in Britain and the United States during the middle war period graphically indicate that Americans had decided that they were a people of natural, and probably inevitable, plenty. When in June 1943 the British were asked in a poll if they wanted substantial postwar reform, 57 percent replied yes and 34 percent said no, with the young and low-income sections of the population in the vanguard of those anxious for reform. Four months later when this question was asked again, 57 percent of Britons polled continued to desire far-reaching reforms, as did 71 percent of the Canadians who were asked the same question. Only the people of the United States were out of step with this popular desire for change. In the first poll, only 34 percent of the Americans favored significant postwar reforms and in the second, only 32 percent. Both of these results were exactly opposite those scored in Britain, and to make the contrast even more striking, among the Americans polled, neither youth nor those with low incomes showed strong support for change. In fact the only group within the United States that looked with favor on basic reform was the highest-income segment of the population!

Even in the way it perceived domestic threats and dangers, the American people were marching to a different beat from the population of the rest of the world. In November 1943, when a poll asked if there were "harmful" groups in the United States which should be curbed, 58 percent said yes, and when asked to enumerate such groups—just as in Britain—Fascists, Communists, Jehovah's Witnesses, and Jews made the list, together with a pair of especially American scapegoats, blacks and Japanese-Americans. But none of the ethnic or religious "enemies" garnered more than 10 percent of the hate vote, and even the Communists only managed to rack up 16 percent, one percent more than the Fascists. The runaway winners in the American "harmful groups" contest were the labor unions, who took 36.6 percent of the negative vote. Even if one is reluctant to accept one public opinion poll as definitive, and due allowance is made for the public's hostility toward wartime strikes, this poll does suggest a degree of American socioeconomic conservatism and a blind faith in the benefits of "natural" economic forces, which could not even be approximated anywhere else.

Since during the war Americans were better off than they had ever been, and their country possessed the productive might which promised to cut a very wide swath in the postwar world, the popular mood of socioeconomic conservatism was not completely shortsighted. Where it definitely did come up short, however, was in the failure to grasp adequately the role of government taxation and spending in producing the great boom in the American economy or realizing that the peculiarity of world conditions had played a fundamental part in making it possible. If individual Americans had been pressed, most of them would probably have conceded that their country's great leap upward owed something to the devastation of the factories and farms of other countries and had benefited from the inability of traditional exporters like Germany, Britain, and Japan to supply their overseas customers in wartime. But such realizations were rarely confronted, and the public generally remained almost completely blind to the government's role, and even more unaware of the international dimensions of the great economic expansion which Americans were counting on for employment and prosperity after the war. Therefore, at war's end, tending to see the United States economic boom as the product of domestic developments and laissez-faire capitalism, rather than as part of greater international changes and the revolution in the economic role of their government, the people of the United States were not ready to assume the world responsibilities that their new wealth and power pressed upon them.

But even during the war the global economic reverberations

of the American economic revolution continued right on their way whether the United States public was aware of them or not. In addition to lend-lease, American commercial exports increased 100 percent during the war years compared with the 1936–1940 average, and imports went up 30 percent. Much of the export rise was due to direct purchases by various Allied belligerents, but there are indications that the United States was gobbling up some traditional European export markets as well, for shipments to Canada and Latin America rose by at least 60 percent. In addition, some wartime changes in the pattern of exports were fraught with future significance. In 1939, "crude food" constituted one-third of total American food exports, with "manufactured food" making up the other two-thirds. But by 1945, "crude food" had slipped to 25 percent of the total, as "manufactured food" exports shot up 450 percent between 1939 and 1945. Obviously, canned tomatoes and Spam built the foreign-trade highways that Coke and Pepsi would travel during the 1950s and that McDonald's and Colonel Sanders would convert into freeways in the 1970s and 1980s.

The 30 percent increase of gross imports into the United States during the Second World War may not at first glance appear to be very significant, especially in light of the enormous expansion of all other aspects of the American economy. But if one remembers that the war virtually cut off imports from some areas, especially Southeast Asia and the Pacific, while European imports were sharply curtailed, the 30 percent figure takes on additional importance. That the incredible production boom in the United States put great pressure on domestic sources of some raw materials gives added weight to the matter of imports. Since by 1943 United States aluminum production exceeded the whole world's prewar output, concern had to arise about American domestic sources of bauxite, and as the manufacturing expansion roared on, similar worries arose about other industrial raw materials, whether they were traditional American exports or were being devoured by the war industries at home.

What the war did to America's petroleum position shows the

situation very clearly. At the start of World War II, the United States was the world's greatest oil exporter, and the war crisis brought an additional 100 percent increase in American petroleum shipments abroad. But during the years 1941–1945, American oil imports also rose 40 percent, with almost all of the incoming shipments originating in the Caribbean Basin. The effect of the feverish wartime export and domestic consumption of petroleum then very quickly revealed itself in a significant reversal of America's raw material position. By 1950, petroleum imports into the United States virtually equalled exports, and five years later, America was a massive net importer of petroleum.

It is not surprising therefore that when the 30 percent figure for the gross increase of imports into America during the war is picked apart region by region, some very symptomatic indicators begin to emerge. By 1945, imports from Canada had risen 120 percent above those for the 1936–1940 period. Some of this increase was due to manufacturers moving portions of their operations over the border and then backshipping into the United States, but a very large proportion consisted of industrial raw materials, especially timber, iron ore, and what would soon come to be known as "strategic" minerals. Latin American industrial raw material producers, such as Mexico, Venezuela, Chile, and Colombia also saw their sales to the United States go up from 75 percent to 150 percent during the war years.

There were no comparable rises in imports from the Middle East, because transport difficulties and the uncertainties created by the war combined to persuade the United States to satisfy its oil needs from domestic and Latin American sources. But the wartime shortages of petroleum certainly did make both the oil companies and the government eager to get control of enough Middle Eastern oil so that after the war domestic reserves could be conserved and the country would still have sufficient petroleum to operate its economy on the large scale which had been developed during the war.

However, it was not necessary to wait until the postwar era to see America compelled to move beyond the Western Hemisphere to secure raw materials to feed the supereconomy developing within the United States. The wartime import statistics for two African territories show the long-term trend at least as clearly as the morning shows the day. Although its gross volume of shipments to the U.S.A. was substantially lower than that of the large Western Hemisphere industrial raw material exporters, the Belgian Congo upped its American sales by 600 percent, in part, of course, because it was then the world's chief source of uranium. But South Africa, which depended for its trade on a broad range of important raw material exports, rather than one vital commodity, did even better, increasing its sales to America between 800 percent and 900 percent during the war. By 1945, the value of South African shipments to the United States already exceeded those from Colombia or Venezuela.

The worldwide flow of raw materials from the underdeveloped countries to the United States was thus already in process by 1945 and together with the enormous increase of America's industrial and farm production, as well as the determination of the people and government of the United States to maintain this swollen economic phenomenon, the three biggest pillars of American domination were in place. Very soon anguished critics would decry the efforts of the United States to solidify its supremacy by making the dollar the basic currency of the "free world" and doing everything in its power during the 1950s to open up the world to its goods and its investment capital. Amid the havoc wreaked by the postwar American development of raw materials in underdeveloped countries with repressive regimes, it has been generally overlooked that this was not a new departure, but merely the natural extension of trends begun, or greatly accelerated, during the war in such places as Chile, the Belgian Congo, and South Africa. What has been denounced as American economic imperialism was not the product of the classic need to export surplus goods and capital. If allowance is made for inflation, the net value of American investments abroad actually fell during the war years, and virtually no one in the United States between 1941 and 1945 was desperate to find foreign customers for their goods.

The United States did make the decisive leap toward world economic domination during the wartime period, but a democratic ideological passion or an anti-Fascist or anti-Communist crusading passion was not the cause. The decisive dynamics were greatly expanded productivity, rising popular expectations, and the need for foreign raw materials to fuel this growth. The classic textbook pursuits of foreign markets and investment outlets would have their day, but they were not the causes of the economic revolution that is called Americanization; they were simply its postwar effects.

Given the complexity and uniqueness of the wartime economic trends, and specifically because they were not caused by ideology, it is not surprising that the American public did not immediately comprehend them, especially if one remembers that these trends still seem to be a mystery to many politicians and historians. The dominant postwar international issue which most occupied the American public in the early and mid-1940s was actually not economic at all. As with the other Allied belligerents, the people of the United States were mainly interested in how to protect their security in the postwar period and at the same time hoped to do everything possible to avoid another major war. It is frequently forgotten that all four of the great Allied belligerents were reluctant warriors who had been forced into the conflict, and they therefore had future security, and the avoidance of a repetition of such events, uppermost in their minds.

As soon as they had overcome the first shock of the surprising and effective Japanese attack on Pearl Harbor, the American army and navy commanders set sections of their staffs to work drawing up plans to stop anything similar happening again. Long before the great Red scare began to focus American military planning on a possible Soviet danger in 1944–1945, contingency plans had been drawn up to meet possible attacks from all and sundry, complete with lists of the most appropriate forces and overseas bases which would best shield the United States from assorted aggressors. Such plans were of course kept secret from the general public, but the polls indicate that the American people were at least keeping pace with the military planners in their desire for new and more effective guarantees of United States security.

Public opinion polls, especially in the mid-1940s, had certainly not attained absolute reliability, but they remain the best indicators of the broad sweep of public opinion, and—in sharp contrast to Britain—in the United States they were frequently given serious consideration by national leaders. Not only did election-minded politicians and businessmen extend great respect to them, but the State Department, on instructions from the White House, actually commissioned its own polls of opinion on what it thought were important wartime foreign policy issues. An American intelligence organization, the OSS, even recruited a prominent poll forecaster—Elmo Roper—into its ranks, and experimented with the use of opinion polls as a device for acquiring intelligence information about foreign countries.

The polls had shown the public strongly favoring the acquisition of additional bases in the Western Hemisphere even before Pearl Harbor, and when American forces began to conquer Japanese central Pacific bases, the overwhelming public feeling was that they should be retained as American defensive bastions. In June 1943, 84 percent of those polled wanted to hang onto the bases conquered from the Japanese, and a year later when Japan's offensive power had definitely been broken, 69 percent still wanted to retain the Japanese Pacific bases. Even in April 1945, with Germany defeated and Japan hanging by a thread, 65 percent of those polled favored acquiring more bases or overseas territory to provide the country with a defensive shield.

Thus, just as one can see a strong public, as well as government, desire in the Soviet Union to create a territorial defensive wall against Germany in postwar central Europe, so one can observe an analogous enthusiasm in the United States for a defensive archipelago in the Pacific to protect the American West Coast.

The overwhelming majority of the people of the United States were converted by the war to a belief, which would have been near to a national heresy in 1938, that armed power was the best safeguard of peace and security. The shock of recognition brought by Pearl Harbor that even the U.S.A. could be attacked, when coupled with the demonstrations provided by World War II of the sorry plight that could befall victims of aggression, probably played the biggest part in converting the American people to a belief in the need for their own armed power. On the subconscious level, the great economic boom may also have played a role, for because of it the United States actually had far more treasure to protect than ever before.

Once in possession of a great military force, Americans came to believe that in most circumstances it should be used without restraint in order to bring victory. Not only did 85 percent of those polled in August 1945 approve of the decision to drop the A-bombs on Japan, a year before 63 percent of the Catholics polled supported the bombing of historic and religious buildings in Europe if the military authorities "believed it necessary." This public support for energetic military measures in times of emergency made it a foregone conclusion that there would be strong backing for maintaining a much more powerful military force after World War II than the peacetime United States had ever previously possessed. Retention of the draft in the postwar period consistently garnered the support of 65 percent to 70 percent of those questioned in public opinion polls from June 1944 to the end of the war. But perhaps the clearest indication of the public's conversion to the belief that security could best be achieved by one's own armed strength came in a poll of September 1943, when the public was asked to choose between general disarmament and the retention of large postwar American military forces. Twenty-six percent of those questioned opted for general disarmament, while 68 percent chose to put their main future trust in the armed forces of the United States.

Not even the prospect of a large United States military shield quieted all the security fears of the American people, however. In June 1944, the month of the D Day invasion, 60 percent of those polled believed that Germany would again attempt military conquest, even if completely vanquished in the present conflict, and in every poll conducted between mid-1943 and the end of the war, a large majority of the respondents supported the idea of holding down the defeated Axis powers by long periods of military occupation. From early 1944 on, the majority of Americans polled favored sending Germans to the USSR to do reconstruction work after the war, with the supporting percentage climbing to 60 percent in mid-1944 and staying there in the spring of 1945. American backing for German forced labor in Russia was always higher in the polls than the comparable support in Canada, and in April and May 1945 when the liberation of the concentration camps produced a mighty anti-German outburst in the United States, the polls showed 80 percent of Americans in favor of sending forced German labor to the East, while only 46 percent of Australian opinion supported the idea.

One suspects that the rising tide of American enthusiasm for punishing aggressors and forcefully preventing a rematch with the Axis was a product of the advancing sense of their country's own military power, which gripped the people of the United States as the war drew to a close. The heavy commitment of American forces in the final European battles of 1944–1945, followed soon after by triumph in what, by all odds, was an overwhelmingly American war in the Pacific, seemed to have put some hard reality into traditional Yankee boasting. Just as the people had been quite realistic—if blinkered—in deciding to try to hold on to what they had gained once they grasped the economic benefits which the war had given them, so it appeared realistic for Americans to start judging their enemies as well as their friends in hard power terms after they were convinced that their country actually had acquired the attributes of a super-power.

In a poll taken in September 1943, when a measure of uncertainty and romance still held sway, 61 percent favored a postwar military alliance with Great Britain, and 56 percent even supported such an alliance with Nationalist China, but only 39 percent wanted to line up militarily with the USSR after the war. But by August 1945, when, if we were to accept the rigid scenarios of some postwar scholars, the cold war fever should already have been spreading throughout the land, only 3 percent of those polled opposed a postwar military alliance with the USSR, while 49 percent had come to favor it. Of course some of this switch was due to end-of-the-war euphoria, and perhaps a touch of optimistic dreaming about postwar prospects. But United States opinion as indicated by the polls had always held that there could be sharp postwar disagreements with the USSR, suspected that the Russians would want to acquire additional territory, and yet by the end of 1944, the polled opinion was still evenly divided on whether the United States should support Poland or the Soviet Union in their territorial disputes. It certainly does not seem accidental that the shift of opinion that came to favor a military alliance with the USSR at the end of the war coincided with a rising sense not only of United States's strength but of the power of the Red Army as well, for at the end of the Pacific war when Americans were asked what they admired most about the Soviet Union, "her military campaigns" won out over any other factor by better than two to one.

The respect which Americans had acquired for military strength (both their own and that of other large, and potentially hostile, countries), the aftershocks of insecurity left over from Pearl Harbor, and the demise of the public's faith in fortress America, combined to shape the population's dominant view of how the postwar world should be organized. Like the Canadians, the average American was initially inclined to fight first, and do the postwar planning later, but old-fashioned isolationism was flattened by Pearl Harbor. The vast majority of the polled population immediately saw the United States destined for a more active international role after the war, and by July 1942, three-fourths had come to look favorably on the League of Nations, which had, unfortunately, expired before the American people changed their minds and decided that they would like to join. Support for a more active United States role in the postwar world soared to 80 percent in the polls by mid-1943, with the new West Coast industrial zone, which had harbored some strong isolationist currents in the 1920s and 1930s, now among the leading areas of internationalism.

As early as December 1941 a poll indicated substantial popular support for the proposition that the United States should play a leading part in maintaining postwar "order," and an October 1943 *Fortune* poll found businessmen favoring by two to one the idea that an international organization should "police" the world after the war. But not until the very end of 1943 did a clear polling pattern emerge in which at least two-thirds of the respondents always supported American entry into a postwar peacekeeping organization. Once established, this trend moved along steadily, culminating in the five-to-one favorable judgment on the United Nations Charter that was recorded in July 1945.

But once one leaves the American commitment to an international peacekeeping organization, backed up if necessary by American armed force, one falls into a quagmire of confusion, disagreement, and blindness about what the United States should do in the postwar world. A *Fortune* poll taken in May 1944 showed that two businessmen out of three believed that America's trading prospects would be improved by the creation of an international peacekeeping organization. But two months earlier, a poll of the general population had indicated that there was minimal support for an international organization like the United Nations concerning itself with tariff restrictions or minimum working conditions, a result which hardly reflects much credit on the vision of the country with the world's highest wage level and the greatest stake in expanding trade.

The United States was still a very large and complex country with the views of a multitude of groups cutting every which way. It is instructive in this regard to note the results of a poll taken immediately after the Yalta conference. The Yalta communiqué issued on 12 February 1945 made no mention of the more controversial points in the agreement that would later cause such an uproar when they became public, such as the territorial concessions to the USSR at the expense of Japan and Poland and the requirement that all Soviet nationals would be compelled to return to the USSR whether they wanted to go back or not. But even though the communiqué concentrated on Allied unity, Four Power plans for the occupation of Germany, and the organization of the United Nations, while only hinting at some special Soviet influence in determining the form of government in Poland and a British role in shaping the future of Yugoslavia, that was enough to reveal the breadth of public opinion divisions which foreign policy could produce in the United States. Although the general response to the communiqué was favorable, businessmen tended to follow their economic biases and believe that the agreement tilted too much toward the USSR, while the black population was inclined to pursue its colonialist fears and suspect that it was overly favorable to Great Britain.

Old habits and attitudes died hard. The majority of the population was unwilling to give up its belief that the United States had been taken by its debtor allies in the First World War, and was also unable to grasp how complete was America's long-term economic triumph in the Second World War. In September 1945, 68 percent of those polled thought that Britain should be required to pay for *all* the military supplies she had received from the United States during the war. In the same month, two-thirds of those surveyed not only opposed granting a low-interest recovery loan to the Soviet Union, an equal percentage was against extending such a loan to the United Kingdom.

Such reactions were frequently seen, especially in Britain, as simply one more proof that Uncle Sam was indeed a miser, and his people completely lost to materialism and greed. If one examines the whole sweep of wartime polls, however, it is clear that simple avarice was not the primary cause of the American public's resistance to postwar international loans, for between 1941 and the summer of 1945 the American public consistently supported giving free assistance to the needy of Europe and Asia, and Congress routinely voted large sums to support the United Nations Relief and Rehabilitation Association (UNRRA).

One might, of course, contend that with its gigantic food production and bulging warehouses, there was an element of self-interest in American expressions of generosity, for presents might grease the skids of trade. But if that might be said of gifts, it was definitely truer of loans, yet the public overwhelmingly approved of the former and opposed the latter.

The willingness to give in the short run, but not to loan in the long run, underscored the American people's limited understanding of why they had emerged from the war rich and strong while others came out poor and weak. Most Americans granted that they had been fortunate to be shielded by their oceans one last time, and this realization persuaded the vast majority that an international peacekeeping organization and a large standing American military force would henceforth be necessary. The same sense of having been so lucky, or blessed, that the bulk of the death and destruction fell on others rather than on themselves, was an additional important wellspring of their readiness to assist others.

But at the same time, Americans did not generally believe that they had gained because others had lost, or that their country had simply been the beneficiary of an enormous infusion of Keynesian pump-prime spending in the form of a mass mobilization and mountainous orders for war matériel. The people of the United States tended to feel that the overwhelming power and prosperity that they held in 1945 had arisen chiefly from their own efforts and the natural economic processes of free enterprise. This attitude had the effect of distancing them not only from the condition, but also from the outlook and general longing, of most of the rest of the world's population, because outside the United States the feelings of the vast majority of people were dominated by bereavement, dissatisfaction with the present, and a desire for radical change. This dichotomy between the Americans and the others inevitably contributed to an initial postwar intensification of the American sense of detachment from the rest of the world and set up an unavoidable foreign policy two-step for Washington in the period following V-J Day (15 August 1945).

Reserve and caution in the use of America's enormous power outside the Western Hemisphere had to be attempted first, but when restraint failed to produce international order, more radical measures had to be used to satisfy the American public's craving for national security and solid protections for the good life that World War II had given to the United States. The new sense of power, prosperity, and wartime achievement was then mobilized in the name of resistance to Soviet communism, and through the cold war, the United States government, and its people, slowly and reluctantly moved on to accept a permanent, assertive role in the political, economic, and military affairs of the whole world.

CHALLENGES
BETWEEN HOT WAR
AND COLD

THE second great war lessened the physical isolation of most societies, due to the great intertwining of armies and navies, the vast expansion of air transport, and the increased awareness of foreign events produced by newsreels, radio, and government propaganda. People everywhere had gained some increased sense of international interdependence from this mixing together of the world's populations, and the dramatic demonstration of the proposition that every individual's life could be seriously, even mortally, affected by events which seemed to have their origins halfway around the world.

In this sense the war made the globe smaller and gave some impetus to the idea that everyone was "a part of the whole and a piece of the main."

But it is at least equally true that due to the differing circumstances faced by each country, and the compelling need to take advantage of the special characteristics of every nation in order to mobilize effectively, the war actually accentuated the peculiarities of all societies. The process of total mobilization showed some common characteristics everywhere, such as rationing and compulsory labor allocation, but in order to wring the most out of any nation, its government had to focus attention on the folkways and mores of that particular country. The wartime posters and cartoons of the various nations are frequently, and quite rightly, cited to show the temper of the times, for to be successful such images as Bill Mauldin's "Willy and Joe" had to encapsulate the country's mood, desires, daily language, and visual perception at a given moment.

Such endless reinforcing of the special qualities of each nation's life, when coupled with the exhilarating experience of participating in a great national cause, inevitably heightened the sense of national identity. This result was then further augmented by the fact that the war handed out a different fate to every society.

The balance sheet of war revealed that Britain and most of the smaller Allied countries were badly strained by their wartime exertions, lamed by both poverty and austerity, and made fearful and envious of the Big Two. The political-economic structure of fragile, old-fashioned, and marginally developed countries, such as China, was wrecked by the war, the traditional ruling groups were weakened, and the door lay open for revolutionary civil war. The USSR (as well as the Axis nations and every other country that had carried out protracted combat on its own territory, such as Yugoslavia) was a shambles, with millions dead and few bright spots except pride and a hope for future security and peace. The U.S.A. alone emerged from the conflict with both its military and economic power greatly enhanced, and its people inclined to feel that they were on top of the best of all possible worlds.

Each nation had therefore undergone very special, and intense, experiences, which made them "more different," and yet had given them contacts with foreigners, contacts which frequently created an increased sense of multinational identity and comradeship. This enhancement of both national and international consciousness would inevitably pose serious challenges for all those responsible for the conduct of international relations in the postwar era.

The war produced another equally significant and troublesome paradox in the innermost cravings of the majority of the world's people. On one hand, a deep longing arose during the war for a quick return to what were perceived as the simple, warm, and pleasant ways that had prevailed before the conflict began. Often such desires were shrouded in distortion, because by any objective measure the 1930s' world of depression, diplomatic tension, and Stalinist purges had hardly been a Garden of Eden. However, most people found that the hardships, shortages, and horrors of war were easier to bear if they kept their hopes focused on an ultimate return to the conditions that had prevailed in some imaginary paradise lost, whether it was a pub with endless pints of bitter, a new Chevy, a joyous reunion in Shanghai, or a satisfying job in the Donets Basin.

Yet side by side with such nostalgic fantasies, there burned within many of the world's warring people a sense that the flaws and failures of the prewar societies had been the spawning ground for the terrible conflict which had swept over the world and thrown their lives into such disarray. This feeling frequently produced a burning sense that fundamental changes were required after the war to make certain that a similar conflict never happened again. In some countries, such as Britain, this feeling extended beyond the realm of the international situation to incline large numbers of people to the view that essential changes at home were necessary as well. In other countries, especially the United States and the USSR, although much less demand for domestic reform existed—or was allowed to express itself—the belief that major alterations were required in the system of international relations seems to have been strong.

Of course a desire to go home and curl up on the hearth with the cat does not necessarily preclude anyone from believing in the desirability of international reform, and indeed, many people went through the war years simultaneously clinging to both of these dreams for the future. But when the shooting stopped, and the authorities faced the necessity of establishing their policies, the dichotomy between those for whom the war had most intensified the desire to push aside great issues in favor of homey or traditional things, and those who wanted to institute basic and far-reaching reforms, became critical. The wartime public's vision of the brave new world that was to follow the end of hostilities bounced so sharply both backward and forward, that no government was in a position to chart a clear route into the future by trying to satisfy the public's deepest cravings.

Yet all the major governments had to begin doing something about the political situation of the world as soon as the war ended because very little had been done during the conflict to resolve basic problems. President Roosevelt and some other political leaders had been convinced that it was best to defer as many controversial issues as possible until after the war, for if political disagreements had divided public opinion in wartime, popular support for total war measures such as the draft and rationing would inevitably have declined. In Roosevelt's view, contention over wartime and postwar policy would not only have exposed an Allied flank to enemy propaganda, it would have undercut the total consensus which produced for the Allies the weapons and military manpower that were required to win the war. Roosevelt's desire to delay making important postwar political decisions, especially those concerned with borders, zones of influence, and occupation policies for defeated enemies, set the tone for wartime Washington, and generally forced London to take the position that winning the war should come first. Moscow and Chongqing were less than enthusiastic about this attitude and repeatedly attempted to gain the support of the two Western powers for their favorite postwar projects, but up until the summer of 1945 few of the basic heartfelt wishes of East or West had been formally satisfied.

In the wartime "Big Two" meetings between Churchill and Roosevelt, the Atlantic Charter principles of no annexations of territory and the importance of there being a popular voice in any newly established postwar governments were accepted by Britain and the United States. In the "Big Three" meetings at Teheran, Yalta, and Potsdam (the latter falling between V-E Day and V-J Day, when Harry Truman was president of the United States and Clement Attlee had replaced Churchill as prime minister midway through the conference) the three most powerful Allied leaders agreed that they should continue to cooperate after the end of the war in order to establish, and guarantee, lasting peace. This basic principle of big-power cooperation was then embodied in the Charter of the United Nations Organization, where the veto in the Security Council was conceded to the Big Three, plus France and Kuomintang China. The acceptance of the United Nations Charter at the San Francisco Conference shortly before V-J Day seemed to proclaim to the world the beginning of a new era of cooperation. But Roosevelt had died even before V-E Day, Churchill would fall from power prior to V-J Day, and the French and Chinese spokesmen had never actually been in the Allied inner circle during the war. Thus the only one of the major wartime leaders who remained was Joseph Stalin, and the principle instrument created during the war to resolve future troubles was a United Nation's Security Council, which required the unanimous agreement of the major Allied wartime powers.

In addition to the big powers' agreement to try to agree during the postwar period, a few other specific, if broadly significant, agreements had also been made during the war. The reorganization of the international monetary system undertaken at Bretton Woods in July 1944 made the American dollar the world's basic currency. In the secret provisions of the Yalta agreement, the USSR acquired a few strategic points in northern Asia, especially the Kurile Islands and Port Arthur (Lüshun), and in the course of various wartime foreign minister and Big Three meetings, the Soviets also secured Western acceptance of a restoration of their 1941 frontier, which meant that the Baltic states and eastern Poland would be part of the postwar USSR. The Allied wartime gatherings had further decided to push the Polish border farther westward at the expense of Germany, and had conceded special Soviet interests in Eastern Europe, hedged in only by vague assurances about the establishment of "democracy," the holding of elections, and consultation with the West. Finally, at Potsdam, the Big Three, later joined by France, pledged themselves jointly to administer Berlin and Vienna (which lay within the Soviet zones of Germany and Austria) and also to run the econ-

omies of the four zones of Germany on the basis of common
policies worked out in the Allied Control Council.

Beyond these bits and pieces, plus the unanimous-rule machinery of the United Nations Security Council, and some proposed meetings of the Council of Foreign Ministers, the Second
World War bequeathed little in the way of positive assistance to
the process of building a postwar system except for the indispensable fact of the defeat of the Axis and some very short memories of wartime harmony. Even most of the specific territorial
and political agreements that had been made during the war
actually settled very little, and by the late 1940s some had
boomeranged and become matters of East-West wrangling that
set off further controversy. Once the secret provisions of the
Yalta agreement regarding Poland and territorial gains for the
USSR became publicly known in the late 1940s, for example,
they unleashed a storm of protest against Soviet expansionism
and led to wild accusations in the United States that American
"Reds" had sold out Western interests to the Russians, thereby
stoking the rising anti-Communist passion of the American
people.

Thus, most of the serious difficulties which World War II had
sent hurtling around the globe, from economic destruction and
instability to a heightened sense of national consciousness, had
not been dealt with during the conflict, but were simply dumped
into the laps of those who held power in the major countries after
1945. Yet the first and most pressing concern of all such leaders
was to try to handle the weighty economic, political, and psychological legacies which the war had deposited in each of their own
countries. As had been true during the war, so in the early postwar era as well, domestic developments within each of the major
powers were therefore vitally important in determining what the
wartime Big Four would do abroad. Once again, the course of
events inside the United States, the Soviet Union, China, and
Great Britain would decide, to an unusually pronounced degree,
the future of the whole world. China fell into economic and
political chaos, Britain slumped to the second or third rank, and

both the United States and the Soviet Union initially sought to look inward as much as possible and solve their own postwar domestic problems in their own way. The inevitable consequence was the creation of an enormous international power vacuum, made even emptier by the failure of the United Nation's peace-keeping machinery. Unavoidably this condition forced the two giants gradually and reluctantly to turn more and more of their attention away from their domestic pursuits, and to swing about facing one another. The great confrontation was thereby created and the era of the cold war begun.

5

Healthy, Wealthy, and Wise?

AMERICA, 1945–1950

For the United States, V-J Day in August 1945 was a more significant moment of national triumph than it was for any of the other members of the Allied coalition. America alone had thrown herself into major wars against both Germany and Japan between 1941 and 1945, and she finished the second of the two in a crescendo of armed might and high-tech warfare which was fittingly, if ominously, capped by the atomic bombing of Hiroshima and Nagasaki. This transcendent display of determination and power seemed to announce to a battered and war-scarred world that the young giant, America the invincible, had taken the fate of the world, and indeed the very atomic stuff of the universe, into its hands.

Wherever the public opinion pollsters could reach in 1945, the result was the same, for the majority of people everywhere believed that the United States would be the most powerful country on earth in the postwar era. But nowhere else was this view so broadly, and fervently, held as in the United States itself, where two-thirds of those polled had concluded even a month prior to Hiroshima and V-J Day that their country would be the most influential in the world after the war. Pride in America's armed might was added to the general satisfaction with the country's newly fulfilled economic promise, to convince the people of the United States that their country was indeed the master of its own, and the world's, fate, and was therefore capable of rather effortlessly leading the way into an era of peace and prosperity.

Between 1945 and 1950, the day-to-day economic experience of most Americans was so rosy that it, above all, set the tone for all aspects of the country's public life. The continuation of the wartime boom into the postwar period, with a high level of employment and massive consumer goods spending, was what the wartime public had wanted most of all. When it actually came to pass, the American public settled into a mood of gratitude, pride, and contentment which allowed little room for concern over domestic or foreign political problems. Difficulties in the rest of the world tended to be viewed as nuisances, threatening to compete with the enjoyment of the domestic economic bonanza which was the public's first love and most heartfelt desire.

The charting of the form and scope of America's postwar domestic economic achievement is therefore to outline the major factors which insulated the American public from facing up to the international obligations that this boom, and the country's power, were actually imposing on the United States.

In 1945, the bloated American wartime GNP figure dipped temporarily as military spending tapered off, but it was rising again in 1947, had equalled the 1945 figure by 1950, and then surged upward throughout the late 1950s. But consumers were not required to wait even a moment to feel the warm glow of prosperity and high levels of consumption. Disposable personal income rose steadily throughout the immediate postwar years, and as rationing ended and more goods came on the market, the level of personal savings fell off 75 percent from $29.6 billion to $7.3 billion between 1945 and 1947. Even those people who did deposit money in banks indicated by their planning preferences that for many the reasons for saving had come to be mixed up with consumer spending. A *Fortune* poll of November 1945 revealed that the traditional motivations for banking one's money, such as preparing for old age or helping with the children's education, had yielded place to creating a down payment for the purchase of a home. Indeed, between 1945 and 1947, while government borrowing rose approximately 12 percent, the amount loaned by banks and savings and loan companies for home mortgages jumped a colossal 33 percent per year.

As soon as new cars and home appliances began to appear in dealers' showrooms in 1946, customers flocked to them with little concern about price or credit terms. They had cash and were eager to spend it. So eager that demand raced far beyond supply, which set off an inflation of 12.5 percent per annum in the first two postwar years, and then brought forth a wave of strikes by workers who suddenly found their real income falling. The sharp inflation spurt tailed off quickly, however, and settled down to a modest rate of 3.5 percent per year in the years 1948–1950.

Federal government policies played a major role both in controlling inflation and in assisting the conversion of industry to peacetime production. The public deserves a share of the credit as well, for despite sporadic complaints, the polls indicate that most people were willing to put up with price, wage, and especially rent, controls until supply caught up with demand. However, the most important phenomenon both in the control of inflation and the creation of postwar prosperity was the speed and efficacy with which American industry and agriculture maintained high production levels while shifting to peacetime markets. This in turn sustained postwar optimism and produced the vital element which allowed the prosperity to perpetuate itself—the abundance of well-paid jobs. In 1945, 66 million Americans were either in military service or were otherwise gainfully employed. By 1947, although the military services held 10 million fewer people than two years before, there was still a total of 61 million people in the United States in civilian employment or military service, while the unemployment rate was held to a modest 3.9 percent.

The retention of a high rate of employment despite the precipitous demobilization of the bulk of the armed forces was in itself a near economic miracle. In part it arose from an unprecedented foreign demand for American goods, which was caused by the wartime destruction and dislocation of overseas production centers, especially those in Western Europe and Japan. The American high production and employment figures were also made possible by the retention of a modest draft in the early postwar years, which gobbled up some of the young school leavers before they attempted to enter the job market. The vast expansion of the higher education system, especially the government's educational assistance for veterans, played an especially important role. In 1949 there were 1.1 million more students enrolled in colleges than in 1938, which itself had been a period of unusually high college enrollment due to job shortages during the depression. One may attribute some measure of the increased postwar college enrollment to a higher technical demand being placed on young people by new developments in science and industry. But the biggest single factor was the G.I. Bill of Rights for veterans, which for the first time opened up the prospect of a subsidized college education to representatives from every class in American society. In 1949, even though the first flood of veterans had by that time already passed through the normal four years of undergraduate study, fully one-half of all males enrolled in American colleges and universities were veterans.

The large number of veterans, and the extensive governmental efforts to assist them, was a phenomenon which affected all aspects of postwar America. In 1940 there had only been 4.2 million veterans in the United States, approximately 7 percent of the male population. By 1947, the total had jumped to 18.2 million, and in that year 25 percent of the total male population of the U.S.A. were veterans. While the cumulative total of government expenditure for veterans from the beginning of the Republic until 1933 had only amounted to $16.2 billion, Washington spent $15 billion on aid to veterans in the years 1946–1948 alone.

Although primarily viewed by the public as a just reward for service rendered to the nation, the huge postwar expenditure on veteran's aid programs was, in addition, an important spur to the country's economic expansion. Assistance to veterans not only kept many returning G.I.'s out of the job market by putting them in college. Such veterans' aid was another instance of Washington's use of public tax and bond money to prod the system into a higher level of economic activity. Just as the New Deal had made use of depression relief spending to help prime the economic pump, and during World War II government-financed military expenditure had drastically expanded the whole American economic system, so in the Truman years the government's help for veterans acted as an important "Keynesian" activating force for postwar "free enterprise."

The enormous outlays for veterans, when coupled with reconversion costs at home and abroad, and the retention of a much larger military and civilian federal machinery than had existed before the war, allowed little room for sharp reductions in the federal budget. The national debt continued to rise during 1945–1947, but at a rate which was less than 13 percent of that for the war years, which meant that it remained slightly below the annual rate of inflation. Inevitably, no sharp decrease in the number of those paying income taxes, or the scale of their payments, occurred. The number of Americans who paid such taxes only decreased 1.1 million to a total of 41.5 million between 1945 and 1947, with a further drop to 36.4 million by 1949. The latter figure still represented a net increase of taxpayers of nearly 1,000 percent during the decade of the 1940s, and constituted a permanent revolution in the relation of the American people to their government and the power of that government at home and abroad. In light of this, the occasional grumbles about the income tax that appeared in the postwar public opinion polls, as well as the scrooge mentality that frequently surfaced in Congress, were in truth isolated spirits of bygone days, for the American people made the leap to paying for a big government with a minimum of discomfort or protest.

It was only the outsiders in American life who lost heavily in the transition from war to peacetime prosperity, and since the crucial element in their loss was the forfeiture of well-paying jobs, their discontent focused on the lack of work rather than on high income tax levels. With the closing of many war industries, and amid a chorus of praise for traditional values and the domestic wonders which waited at home for wives and mothers, large numbers of women were moved out of the work force. But this was far from a total exodus, for the female labor force in 1947 was 2.5 million larger than it had been in 1940, an overall rise of 17 percent. There were not only more working single women than there had been before the war, there were far more two-income families, and this made a substantial contribution to the high rate of purchase of consumer durables and the general appearance of prosperity.

Minority group members also lost ground in the postwar period, as the principle of first fired and last rehired came into full force. But the level of employment of blacks and other minorities in industrial jobs was still much higher than it had been before the war, and the migration of the black population from the rural South to northern and West Coast cities, as well as to those in the South itself, continued unabated. Therefore, World War II's contribution to solving a basic economic problem, which had defied solution for generations, gradually became permanent. In the postwar era, the drag which the impoverished rural South had imposed on the nation's economy was steadily lessened by means of a simple and crude process of depopulation. Even though the movement of poor blacks and whites to more developed areas did not break the age-old barriers of discrimination and segregation, or the handicaps of poor health and education, it did convert those who had moved into relatively more effective producers and consumers. Whatever the hardships and injustices involved in this process—and there were many—the general economy benefited, and there are even some signs that the war encouraged at least some whites to think that minority people needed a helping hand. An October 1947 poll, for example, revealed that 50 percent of the respondents believed that some Americans deserved "a better break," and among the groups specified as meriting help, blacks exceeded every other group by nearly four to one, even in the South.

Yet such well-meaning pieties failed to produce any significant reform measures in the immediate postwar years except for the desegregation of the armed forces. Furthermore, within a generation the concentrations of young unskilled black victims of discrimination in urban areas would constitute as serious a drag on the economy of the 1970s and 1980s as southern rural stagnation had done on that of the 1920s and 1930s.

Such considerations lay far beyond the horizon of the late 1940s, however. With statistics by the end of the decade showing an increase of five million in nonfarm work to set off against the loss of three hundred thousand agricultural jobs, the great American economic machine seemed to be working smoothly. New medical technology, more hospitals, and the means to increase nearly everyone's food intake combined to produce a drop in the death rate. At the same time, the baby boom, general affluence, and improved pre- and postnatal care did wonders for the birth rate. The combination of the dip in the death rate and the rise of the birthrate produced a steady increase in the population, which confounded those demographers who had predicted that population size would fall or remain constant in highly developed societies. The population boom thus seemed to add the blessing of biology to an America already confidently beaming about its prosperity and world power.

Not surprisingly, most public opinion surveys taken during the late 1940s showed Americans contented and confident. Eighty-six percent of those polled in January 1949 indicated that they were satisfied with the community in which they lived, and 77 percent expressed themselves as being generally content with their lot in life. In January 1947, 69 percent of all poll respondents thought their chances in life were better than their fathers' had been, while only 12.5 percent did not. Even 67.8 percent of the black people polled believed that they had more opportunities than their parents. Furthermore, as befitted a satisfied, optimistic, male-dominated society, 62.1 percent of the general population, and a full 75 percent of the black population, believed their *sons* (no mention was made of daughters) would do even better than they had done.

There was nearly as much pleasure taken in American realities as there was in the American dream. In the spring of 1949 when a poll gave people an opportunity to pick the place in the whole world which they would most like to visit during their holiday, 52 percent chose California or Florida, 12 percent selected other parts of the United States, and only 28 percent picked a location beyond America's boundaries.

Considering that most of the rest of the world was in a condition of general misery in the late 1940s, Americans showed rather good sense in wanting to stay at home, at least for the time being. The national vision was much less clear, however, regarding the role which the war and government expenditure had played in creating their happiness, but the leaders were probably more responsible for this than was the general public. No government or business opinion maker found it desirable to point to the war as the chief cause of the country's rise to power and contentment; it always seemed better to refer to some political program, economic shibboleth, or moral platitude as the main cause of the nation's great awakening. Not even the admirals and generals were bold enough to proclaim to the American people that the war had been good for them. Therefore in late 1948 when the pollsters dutifully asked if it had been necessary for America to enter World War II "to *keep* this country, the way you want it," 78 percent of the respondents just as dutifully replied yes (emphasis added).

Despite all the changes produced by the war, traditionalism was still strong enough to feed people's dreams. In November 1945, when people were polled on their favorite spare-time occupation, reading easily came out first, besting even sports by nearly four to one. Three and a half years later, in May–June 1949, poll results showed that 56 percent had never even seen a television program, much less owned a set.

The widespread reading of newspapers inclined all governments to take press impact very seriously. A British Foreign Office briefing for the foreign secretary in October 1945 went so far as to claim that by "publishing the facts" about the USSR's "deliberate policy of non-cooperation," British newspapers had only required two months to deflate "much of the pro-Russian emotionalism" which had been built up in Britain during the war. But the polls suggest that governments on both sides of the Atlantic exaggerated the ability of the press to alter public attitudes quickly. As late as the end of 1946, an American poll showed that while 21 percent thought that the newspaper which they usually read presented a fair picture of the USSR, 17 percent believed they were given too rosy a view and a full 42 percent held that their regular paper painted the USSR blacker than it really was.

Along with public skepticism, the impact of the American press was lessened by the populace's general ignorance of facts and concepts related to complicated developments at home and abroad. In May 1949 nearly half of those polled did not know the meaning of the word *lobbying.* A December 1948 survey found that despite the Truman Doctrine, the Marshall Plan, and the Berlin blockade, 46 percent did not grasp the meaning of the term *cold war,* and in March 1950, two months prior to the outbreak of the Korean conflict, 42 percent still did not know what "cold war" meant.

Changes had simply come too rapidly for the people to take everything in, and they looked toward the familiar, and what was working well, for security and succor. In material matters, God seemed to have taken special care of America, and the population responded by giving its heart and its loyalty to what it saw as the primary cause—the American system of minimally regulated capitalism. In January 1947, a poll found that only 19 percent of *union members* favored the closed shop, while 35 percent preferred the union shop, and a full 41 percent believed in the open shop. Of course not all parts of the American labor movement had such complete faith in the "free market" economy, but Ernest Bevin was surely correct when he declared in September 1945 that any effort to establish a worldwide minimum wage would founder on the opposition of the United States as well as that of the Soviet Union.

Since much of Americans' postwar optimism rested on the high performance of their economic system, it inevitably followed that initially their most pressing fears and forebodings focused in this same area. Throughout 1946 and 1947 American surveys revealed repeatedly that at least 60 percent of those polled anticipated a massive depression within ten years—perhaps as punishment for their sins of indulgence—while comparable polls in austerity-plagued Britain only found half as many prophets of economic doom. The pattern of American worries which emerged in the quarterly polls between 1945 and 1950 traced a clear, orderly shift as the people gradually put apprehension about the stability of their prosperity behind them, and simultaneously became more worried about the dangers that existed beyond America's boundaries. Between the fall of 1945 and that of 1946, the top three worries in every poll were domestic matters such as jobs, strikes, and inflation. Not until August 1946 did an international item, namely "peace," manage to reach third place. By early 1947, "international problems" had moved into second, with strikes and labor problems still first, and inflation third. Inflation managed to move up to first place in late 1947 and early 1948—just at the time it was actually abating—but from then on, in the era of the Marshall Plan and the Berlin blockade, international issues such as "peace," "Russia and Europe," and "other foreign issues," always held at least first and second place in the American anxiety ratings.

It is noteworthy that the polls indicate that the American public's apprehensions moved from domestic economic matters to foreign political matters between 1945 and 1948. The population saw quite rightly that most postwar domestic political divisions were relatively superficial, and it grasped further that in the late 1940s, the crucial American vulnerabilities abroad were still more political than economic. Despite some expansive talk in

corporate boardrooms, and the efforts of the State Department
to get other governments to follow trading and raw material
policies that would coincide with the interests of the world's
largest producer and trader, there was actually no great American economic explosion abroad in the late 1940s comparable to
that which had occurred during the war, or was actually taking
place inside America between 1945 and 1950. Exports did mark
up solid gains of 10 percent to 15 percent above 1945 by the year
1947, but if measured in real terms, they then actually fell by a
third between 1947 and 1950. Imports tended to follow an in-
verse pattern, rising less than 10 percent until 1947, and then
jumping an additional 30 percent by 1950. Overall American
imports from Canada and Africa did show healthy increases in
the first five postwar years, while those from Latin America did
not proportionately increase as much. The great exception lay in
the Latin American petroleum-exporting countries such as Mexico and Venezuela, which, along with the Arab nations, secured
strikingly higher sales to the United States between 1945 and
1950.

But before rushing to the conclusion that oil imports had already reached a position to exert decisive influence on American
policy—not to speak of American life—it is important to note
that on every Arab-Jewish issue that emerged in Palestine during
these years, the United States always came down on the Jewish
side. Furthermore, the statistics have a sober warning sign for
those who wish to maintain that the driving force in American
immediate postwar policy lay in a determination to advance
capitalism, exports, and raw material imports, for among the
countries with which American trade actually made the greatest
percentage gains was the Soviet Union, whose import-export ties
with the U.S.A. were over 100 percent higher than prewar until
the year 1949.

America's comparatively sluggish international economic role
in the immediate postwar period shows up especially strikingly
in the matter of investment. In the years 1945–1947, inflation-

adjusted overseas investment by the United States government increased by approximately one-third, but long-term private capital investment fell slightly, and the total of all private American foreign investment remained approximately even. The next three years showed a sharp change in the activity of the various types of American investment but no significant shift in the overall pattern. The American government's overseas investment only increased 5 percent between 1947 and 1950, while long-term private, and overall private, investment went up by one-third. During the whole five-year period 1945–1950, Canada continued to be the chief recipient of American private investment capital, with the dollar inflow there rising by 33 percent. Latin America was another zone of heavy new American private investment (a rise of 50 percent), with the petroleum-producing countries showing especially large increases. Outside the Western Hemisphere, the Middle East and Africa led the list of areas to which American capital funds found their way in the last part of the 1940s. Obviously oil was again the important factor in the Middle East, and in Africa the wartime trade increases with South Africa had been so enthusiastically followed up by the U.S.A. that in 1950, the Union of South Africa held 25 percent of all American investment on the African continent.

Even so, the general picture fails to reveal evidence of a broad American foreign investment campaign. Instead, there were only a few places where American private capital was prepared to enter enthusiastically of its own free will, as in the oil-producing regions and South Africa, while the rest of the world was either ignored or left to the uneven mercies of United States government aid and investment. In Western Europe, for example, where American government grants and loans were most extensive, and have received the most publicity, American private investors responded to the opportunities which such aid provided by actually *decreasing* their real gross investment level between 1945 and 1950. On the other hand, when the United States government refused Latin American requests for a "Marshall Plan" for the Southern Hemisphere, the State Department tried, with considerable success, to encourage private investors to send all possible capital south of the Rio Grande.

So, though to a war-torn and disorganized world, American trade and capital seemed enormously important in the immediate postwar period, they were peripheral to the United States both in terms of domestic economic statistics and public opinion. American producers and investors had not yet broken through their traditional reluctance to raise their sights much beyond the huge United States domestic market or to send their money to distant places with unpronounceable names that lacked the guarantees of stability present in Long Beach and British Columbia. The modest increase in America's international economic activity between 1945 and 1950 was actually a valley between the enormous World War II economic explosion and the great expansion in trade and overseas investment which began in the mid-1950s. Only in the latter period, when cold war passions had smoothed the way, was it possible to create a government and business campaign to employ a full range of private and public economic weapons as cold war instruments which would reap substantial gains both for an assertive worldwide American foreign policy and for the domestic economy.

Consequently the American public's international economic consciousness barely expanded at all in the early postwar period of 1945–1950. By mid-1947 the polls indicated that the majority had put the extreme isolationist high-tariff inanities behind them, and were even ready to accept the proposition that such ex-enemies as Japan should be allowed to sell their goods in the United States on the same basis as other countries. But in regard to America's general economic relations with the rest of the world, the average American seemed unable to move much beyond the dictates of human kindness and charity because of fears of international entanglements.

Between 1945 and 1947, in addition to UNRRA aid via the United Nations, the United States government provided Europe with ten billion dollars' worth of economic assistance, which actually worked out to a larger amount per annum than that which would be provided under the Marshall Plan during the height of the cold war. Not only did the American people not object to such humanitarian aid programs, the polls indicate that just as during the war, they would have been prepared to go even further. Between the spring of 1946 and the fall of 1947, a series of public opinion surveys put the people's international generosity through a series of stiff tests. In March 1946 they were asked if they would eat less in order to send more food to Europe, and 67 percent replied yes. A month later they were questioned on whether they would be willing to undergo rationing again to aid their wartime allies, and 67 percent again said yes. In May 1946, when the issue was put in an even broader form, proposing the reintroduction of rationing to aid all peoples in need, the number in favor rose to 70 percent. After two years of giving for postwar assistance, 65 percent of those surveyed still favored spending four hundred million dollars for food relief in the fiscal year 1948.

For those inclined to write this off as cold war calculation masquerading as generosity, in July 1947, two months *after* President Truman's announcement of his militantly anti-Communist aid program for Greece and Turkey, the majority of those polled believed that relief assistance should even be sent to needy countries whose governments were "unfriendly" to the United States. Even up to the very eve of the Korean war, after five years of rising international tension, 73 percent still supported aid programs for underdeveloped countries.

However, again just as during the prewar and war periods, when the questions were turned to ask whether the United States should make foreign loans, with their implication of more international entanglements, the public showed strong opposition. Throughout late 1945 the surveys revealed that the public was as firmly opposed to granting a loan or "free recovery aid" to Britain as it was to extending credit to Soviet Russia. In March 1947 when asked whether they were inclined toward balancing the budget or cutting military expenditure, 71 percent of those questioned preferred to keep up spending on the armed forces even at the cost of unbalancing the budget. But when the question was shifted to a choice between balancing the budget and making foreign loans, only 14 percent favored the loans. Nor did the tensions of the early cold war do much to overcome the American public's hostility to extending foreign credits. When asked in September 1949, after even the NATO pact was in existence, whether they would approve of a new loan to Britain, only 12 percent were in favor, while 50 percent had no opinion and 39 percent were opposed.

To some degree, this resistance to loans betokened the traditional American suspicion of foreigners. In July 1947, 71 percent opposed allowing any European displaced persons to enter the United States, and it must be allowed that for all the international understanding prompted by the war, returning G.I.'s frequently brought back bucketfuls of disdain for various other nationalities and an exaggerated vision of American superiority and virtue. In the late summer of 1945, even the president of the United States rocked a British diplomat back on his heels by off-handedly dismissing the French people as "listless and waiting for outside relief," and then going on to characterize Charles de Gaulle as "a pinhead."

But far more important than the simple phenomenon of xenophobia in the opposition of postwar Americans to what they saw as political-economic entanglements, was the people's deep distrust of every government in the world except their own. That in the late 1940s they should harbor suspicions regarding their former Axis enemies or the Soviet Union is not cause for wonder, but the degree of mistrust shown toward the British government, as well as that of other "Western" countries, was indeed noteworthy. Between March 1946 and March 1947, as has been frequently noted, the polls showed that the percentage of Americans who thought that the USSR wanted to dominate the world rose from 29 percent to 52 percent, while that for Germany dropped from 14 percent to 10 percent. But what has not been indicated is that in the spring of 1946, 12 percent of those questioned thought that poor bankrupt Britain was out to dominate the world, and 9 percent still clung to that curious view a year later. In February 1946, those registering suspicion of the United Kingdom stood at 41 percent while the percentage of those doubtful about the USSR was only eleven points higher. Two months later, after Churchill's "Iron Curtain" speech at Fulton, Missouri, only 18 percent of those surveyed were ready to line up with the United Kingdom against the Soviet Union. By September 1946, with the troubles in Palestine added to traditional Anglophobia, while 53 percent declared themselves as friendly to Britain as they had been a year previously, 30 percent were less friendly. Two months earlier, when asked which country most needed to receive American propaganda broadcasts, Britain came second to Soviet Russia, and *ahead* of defeated Germany.

As the cold war gained momentum, British and American officials continued to have good reason to worry about the strength of Anglophobia in the United States. When in May 1947 the pollsters asked which countries in the world were democratic, 88 percent of the American respondents said the U.S.A. No other country received even 50 percent, although Britain did manage to stagger in second with 48 percent yes and 35 percent no. On the even more significant weather vane issue of military security, Americans were extremely cautious. In September 1949, after a series of spy scandals and the Soviet detonation of an atom bomb, only 19 percent of Americans surveyed approved of sharing atomic secrets with the British despite the wartime collaboration of the two countries and Canada on the original atomic bomb project.

Given their doubts about other states, the people of America were naturally inclined to safeguard their postwar security by maintaining large military forces of their own. This inclination was strengthened by the codification of a popular myth that in 1941 a shy and retiring America had been innocently minding its own business until driven into World War II by the completely unprovoked "surprise attack" on Pearl Harbor. By the end of World War II the public memory of pre–Pearl Harbor lend-lease aid to the Allies, the oil embargo on Japan, and other assertive American prewar policies had nearly evaporated. In March 1946 when asked if the United States should have been attempting to stay out of World War II in 1941, 79 percent of the respondents said yes (and 8 percent no), and in response to the follow-up question whether Franklin Roosevelt had actually been trying to keep the United States out of the war in 1941, 65 percent said yes, and only 16 percent no. While granting that the Pearl Harbor congressional investigations were then in process and may have helped to unsettle the public mind, this result is still quite startling. After all that the United States had been through since 1941 one would have anticipated that more than 8 percent would think direct intervention in 1941 had been justified, and that more than 16 percent would have grown beyond the fiction that prior to Pearl Harbor the leaders of the United States government had been acting like directors of a children's crusade for peace.

But the view that the United States had been a totally innocent victim in 1941 (and perhaps 1917 as well) triumphed so completely that the absolute bedrock of the postwar public attitude toward foreign relations was that henceforth American armed might must be powerful enough to defeat all comers. The old belief that standing armies were a threat to democracy was almost totally swept away in a public resolve never again to be caught by susprise or be so poorly armed that the country could not defend itself. In eight public opinion polls taken between November 1945 and March 1949 those approving a universal one-year military training system were 72 percent in the first poll and 73 percent in the last, with the votes for such training never falling below 63 percent (May 1946) and peaking at 77 percent in April 1948 at the time of the Berlin airlift. Whenever the public was asked whether it wanted an increase in the size of the regular military forces, as occurred in December 1946, May 1948, and June 1950, the response was always strongly affirmative (70 percent, 81 percent, and 63 percent). On the first and last of these occasions those surveyed indicated by large majorities that they wanted no cut in the armed forces to make possible a reduction in taxes, and in June 1948 and February 1949 strong majorities indicated a willingness to pay higher taxes if necessary to give America more armed power.

By the end of the 1940s not even the dangers of an atomic weapons race with the USSR could deter American opinion from its basic commitment to the view that America's security had to rest primarily on its own armed forces. Seventy percent of those polled in August 1949 favored continued manufacture of A-bombs, and in February 1950 (five months after the Soviets' first atomic blast), 77 percent wanted the United States to go ahead and develop the H-bomb. In addition, although during the Korean War a poll found 60 percent opposed to use of atomic weapons in that conflict, an equal percentage in both 1949 and 1950 gave their stamp of approval to the use of the A-bomb in a general war, perhaps even on a first-strike basis.

But even in the face of this picture of a defense-minded American public stumbling into support for an atomic weapons race with the USSR, there is an indication of another very important current in the American people's postwar view of the world. In the February 1950 polls in which those responding overwhelmingly endorsed manufacture of the H-bomb, they were also asked if a control arrangement with the Soviet Union should be sought before work on the superbomb began. Over 50 percent said yes, and as if to show that this was not a fluke, when the question was tried again the following month, two out of three endorsed trying for a control agreement before any go-ahead was given for new nuclear weapons.

It is significant that even at this late date, after five years of cold war events and waves of anti-Soviet propaganda, the public had not abandoned all hope of a general settlement. The polls indicate that at every stage in the five years following V-J Day, the public operated on the belief that if the U.S.A. remained militarily strong, an arrangement for general peace would ultimately emerge through the offices of the United Nations. Considering American doubts about foreigners, and especially foreign governments, this may seem to have been a very peculiar phenomenon. But it appears that just because the American people were so pessimistic about the desire and ability of other countries to keep the peace through the old system of independent states and alliances, they concluded that salvation would have to come through American armed might and the United Nations.

Of course these initial starry-eyed hopes for an immediate transformation of swords into plowshares was soon followed by a slump in the rating of the United Nations in both American and British polls. But in May 1947, two months after the Truman Doctrine, two out of three Americans surveyed still believed that it would be better for the cause of peace to keep the USSR in the United Nations rather than attempt to exclude her. A February 1948 poll then found 51 percent pinning their hopes for peace on the U.N., 21 percent on a future system of world government, and only 13 percent inclined to put their trust in military alliances. In September 1948, 67 percent thought the United Nations Organization was an important force for peace, and in October 1949 after everything had happened from the Prague coup to the establishment of NATO, 61 percent continued to believe the United Nations was at least a partial success while only 19 percent considered it a failure.

The American public's desire to put its international faith in the United Nations and America's own military shield, while remaining cool toward military alliances and an aggressive global economic policy, was neither very profound nor very realistic. It failed to take into account the complexities of the world situation, the general devastation and disorganization outside America's borders, and the economic interdependency imperatives which underlay any hope of a long-term perpetuation of America's great post-1940 economic bubble. Furthermore, to rest a superpower's foreign policy on the twin pillars of support for the United Nations and acquisition of the maximum number of overseas bases was not very consistent, for as Ernest Bevin remarked in January 1946, in a classic piece of understatement, it was difficult "to mold these two things together."

All these criticisms of the postwar American public's attitudes are surely correct, but with four decades of hindsight it is nonetheless difficult to judge them too harshly. The enormous wealth and power which the American people had gained from the Second World War had not stifled their generous impulses nor inclined them, despite their feelings of economic insecurity, to use their strength to dash into every corner of the world grabbing raw materials and foreign markets. They had abandoned their dream of national security via isolationism without developing an appetite for incessant meddling or endless crises. They wanted a general settlement, a war deterrent, a machinery for resolving serious disputes, and they had come to believe that they would have to work in the world for international peace. In that sense, the public's conversion to a belief in the United Nations and the maintenance of strong military forces was about as much headway as anyone had a right to expect from one generation.

The basic difficulty was that in addition to a great global clamor calling on the American people to go further in varied and sundry ways, two branches of the United States government were also anxious to push the public in directions that it was not eager to go. Because Congress controlled the budget and the power to ratify treaties, it easily moved on to proclaim that it was the fulcrum of the people's will. Following the election of the highly conservative Eightieth Congress in November 1946, this claim was given a sharper cutting edge as the Republican majority waged a fierce political, and partially ideological, war against the Democratically controlled White House. So powerful did Congress appear that astute foreign observers believed it to be the critical element in American society. As the new British ambassador to Washington, Archibald Clark Kerr, reported to London in July 1946, "ultimately it is this lot that counts . . . so much more than the press that I have determined that my first and supreme duty here must be to do my utmost to nobble the members of the Senate and the House."

This was "no easy job," as Clark Kerr realized. The troubles with the Congress in the late 1940s, however, went well beyond the usual complaints about its provincialism, inefficiency, and death-defying slowness, for the polls suggest that both the Seventy-ninth and Eightieth Congresses were frequently marching to a different drummer than the majority of the public. The survey results consistently showed the population far more inclined to grant humanitarian aid abroad than the Congress, and the public was also more enthusiastic about the United Nations and more prepared to turn away from armadillolike interwar isolationist policies. Ironically, although most congressmen liked to parade their commitment to upholding America's image and power, the public was willing to pay for larger military forces than the representatives of either political party in Congress.

But if Congress was out of step with major elements of public opinion, so was the White House. On first glance, the Truman administration should have been the apple of the public's eye. Not only was this administration a successor to that of the highly popular Franklin Roosevelt, but the postwar president of the United States embodied many of the attributes of the common man at a time when the "age of the common man" had supposedly dawned, and when the positions of greatest authority over foreign policy had in fact fallen into the hands of such common men as Ernest Bevin and Joseph Stalin, as well as Harry S. Truman. The new president spoke simply and directly, and as George VI said after their first encounter, he was "short, simple and looks one straight in the face." Harry Truman was optimistic, "self-possessed," inclined to see things in "blacks and whites," and always ready to make crisp decisions. All this was true-blue American, and since the new president managed to put some illustrious, if tired, men such as George C. Marshall into positions of authority, he might have been expected at first glance to reap a public relations harvest.

But Harry Truman depended on his old Missouri and Senate cronies, many of whom clung to beliefs about international relations which lagged miles behind those of even the humblest citizen. Indeed, a man like the president's personal aide, General Harry Vaughan, had political views, which, sympathetic observers granted, could only be characterized as "American Legion Baroque." Nor did the president succeed in removing a number of intransigent individuals from positions where they could easily impede moves toward an innovative foreign policy. John Foster Dulles exercised a near-veto power over the secretary of state at international conferences as early as the summer of 1945, and General Douglas MacArthur possessed the authority to do and say nearly anything he wished all through the late 1940s. The American proconsul in Tokyo never hesitated to pour out his most outrageous views regarding sensitive American domestic matters to foreign emissaries. For example, in December 1947, he told a visiting British military man that the regular Republican presidential candidates, Dewey and Taft, could be easily "licked" because they were "shopworn," while among the Republican party military hopefuls for the White House, he stood in a better position than Eisenhower, whom he alleged had "Jewish blood in his veins."

But even this picture of Mr. Truman as a man of muddle who gladly tolerated mediocrity and eccentricity was not the most fundamental aspect of his foreign policy troubles. Due to the complexities of the international situation and the intransigence of the USSR, he could not give the American people what they wanted most, a quick and clean general postwar settlement. Secretary of State Byrnes failed to move Molotov by brandishing the A-bomb at the London Council of Foreign Ministers in the summer of 1945, and he was equally unsuccessful in December at Moscow when he tried to use his senatorial talents to "jump in quick" and clinch some kind of compromise. Stalin would not be hurried and obviously saw no reason why he should make things easier for the Truman administration. Therefore neither Byrnes nor Truman was able to point to the achievement of a general agreement for peace, and the administration had no choice but to attempt simultaneously to wrestle with an unstable world and the American public's preference for a simple policy based on support for the United Nations and the buildup of a large deterrent military force.

At the United Nations the Soviets again blocked the way, with vetoes and *nyets* making it impossible for the administration to point to any effective machinery there which would actually make the world stable and safe. Mr. Truman's own fiscal conservatism, when coupled with that of his old congressional colleagues, barred the way to giving the American public a large, visible, military force, which might have provided them with a greater sense of pride and security. After yielding to the initial public clamor to bring the boys back home, Mr. Truman was so tormented by the size of the national debt and the high level of taxation that he cut down military appropriation requests, and thereby forfeited any chance of winning popular support by creation of a large, and truly comforting, security blanket.

The postwar armed forces, numbering 1.7 million in 1947, were not large enough either to scare the Soviets or to reassure the public. But this force, which was five times larger than that of 1939, was certainly big enough to permit tens of thousands of military staff planners to be spread through the Pentagon, military installations in the U.S.A., the armies of occupation in Germany and Japan, and the multitude of new American bases around the world. Included among the 2.1 million Federal civilian employees in 1947, there was another large group of foreign affairs planners distributed across such departments as that of War, Navy, and the Treasury. These civil and military planners conceived their principle job to be the appraisal of the world situation and the development of schemes to deal with real or possible problems from Tijuana to Transylvania. Army planners had already begun staff studies for possible future world wars even prior to V-J Day, and G-2 began to focus on the Soviet Union as the most likely future general war opponent soon after the end of hostilities. Paradoxically, the postwar military's passion for contingency and emergency plans was partly caused by the generals' angst at the speed of the immediate postwar demobilization, for it had brought to mind disquieting analogies with the weak military forces which had made the United States so vulnerable between the wars.

Because the State Department nursed its own past grievances and sensitivities, it too was anxious to display planning and "crisis management" mettle in the immediate postwar years. Throughout most of the nineteenth and twentieth centuries the State Department and the diplomatic service had performed few roles except to act as humble message carriers and serve as the butt of numerous tired jokes about useless people who wore striped pants and spoke with affected accents. During the few moments when the United States had played forceful roles in world affairs, especially during the last part of World War I and nearly the whole of World War II, the White House staff, rather than officials of the State Department, made and executed basic American foreign policy. But then in April 1945, along came Harry Truman with his devotion to orderly administrative methods and a textbook view that the nation's foreign policy should be formed and executed chiefly by the Department of State.

The moment for which State Department activists had dreamed for 150 years had finally arrived—the department was to take the lead in asserting American influence to secure a worldwide settlement, protect American security, and advance what it saw as American interests. Young regional specialists in the department like George Kennan and Charles Bohlen, who had spent years trading position papers that actually led nowhere and only occasionally had found themselves brought into the bright light of White House attention because they had been needed to translate for some special emissary or the president, suddenly found themselves courted and treated like oracles. This was heady stuff, and the department exhibited such gusto in rushing forward with it that within three years it had convinced the public that it actually did run the nation's international relations. When in September 1948 a public opinion poll asked who the population thought was most responsible for American foreign policy, 43 percent replied the secretary of state, 21.4 percent believed, perhaps drolly, that it was Senator Vandenberg (the Republican chairman of the Foreign Relations Committee), and only 9.4 percent named Harry Truman. Such a development must surely have led to rustling in the graves of both Woodrow Wilson and Franklin Roosevelt.

As if the military and State Department did not have enough international planners and analysts in the early postwar years, a third major group was provided by various intelligence organizations. Although CIA was not formally created until 1947, World War II had left behind a large number of intelligence analysts, many of whom were put to work in various transitional units in the War and State departments during the years 1945–1947. Like the State Department, the intelligence organizations won their Madison Avenue effort to woo public opinion, 77 percent of those surveyed in March 1946 indicating that they favored a permanent American intelligence set-up and a global network of secret agents. The spooks actually went to work so quickly that by the end of the year 1946 the British foreign secretary had to demand that his embassy in Washington put virtually everything into cipher, because the United States government was obviously tapping into the transatlantic telephone traffic of what were supposed to be "friendly governments."

Although the postwar American military, intelligence, and State Department planners were long on numbers and money, the system was badly organized, and the planners lacked experience in coping with complex peacetime conditions, continuous high-level relations with major powers, or the kind of interconnected labyrinth of worldwide difficulties that had been left behind by the Second World War. The analysts therefore made frequent errors about specific problems in various parts of the world, but what was more serious, in their inexperience they were too inclined to seek answers in strained historical analogies. The notion that postwar Russia was rather like prewar Nazi Germany, and Stalin was really a Hitler with a large mustache, gained such credence in Washington even by the end of 1945, that the notion of an inevitable replay of the "expanding aggressor" scenario of the 1930s had virtually taken possession of the bureaucratic mind.

Furthermore, due to their want of experience as well as the

feeling of relative military weakness, the foreign policy and defense staffs showed an inclination to move issues too quickly to a level where the threat to employ extreme military pressure, especially the use of atomic weapons, might possibly resolve them. Such an all-or-nothing approach tended initially to find favor with a public which pined after quick settlements and believed in the efficacy of armed deterrence. But it boomeranged, not merely because the Soviets saw through it and refused to be frightened, but because the United States government simply did not have a formidable atomic weapons arsenal in 1945–1946. As late as 1947, there were only a dozen atomic bombs and twenty-eight heavy bombers equipped to drop them. Therefore, American "nuclear diplomacy" never had a chance of cornering the Soviets or making the American public believe that the United States possessed an effective international security weapon.

Having failed to tidy up the postwar international disorder quickly or tame the Soviet Union by any relatively simple or direct method such as the United Nations, re-creation of a huge expensive military machine, or atomic bluff, Washington's new international security establishment fell back on the policy of "containing" Soviet expansion by a combination of global diplomatic activity, economic pressure, aid programs, military alliances, and covert operations. This approach, which its creator, George Kennan (who set forth its basic principles in his "Long Telegram" from Moscow in early 1946, and under the nom de plume "Mister X" later presented it publicly in an article in *Foreign Affairs*), contended would limit Soviet expansion chiefly by political and economic pressure rather than military means, seemed both reasonable and unavoidable in Washington. But containment did not have much appeal for the rest of the country, because it involved continuous American governmental activity in the four corners of the world, which every postwar opinion poll makes clear was about the last thing that the bulk of the public, caught up in its postwar spending bonanza, had in mind.

The government was able to hide most of its covert enterprises (such as the effort to tip the Italian elections away from the

Communists) so these never had to stand the test of public opinion in that period. But containment's foreign aid and alliance programs could not be kept secret because they required tax money and, in some cases, Senate treaty approval. It is therefore easier to judge through the polls how the public reacted to them. The first major program, the Truman Doctrine of economic and military aid to Turkey and Greece in 1947, secured a small majority in favor of the general idea, but then an equally large group disapproved of actually sending any American weapons or military advisers. The Marshall Plan, which emerged in 1947–1948, seemed to do rather better. Two-thirds of the respondents who were familiar with the plan approved, but even at the end of September 1947, 50 percent of those polled had never heard of it, and when a year later the public was asked whether armed strength or the Marshall Plan was the best way to avoid war, military power still won by better than two and a half to one.

By 1948, in most polls, the majority had come to approve the creation of a military alliance system in Western Europe, and generally even agreed that American military forces should be used to stop Communist coups in major Western countries. But a suggestion that two billion dollars' worth of military assistance actually be sent to Western Europe was beaten two to one in a December 1948 poll, and six months thereafter (May 1949), over a third of those responding to a major survey believed that creation of NATO had actually increased the risk of war.

For Asia too, despite subsequent fantasizing by the China Lobby—that fanatical band of Chiang Kai-shek's American supporters, such as Congressman Judd and Henry Luce of *Time* and *Life,* who in the 1950s would accuse "Reds" in the State Department of "losing" China to Mao—the American public actually had substantial doubts about containment aid and alliance support for Kuomintang China. An April 1948 poll found opponents of aid to Chiang ahead nearly two to one. Eight months later, although 28 percent of those polled did not even know that there was a civil war raging in China, among those who did, opinion had swung around so that almost two out of three supported aid to the Kuomintang. However, this support immediately evaporated when the pollsters actually suggested a figure of five billion dollars in assistance to Chiang, for then 34 percent opposed, 40 percent were doubtful, and only 28 percent approved. By April 1949, with Mao's victory at hand, the majority had concluded that it was best to keep American hands off China. Just before, and just after, the Communist triumph in 1949, although those who opposed diplomatic recognition of Mao's regime steadily exceeded those in favor by majorities of two to one, on the issue of trade, opponents only held a slim advantage in both an April and November 1949 poll.

But then North Korea invaded South Korea in June 1950, and the United States responded by leading a United Nations crusade to protect what was seen as a victim of Communist expansion. American intervention was soon countered by Red China's entry into the war on the side of North Korea, and three years of bloody fighting, plus thirty thousand American battle dead, were required to achieve even a stalemated armistice in June 1953. Of course this eliminated any possibility of accommodation with Mao's China for the foreseeable future, and it simultaneously accelerated the evolution of American opinion toward favoring the rehabilitation of Japan and Germany to help serve as counterweights to the Communist powers in Europe and Asia. But it took this actual combat, and the bloodying of American forces, before the polls showed a steady near-unanimity of opinion in favor of a containment policy and the extensive military aid programs which accompanied it. Until that point, substantial popular doubt had remained. In August 1949, after NATO had been established and at the very moment of Mao's triumph, when a poll had asked whether the United States should send military assistance to any country which wished to defend itself against the Soviet Union, the result was 14 percent with no opinion, 40 percent against, and only 46 percent in favor.

By this time the public had seen a series of Soviet repressive regimes imposed on Eastern Europe, the Czech coup, the Berlin blockade, the paralysis of the United Nations, and what the China Lobby called "the loss of China." It had been subject to an intense anti-Communist and anti-Soviet propaganda campaign waged by a series of private Red baiters as well as the government itself. Even during the Second World War the public had been restrained in its enthusiasm for its Soviet ally and favored doing everything punitive to domestic Communists short of drawing and quartering. The great Red scare of the late 1940s and 1950s, which fed on the apparent failures of America's "soft" postwar foreign policy, went further in whipping up hatred of "Reds" and "pinks," and shredded the civil rights of many American citizens. It convinced most Americans that Soviet Russia was at least as aggressive and untrustworthy as Nazi Germany had been, and in head-to-head confrontations, such as the Berlin blockade, up to 85 percent of those polled were prepared to stand firm against the USSR, even at the risk of general war.

But despite the best efforts of the government's containment enthusiasts, as well as the exertions of those preaching the dangers of the Red peril, prior to the Korean War, occasions on which the polls showed Americans closing ranks about what should be done regarding the USSR were extremely rare. The public did not warm to the prospect of leading an eternal global economic and political-military struggle against the Soviet Union or what it was taught to see as Communist subversion in Europe and the Third World. It reluctantly gave up its simplest dreams and gradually adapted itself to the inevitability of one military assistance and overseas investment program after another. But it never did so enthusiastically. In their hearts, the American people were very limited internationalists, who much preferred to stay home and enjoy their economic prosperity.

The war had given the United States such an overabundance of economic and military power that no lasting postwar settlement was possible without the active participation and support of the U.S.A. The great midcentury conflict created in Washington a governmental machine whose members grasped this fact, and were prepared to go beyond public opinion in order to find the means through which a system of economic and political stability could be established in at least most of the world. But the public never understood the international underpinnings of its own economic miracle, and failed to be touched by the magic wand of imperial delight which would have made it enthusiastic about the establishment of the *pax Americana.*

The postwar United States remained an enormously powerful and erratically assertive giant, but ultimately it was a reluctant one, and the rest of the world therefore simply had no choice but to do the best it could with that.

6

The Walking Wounded:
THE USSR, 1945–1950

In May 1945 the supreme Soviet leader and the people of the USSR stood up proudly amid the ruins of their country, having triumphed in the bloodiest war of endurance in modern times. With good cause the people believed that their fortitude and their ability to absorb punishment had been the most basic element in the ultimate Allied defeat of Hitler. They wanted their achievement to be recognized and honored, and the opportunity provided by their triumph to be so used that the USSR would henceforth be powerful, secure, and totally immune from any more surprise attacks such as the calamity which had befallen them on 22 June 1941.

Stalin and his associates had, however, always been highly suspicious, and had routinely employed repressive measures that appeared to be extraordinarily barbarous by Western standards. They carried within themselves a heavy baggage of Marxist-Leninist distrust, a long history of brutal factional fights lost and won, and a withering record of domestic political atrocities. Coming on top of that heritage, there was little chance that the dangers and generalized savagery of the war in the East would incline such men to lie down quietly with lambs, or other lions. The war may actually have exaggerated the extreme statism of

168

the USSR and intensified the leaders' suspicion of everything which transpired outside the Soviet Union's borders.

Their country had been ravaged, many of its people and productive facilities decimated, and they were still faced with the same old problems of backwardness, distance, and weather, as well as eight to ten capitalist countries surrounding their zone of influence and the American colossus with its atomic bombs and overwhelming economic power standing just over the horizon. The surviving Soviet population had been pulled together displaying much of the pride and power of a tribal band, and the Red Army had shown itself to be an awesome fighting force, but given the circumstances that prevailed in 1945, there was no possibility that such relatively modest developments would have been sufficient to make Stalin and his colleagues put their combative distrust behind them.

The sharp limits which existed to the postwar possibilities for cooperation between the USSR and the Western powers were made graphically clear from some of the earliest postwar exploratory discussions with Stalin. The secret police repressive system that the Soviets erected behind their advancing armies in Eastern Europe was the main danger signal for such people as the American secretary of war, Henry Stimson, but no Western leader ever came remotely close to actually negotiating with Stalin about whether the NKVD operations and the Gulag would be continued. The initial sticking points on which the Soviet leader refused to give an inch were far pettier than that. Stalin rejected all Anglo-American efforts to initiate commercial air services from Western cities through to Moscow, demanding that every flight terminate in Berlin, where passengers would have to be transferred to Soviet aircraft. Even more suggestive was Stalin's insistence, not only that every Soviet national who had been left in Western hands by the war should be forcibly returned to the USSR—the so-called victims of Yalta—but that no Soviet citizen should henceforth be allowed to leave the Russian homeland. British leaders tried repeatedly to persuade the Soviet government that the twenty-two Russian women who had married

British diplomats and soldiers during the war should be allowed to join their husbands in the United Kingdom. In 1946, Molotov rejected such an appeal because the exit of these twenty-two people would be "extremely dangerous," and when Field Marshal Montgomery raised the matter in an unusually warm and friendly discussion with Stalin in January 1947, this was the only subject on which the Soviet leader gave the field marshal no encouragement. When the British foreign secretary, Ernest Bevin, tried again two months later, Stalin declared that he "did not think anything could be done," and then donning his old costume of the well-intended Uncle Joe who was hemmed in by a nasty Politburo, he told Bevin that "he had twice been hardly dealt with in the Supreme Soviet for raising this subject." Every citizen's labor was seen as essential, all were potential traitors and spies, and therefore no one could be allowed to turn away from the system, or escape from it.

So, no matter what course diplomacy had followed in the postwar period, the USSR would have remained more cut off, more repressive, and more self-sufficient than the Western states. At the best, some balance and some interaction between the two systems might have been possible, and perhaps a measure of trust could have been generated based on accepting the differences and playing a vigilant game within hard-edged rules. Better than that there could not have been, but as Stalin pointed out to Ambassador Harriman as early as December 1945, things could be made much worse. The Soviet Union could become, in the Soviet leader's word, "isolationist," by which he presumably meant that she could seal off herself and her zone as completely as possible, cut her trade and contacts with the West to a trickle, refuse to play the rest of the world's game, and make use of Communist parties and intimidation to weaken other countries and keep them off balance.

For the Soviet Union as for the West, there were solid reasons to avoid going along the East-West "isolationist" route if it was possible to avoid it. The people everywhere longed for peace and security after the ravages of the war, and nowhere was this feeling stronger than among the long-suffering population of the Soviet Union. In addition, a new arms race was hardly in the interest of a country as badly battered as the USSR, especially when its neighboring states were in a condition of such destruction and disruption that they posed no immediate danger. But it was the breadth and depth of the injuries that Soviet society had sustained that surely was the biggest factor beckoning the Soviet leadership toward exploring possible benefits from limited cooperation. Canny as he was, Stalin must have realized that even his best efforts could not completely hide the degree of the USSR's domestic destruction from foreign governments. For example, when Bevin returned from Moscow in December 1945, he declared that although he had not been allowed to see much, he "understood" that seventeen hundred towns and sixty thousand villages had been "completely knocked down," and that "we have no measure at all" of the terrible conditions "under which her people are living."

Ironically, it was Stalin's Marxist-Leninist vision, as much as anything, which blocked a significant early postwar arrangement for economic cooperation going beyond expanded trade and perhaps leading to bigger things. The Soviet leader seems to have been firmly convinced that the postwar West, especially its American capitalist heartland, inevitably had to fall victim to a quick depression if it did not immediately secure large foreign markets to absorb the surplus output which had been created during the war. Therefore, in his mind, he was doing the West a favor by offering to accept a loan to purchase American goods, because he would be making a major contribution to at least delaying the economic debacle which was hanging over the United States. Needless to say, Washington was not inclined to see matters that way, contending that to merit a loan the USSR would at least have to mend its repressive ways, if not make substantial concessions. This impasse quickly led Washington to avoid all further mention of a possible loan after Harriman's offhand 1945 suggestion to the Russians that it might be possible, and the United States soon joined the British in concluding that tendering loans was no way to exert pressure on Moscow.

Therefore the economic path to possible closer East-West cooperation was quickly lost, and the unilateral recovery course on which the Soviet Union embarked soon made matters worse. At that time all industry, in both East and West, depended on masses of labor, and the productive strain put on the USSR by the sheer wartime loss of manpower is now difficult to appreciate for people who live in societies in which surplus labor and mass unemployment are among the major national torments. But Soviet Russia's heavy wartime population losses caused productive labor decreases that would plague the economy for generations. The 1946 birthrate in the Soviet Union was only 75 percent of that for 1940, while births in 1950 were still 20 percent below the prewar level.

The heavier losses by the Great Russian population, compared with those of other nationalities in the Soviet Union, put a limit on the amount of conquered border land which could be annexed to the USSR without undermining Russian predominance. This, along with other factors, forced the USSR to base its new security zone primarily on a system of satellite states rather than simple annexation. The resulting stresses and strains, and the obvious Soviet manipulation and repression, inevitably increased Western criticism of the USSR.

Whether annexed or not, the populations in the satellites provided manpower for the Gulag, as did Soviet dissidents, common criminals, those returning from German captivity, and the people forcibly repatriated by the Western governments. Surely the major reasons for the creation and maintenance of the forced-labor empire were the paranoia of Stalin and the bureaucratic imperialism of Beria, but in addition, the Gulag constituted a significant labor force in the USSR's postwar economic recovery campaign. The use of a large number of German POWs as forced reconstruction labor—a policy which had been warmly applauded by American wartime public opinion—also played a part in speeding up Soviet recovery, as did the eight hundred thousand Japanese who had been captured in Manchuria in August 1945 and were still toiling in Siberia three years later.

Harsh Soviet exploitation of Gulag and enemy POW labor certainly did not help to improve relations with the West, and the policy which Stalin followed regarding the size and disposition of the Red Army made things even worse. It was impossible for the USSR to retain its huge World War II military force intact, and most Western analysts now accept that the Red Army was down to 2.8 million men by 1948. This was still a substantially larger force than the American—one million in the army in 1947—though American superiority in air power went a long way to offsetting Soviet strength in manpower and tanks. It should be noted as well that although many of its forces were scattered over the empire, the British army was larger than the American in 1947, and Britain had a higher percentage of its manpower in the armed forces than did the Soviet Union.

Having substantially reduced the size of the Red Army in order to free labor for economic reconstruction, Stalin then did his best to secure additional political and economic benefits from those who remained in uniform. Large Soviet military units were stationed on satellite territory, where much of their support could be paid for from the local economies. The Red Army units in East Germany and the other satellite territories overawed the local population and simultaneously filled the West with fear that what was widely, and erroneously, believed to be a ten-million-man Soviet armored machine might one day simply roll forward to the Channel.

Whether the destabilizing effect of this policy on Western Europe provided the USSR with enough political benefits to counterbalance the dangerous alarm which it produced in Washington is a matter of continuing debate. But it should be noted that the concentration of Soviet armed power in her European dependencies was but one aspect of Moscow's broader decision to exploit the satellites for the sake of a faster unilateral economic recovery in the homeland. The economies of Eastern Europe,

and of Manchuria, were immediately stripped of transport, industrial, and agricultural equipment, which was hauled back to
the USSR to assist in reconstruction. This policy coincided perfectly with Stalin's security mania and the system of building
socialism in one country, which he had championed since the
late 1920s. But it created deep resentment among the Western
Allied administrators in occupied Germany and Austria, who
saw such looting as inimical to any hope of creating successful
joint occupation administrations in the defeated Axis countries.

Soviet looting, rigged trade agreements, barriers to trade with
the outside world, and the imposition of the heavy burden of Red
Army occupation costs kept Eastern Europe as a near wasteland
in the immediate postwar years. This was hardly the way to win
friends and influence people, because it was viewed, quite rightly,
as Soviet economic exploitation. The resulting ill will extended
beyond the local conservatives in Eastern Europe and such Western businessmen as those who lost their oil investments in Rumania, to embrace many Socialists and even such Communists
as Mao Zedong and Tito, who ultimately saw that their countries' economic needs were being sacrificed to those of the USSR.

The unwillingness, or inability, of the Soviet authorities to
come clean with the rest of the world at an early date and explain that much of this was made necessary by the severe damage
which the Germans had inflicted on the USSR, locked all parties
into a vicious circle of suspicion, anger, and further repression.
On one occasion, fairly late in the day, Stalin actually let the cat
out of the bag in a discussion with Secretary of State George
Marshall. In Moscow during March 1947, the Soviet leader con-
fessed, "they were very busy here because they had suffered such
great losses in the war" that "they were only learning every day
how badly hurt they had been." The Soviet leader went on cautiously to reopen the question of a possible loan from the U.S.A.
and to ask again for a better break on reparations. "The United
States and England might be willing to give up reparations,"
Stalin observed, but "the Soviet Union could not." The USSR
had simply suffered too much, "and while reparations might not

be popular in the United States and England, ten billion dollars of reparations were very popular in the Soviet Union."

Marshall got the message and actually explored the possibility of trying to cut a new reparations deal in an effort to entice the USSR into gentler and more cooperative ways. But by 1947 Marshall's associates in Washington had already gone too far down the hard-line road to back away—the Truman Doctrine had already been announced—and the British government was so strapped for funds in the winter of 1947 that it would not consider any diplomatic initiative that would require further financial sacrifices by the United Kingdom. So the USSR was left to recover as well as it could by grabbing whatever was available in the satellites and imposing further economic sacrifices on its own people.

The initial industrial and agricultural recovery program was naturally concentrated on the western regions where prewar development had been greatest, and wartime losses had been most severe. By 1948–1949 a large portion of the productive equipment which had been transferred to the Urals was moved once again to the west, and throughout the whole first postwar decade, the western region received the bulk of new investment. After a shaky, and what seemed to the Soviet people a depressingly slow start, signs of recovery began to appear. The GNP and national income levels of 1940 seem to have been reached again by 1948–1949, although the statistical evidence is spotty and unreliable.

Since this was Stalin's Russia, the heavy industrial sector clearly made a substantial recovery by 1949, and just as clearly, agriculture had been given short shrift. The number of agricultural tractors, trucks, and related farm equipment had probably surpassed the prewar numbers by the mid-1950s, due to a short-term increase of capital investment. But this was merely an emergency response to the combination of war loss and drought, which had triggered a major agricultural disaster in the USSR during 1945–1946. The suffering of the rural population was so intense in those years that famine, and apparently in some areas even cannibalism, occurred, and these left the then-Soviet chief of the Ukraine, N. Khrushchev, moist-eyed for the next twenty-five years. But even these were in part crocodile tears. Khrushchev himself had played a part in the Ukrainian agricultural debacle, and despite some emergency relief, Soviet agriculture continued to lag far behind industry. Gross agricultural production in 1950 was still below that for 1940, and the average yield for most crops in the years 1949–1953 was under what it had been in 1913.

Even to achieve this level of output, the USSR had been compelled to retain very large portions of its working population on the land. As late as 1959, 31.4 percent of the Soviet work force was still on the collective farms, while the percentage of the American labor force employed in agriculture had already fallen to less than 16 percent by 1947. This inefficient use of labor was a serious obstacle to rapid economic growth, and the drag on output lessened the USSR's ability to trade abroad to secure the industrial goods she needed to speed her recovery. As Stalin admitted to Bevin in March 1947, he could only consider selling grain abroad "if there was no drought." There were no agricultural reserves in the Soviet Union, and the system of secrecy and security-mindedness made it impossible to embark on economic policies which might encourage too much interest from outside governments if anything went badly wrong.

This disjointed economic program did permit the USSR to get onto its feet largely by its own efforts, but it was a defense-oriented reconstruction with low, and only very slowly improving, standards of living. The odd balance of backwardness, military power, and pride in the sacrifices and achievements of the USSR that resulted from the system inevitably exploded in various forms of popular xenophobia and fear. At the same time, by stressing that this was a national Horatio Alger story in which the Soviet people and the Communist party had achieved recovery on their own, Stalin acquired a number of highly potent political cards to be played at home and abroad. With one stroke, even the limited economic interdependence which did exist was removed from public view. Wartime lend-lease aid, and the enormous quantity of UNRRA assistance which had poured into Eastern Europe between 1945 and 1947, were dismissed as of marginal importance. The economic exactions from the satellites, which constituted the biggest single element in the nominal 600 percent increase in Soviet "foreign trade" by 1949, were also swept under the rug. Since no clear picture of the country's economic condition or military power was allowed to appear, Stalin was able to present to foreigners, and his own people, any image of the USSR that he found appropriate. The pictures of Soviet Russia which he displayed in his magic lantern show ranged from that of a land martyred in the Allied wartime cause to a country so prosperous and strong that nothing lay beyond its power.

By using such tricks and playing on the ignorance and worry of concerned foreigners, Stalin was able to turn his own person into a hall of magic mirrors, alternately emerging as an ideological fanatic, a practical realist, an all-powerful dictator, and a kindhearted man hemmed in by difficult conditions and intransigent associates. For a tough old trade unionist like Ernest Bevin, attendance at only one Kremlin performance was enough to expose the whole show. Asked by a *Daily Telegraph* reporter to comment in a secret press briefing following the Moscow Council of Foreign Ministers meeting on "the relations between Stalin and Molotov," the foreign secretary snapped back, "One does what the other tells him. Stalin is the boss." A year later, when Field Marshal Montgomery, who had given and received a few orders in his time, had his first direct experience of the actual workings of the Kremlin, even he was rather shocked to discover what real authority looked like. Finding himself in a formal dinner hosted by the Soviet leader, he learned that it was extremely difficult to strike up a conversation even with the highest Soviet officials, for as he reported to London, "the Marshals, Ministers (including Molotov and Vyshinsky), and Generals, are all in the greatest awe of Stalin and shut up like an oyster in his presence."

The reality of Stalin as powerful and ruthless dictator had been too hard a pill for most Western officials to swallow during the war, and led enthusiastically by Roosevelt and only a bit less enthusiastically by Churchill, they had burnished its edges with the hope that the Soviet leader might be just moody, or an actor whose actual position resembled something akin to that of an American big-city machine politician. Initially Harry Truman tried to fit Stalin into the spectrum of tough American political leaders, likening him in May 1945 to "Frank Hague or Tom Pendergast," and then drawing his imagery from the opposition party, suggesting that just like "Joe Martin or Robert Taft," he merely wanted to arrange things to his advantage and protect his own power in his "bailiwick." After Potsdam, however, Truman concluded in a shower of expletives that Stalin was not only a dictator, but a cheat, and a man against whom only power could have much effect. By this time too, a number of American and British generals and civil officials had come to the view that the Soviet people and their leader had not evolved much beyond the level of Cro-Magnon man.

However, there were other strong voices in the West who refused to believe that the kind of cooperation which had existed in wartime was irretrievably lost. Such people existed far beyond the Left wing of the Labour party or the circle around Henry Wallace, for failure to effect an Allied compromise following such a terrible war seemed too horrible a fate for most people to accept. But as Soviet negotiators led by "iron pants" Molotov and Andre Vyshinsky—who had previously distinguished himself as chief prosecutor during the 1930s purge trials—filled the postwar air with rudeness, abuse of the West, and refusal to make concessions, those Westerners longing for a settlement transferred their final dream of success to an intervention by Stalin, who, it was hoped, would overrule his ill-behaved subordinates and make a deal. This idea lay behind Secretary of State Byrnes's unilateral bid for a late 1945 foreign secretaries meeting in Moscow, because Byrnes hoped to get around Molotov's intransigence by making a personal appeal to the supreme Soviet leader. Traces of this same hope that personal contact with Stalin might yet save the situation also appeared in the American public opinion surveys as late as 1948–1949, when two out of three of those polled consistently favored a summit meeting between Stalin and Truman. Even as suave an aristocratic diplomat as Harold Nicholson displayed a surprising degree of determination to hold onto his belief that Stalin alone had a wonder-working capability, for in a conversation with Victoria Sackville-West in March 1946, he ascribed the declining prospects for a long-term peace primarily to what he saw as the fact "that the pan-Slav and world revolution elements have gained the upper hand in Russia and that Stalin has ceased to count."

That postwar opinion in the West was soon divided between those who saw Stalin as an all-powerful villain and those who believed he was the world's last, if not morally best, hope for peace, obviously played into the hands of the Soviet leader. Whichever end of this seesaw one chose to sit on, Stalin rose up on the other. Either as war- or peacemaker he had been placed in a position of ascendency both at home and abroad which surpassed anything he had achieved during either the wartime or prewar periods. Until 1948, when Dijilas and others noticed the slips of memory that pointed toward approaching senility, Stalin played his strong hand with the skill one would have expected of a man who had learned during the war to play the international game in terms of both objective and real reality.

Stalin was a master of the direct, no-nonsense approach to personal diplomacy. When, upon arrival at the Kremlin in early 1947, Montgomery presented Stalin with a copy of each of his books and a case of whiskey, the Soviet leader looked him straight in the eye and said with a smile, "You bring me these presents, now what do you want out of me?" Although he generally briefed himself very well, when a relatively obscure matter such as international control of Danubian water transport arose in discussion with a high foreign official, he did not hesitate to admit that he was unfamiliar with the question and ask for time to consider it. On occasion, he could even to some degree grant the defects of his own regime, conceding to George Marshall with masterful understatement in 1947, that "there was occasional sloppiness in the operation of the Soviet Government."

But no sooner did the Soviet leader make such an admission than he usually managed to turn the same point back the other way, as when he observed slyly to Marshall that it was "possibly due to sloppiness on the part of the United States Government" that Moscow had not heard anything more about the proposed American loan for a period of nearly two years. Stalin possessed an unusual measure of barefaced gall, which allowed him to advance the most absurd justifying arguments for a position he was determined to maintain. When in December 1945 he declared that large Soviet forces had to be kept in northern Iran to protect the Baku oil fields, Bevin teased the Soviet leader about the amount of damage which the Persian militia could be expected to inflict on the Red Army, which was, after all, the largest in the world. But Stalin stuck to his ludicrous position, declaring that there was nonetheless great danger from Iranian "diversionary" activities.

Such a stubborn, yet adroit, negotiator had no difficulty assuming the role of the ill-treated and abused comrade when it suited his purposes. In December 1945, after Bevin had given him a long and misleading explanation to justify Britain's opposition to granting to the USSR a trusteeship in Tripolitania, Stalin replied that he noted "the British were not prepared to trust the Soviets in Tripolitania . . . he saw the situation, the United Kingdom had India and her possessions in the Indian Ocean in her sphere; the United States had China and Japan, but the Soviets had nothing."

In addition to such theatrics, the Soviet leader was prepared to walk softly or even take a tactical step back, when it suited his purposes. Although the West failed to take due notice, during the 1945–1947 period the Soviet occupation system in Hungary, Czechoslovakia, and even Poland—the three most Western and highly developed of the satellites—was markedly gentler than that which was used in Rumania, Bulgaria, or in the Soviet Union itself. Presumably Stalin was attempting to signal to the West that some variety would be possible within the Soviet sphere, and he may have felt that a few silken fingers, even if they were not the whole glove, might make adjustment to Soviet reality easier for the most marginal satellites.

Across the world in China during 1948, Stalin offered to mediate in the civil war at a time when Chiang was already on the run. Obviously, on that occasion it is possible that he was mainly trying to wiggle himself into a controlling position that would give him a halter on Mao, as well as the Nationalist leaders, but it must be recognized that although he did not go as far as the old German Socialist leader, Friedrich Ebert, who reportedly "hated revolution like sin," Stalin was no friend of confusion and disorder. In December 1945, he remarked to Bevin that he was not anxious to have the British evacuate all the territories they held, and gave the British foreign secretary to understand that he accepted the need for a British policing role in Egypt. A year and a half later he went out of his way to remind Bevin that "he had once said [to him] that if Great Britain had not been in Egypt, the Egyptian Government might well have turned Nazi."

Regarding India as well, Stalin did not pursue an energetic revolutionary course or try to crucify London for the postwar policy which it followed in the subcontinent. After initially refusing to allow into the United Nations Organization an Indian "government" which was obviously a mere tool of Britain, the Soviet chief immediately changed tack and offered Bevin a swap whereby both India and the Baltic States would be allowed into the General Assembly. Fifteen months after Bevin failed to take up this offer, and the process leading to independence had begun, Stalin twice stressed to the foreign secretary that regardless of their other difficulties, there was no division of view on the subcontinent, for the USSR wished "success to Great Britain in the enterprise she has started in India."

These expressions of realism, and willingness to cooperate in areas which the USSR did not consider vital, of course did not mean that Stalin was an old softie at heart, or that he was ever willing to be hurried into a settlement. When he held high cards, the basic trademark of his style of play was to delay, be difficult, drag out matters as much as possible, and hope that impatience would cause his opponent to make a serious mistake. Yet it seems clear that in the immediate postwar period he did not want to follow this technique so far that the West would break off. When George Marshall told him in March 1947 that Washington was so angered by Soviet noncooperation in Germany that it was ready to scrap the Four Power control machinery and go it alone, Stalin replied with a reassuring, and highly revealing, view of the way he conducted his business:

He did not think the situation was so tragic and he was more optimistic than Mr. Marshall. After all, these were only the first skirmishes and brushes of reconnaissance forces on this question. Differences had occurred before on other questions, and as a rule after people had exhausted themselves in dispute, they then recognized the necessity of compromise.

But on some issues in addition to Soviet security, there was never any basis for real compromise with Stalin. At home and abroad, he never forgot a slight or forgave even an "objective" enemy. As is well known, nothing Churchill could do was able to erase his anti-Communist past from Stalin's mind, and when in 1946 the former prime minister returned to an anti-Soviet public stance, the attacks of the USSR upon him set new records in vitriolic abuse. Bevin discovered, even in 1945, that practical politics and man-to-man talks with the Soviet leader were not enough to wipe out his past sins. As the old Bolshevik, Mme. Kollontai, confided to British Ambassador A. Clark Kerr, "there were those at the Kremlin" who would never forgive Bevin for having been a member of the "old" international and not supporting the Bolsheviks in 1917. But the British foreign secretary had earned additional heavy black marks from the Soviet leader because he had strongly attacked Soviet Russia in the House of Commons, and as Stalin told the British ambassador, this kind of behavior by a sitting minister was an unfriendly act, and had therefore offended him.

Even after subtracting the inevitable element of drama from Stalin's reaction, there remains a kernel of validity in his lament about the wounding nature of public attacks on the USSR by foreign governments. Nearly every page of the memoirs of Stalin's loquacious, but equally thin-skinned, successor, Nikita Khrushchev, suggests that the regime was obsessed with its international image and believed that being treated "with respect" was an essential element in the protection of Soviet security. It therefore seemed obvious to Moscow that in the deployment of postwar political probes against the West, a diplomacy of uncooperative delay should be supplemented by abuse from *Pravda,* and bitter political condemnations by Molotov, Vyshinsky, and Gromyko. Inevitably, as the difficulties between East and West intensified, the level of Soviet noncooperation and vilification was stepped up until it reached a level which Roy Medvedev has aptly called a Stalinist "policy of reconnaissance in force."

However, the campaigns of psychological warfare missed their targets in the West, and instead of inclining Western leaders to deal more on Soviet terms, abuse by the USSR merely increased suspicion and made compromise more difficult. As Gladwyn Jebb observed at the time, Stalin, and Hitler before him, were terrible judges of foreign public opinion or "mentalities different from their own," and they therefore "always miscalculated the effect of their actions on other countries." Looking back from 1953, Harold Nicholson believed that in the immediate postwar period the Soviets had been handed "a real opportunity of winning Europe for Communism," but they had thrown it away by "their lies and cruelty" and "the incredible stupidity of Russian policy," which "lost them all sympathy and discredited the Communist cause."

Be that as it may, the Soviet political warfare offensive in Europe certainly did play a major role in raising Western apprehensions to the point where two "isolationist" blocks were created that henceforth confronted each other breathing deep suspicion and hostility. But the aggressive Soviet propaganda offensive that misfired between 1945 and 1948 was not an essential or inevitable outgrowth of Soviet communism, or even due to the flawed characters of its leading practitioners, as has been frequently asserted. As even a man like Molotov knew, political abuse was merely a tactical weapon, frequently made up of bunkum. The Soviet foreign minister was "certainly an odd man to deal with," as Harry Truman once remarked, and he was unashamedly amoral in his approach to international relations. In August 1945, for example, A. Clark Kerr observed with genuine wonder the "obvious pride" which Molotov showed when informing the ambassador that the USSR had punctually fulfilled the promise which Stalin had made to the Anglo-Americans at Yalta to abrogate his nonaggression pact and had gone to war against Japan without warning precisely three months after the end of the European conflict. The Soviet attack on Japan in August 1945 certainly did not reflect great moral credit either on those who made it or those who had requested it, but it does not mean that Molotov was simply "a modern robot" who personified the thoughtless malevolence of the Soviet system.

On one level, Molotov and his diplomatic associates were merely Stalin's instruments abroad who rightly lived in terror of taking a false step, which might call down the wrath of the dictator. But they realized that their tough and abusive public stance was merely a preparatory device to put the other side on the defensive before serious horse trading could take place. When, in August 1946, a deeply offended Alcide de Gasperi protested to Molotov about the insulting references which the Soviet foreign minister had made to him in a public speech, Molotov replied, "Oh you must not take that seriously, that was just polemics." A year later, when during a private dinner at the Soviet embassy in London Lord Pakenham complained about the "ceaseless" Soviet propaganda attacks on Britain, Vyshinsky replied that "there were no attacks on the British people but only on 'certain groups' in Britain." The Soviet Union's chief spokesman

at the United Nations went on to explain to both Lord Pakenham and Bevin "that ideological war between parties was natural, and did not involve 'the people.' "

Such explanations probably provided few consolations for
Western diplomats, but they do show that in his own way Molotov was more dramatist than automaton. In fact, when he
thought he had been really cornered, the Soviet foreign minister
could be quite candid. During the Foreign Secretaries Conference of November 1946 when Byrnes lost patience and threatened to break off unless the Soviets stopped nit-picking and
shouting abuse in public, Molotov seemed completely deflated
and pleaded for understanding because "Mr. Byrnes did not appreciate his difficulties." He too had a great number of behind-
the-scenes pressures on him, and at that moment was being compelled "to do something for Yugoslavia" in regard to Trieste.

Despite possible theatrical exaggeration, this incident could
have occurred anywhere, and was as applicable to Western as
Eastern diplomatic life. It was primarily in public that Molotov
and his colleagues appeared extremely odd; behind the scenes he
worked diligently and efficiently as a negotiator and tried to
make use of confidential private gatherings to discover how the
strange Western world actually operated. In off-the-record dinner conversations with Bevin, he sought to learn about such ar-
cane matters as the difference between a regular cabinet and a
war cabinet, as well as the best way to predict the outcome of
American congressional elections. Understandably, he was not
always able to put questions whose answers would throw highly
significant shafts of light on the workings of the Western system.
During a private dinner in late 1947, the informational treasure
which seems to have made the biggest hit with both Molotov and
Vyshinsky was the fact that Herbert Spencer and Karl Marx
were buried in the same cemetery in Highgate.

But aside from the acquisition of such occasional flashes of en-
lightenment acquired "off the record," the basic question remains whether the Soviet Union actually secured significant benefits from its five postwar years of pushing, shoving, and abusing

the West. To deal with that question it is necessary to ponder on Stalin's intentions, and that in turn brings one immediately up against the fact that virtually no Soviet archival materials may be examined by Western scholars. American historians, accustomed to leafing through mountains of State Department and Joint Chiefs of Staff documents, frequently advance the dubious contention that the unavailability of comparable archival material in the USSR means that all considerations of Soviet intentions are little more than playful exercises with minimal historical value.

But one cannot merely sweep aside the question of Soviet intent, for in the mid-1940s Western speculation about the nature of Soviet aims and methods was itself one of the vital factors in creating what we now call the cold war. Nor can one rest content with the view that we are stymied by having all the Western materials and none from the USSR, for the available Anglo-American postwar documentary hoard is not complete since large quantities of material have been withheld by the two Western governments on security grounds. In addition, since the Soviet system did not formulate policy by means of committees struggling for a consensus, no mound of policy papers comparable to those which were developed in the West ever existed in the Soviet Union. Finally, as anyone can testify who has worked on the heap of Nazi German documents captured after World War II, one frequently finds that when studying an authoritarian system even possession of nearly all the documentary evidence does not always provide clear clues as to when, or why, the leader made his most basic decisions.

Therefore, when we attempt to appraise Stalin's postwar intentions on the basis of the broad sweep of what the Soviets did and said, as well as the estimates of perceptive outsiders who had to deal with the USSR, we are following sound historical practice, and are probably on thicker ice than most Western, or even many Soviet, officials were at the time. Surely, as Ernest Bevin grasped early on, Stalin's first goal was to solidify his position in the Eastern European and northern Asian territories that his military forces, supplemented by diplomacy, had acquired during the war. He wanted to hold on to these areas, not only because they were economic assets, but because they would act as security zones providing the USSR with an additional shield in the event of a future attack from either west or east. Even though atomic weapons and the ultimate development of a worldwide system of at least moderate economic interdependence would make Stalin's idea of territorial defensive zones increasingly archaic, the USSR acquired through its own efforts what its leader saw as a security asset, without either changing the system or clearly revealing Soviet Russia's basic postwar weaknesses.

Bevin may very well have been right again when he concluded that Stalin's second priority was to make use of the opportunity provided by initial postwar instability to force Turkey, and perhaps Iran, to make concessions that would strengthen the USSR's southern security zone while pulling the cork out of the Straits of the Bosporus, thus providing the Red Navy with easy access into the Mediterranean. This possible Stalinist goal rested on as old-fashioned a view of surface naval power as his Eastern European policy depended on the importance of mass land armies, and it may have owed a good deal to the Soviet leader's Georgian and Great Russian historical enthusiasms. But when he was met by firm Anglo-American diplomatic, economic, and measured military and naval counterpressure, Stalin gave way, and therefore it is impossible to judge where precisely he was headed or what he hoped to accomplish there.

In regard to Stalin's sensitivities about what happened in central Europe beyond the range of the Red Army, we are on firmer ground. That Stalin genuinely feared the revival of German military-industrial power either as an independent force, or especially if tied to that of the Anglo-Americans, was, as he himself indicated to George Marshall in 1947, self-evident. "Perhaps even more than anyone" else, Stalin stressed, he "did not wish to see Germany rise again as an aggressive power"; he had "no pity, sympathy, or love for the Germans," because the Soviet Union "had suffered too much from the Germans for any such sentiments to be conceivable." But he was caught on the horns of a real dilemma, for although he wanted a free hand to do what he wished in the Soviet zone of Germany, he desired large reparations payments from the rest of the country and was afraid that if Germany were dismembered into four permanently separate occupation zones, the victors would end up "losing control of the instrument of German unity."

For Stalin, the Western powers' treatment of the reparations question and their position on West German economic and political revival were two of the most important touchstones of their long-term attitude toward the USSR. As he indicated in his questions to Field Marshal Montgomery in January 1947, two other highly significant matters for him were the possible standardization of weapons in the British and American armed forces, and the retention of the wartime system of the Combined Chiefs of Staff, because to Stalin's mind, these would be the essential first steps in the creation of any formidable Western military bloc aimed against the USSR.

But virtually none of the immediate postwar developments gave credence to the great Western cold war fear that Stalin was a fanatical Marxist-Leninist revolutionary with a master plan for world conquest whose first stage would be the seizure of Western Europe either through Communist party disruption or armed force. Stalin certainly considered himself a Marxist-Leninist, but much more significantly, he was a devoted Marxist-Leninist-Stalinist, and the basic tenet of that creed was that the strengthening of the revolution depended fundamentally on the defensive power of the Soviet state. He was in this sense always a "statist," not an international Communist party revolutionary, and from all indications he had little more faith in the foreign postwar Communist parties, especially those in France and Italy, than did the bourgeois governments of those countries. It is true that on occasion he tried to use the Communist parties for overt disruptive activities, especially to undermine the Marshall Plan, but that they failed in their task probably did not surprise him. Similarly, although for a brief moment in 1945 he gave his support to the Communist party enthusiasts within the USSR in their battle with the military, technocratic, and governmental bureaucracies, which had expanded during the war, this was as Professor McCagg has cogently argued, primarily "an exercise in control," another example of Stalin's old trick of playing one group off against another. Once the party zealots had brought back into line all those emboldened by their wartime achievements, Stalin quickly slapped down the party, and returned to the kind of "statist" rule that suited him best.

The postwar period saw no great purges such as had occurred during the 1930s, although the intellectuals suffered cruelly, some executions took place, and tens of thousands went to the Gulag. It is likely that in his senile and mindless final phases during the early 1950s, another mass purge was in the making, but overall, postwar Stalinist Russia, although a very difficult place in which to live, was not nearly as ominous as during the thirties. It had become a very tough, generally predictable, and nearly "normal" repressive regime, which contrasted noticeably with the mad hatter's execution party that had existed a decade earlier.

Therefore, those worried Western postwar pundits who studied Marx and Freud in an effort to understand Stalin were largely wasting their time. Until 1950, Stalin was probably mentally healthier than he had been for a quarter of a century, and no definite Bolshevik, or even Stalinist, plan for universal conquest existed. In fact, it is difficult to identify any fixed plan for general world conquest in modern times, for even the most likely candidate, the passion of Adolf Hitler to tame the West and then carry out butchery in the East, lacked the precision and rigor suggested by the word *plan*. Stalin's expansionist tendencies appear from all indications to have been more tempered, and much less precise, even than those of Hitler. Once having acquired his security zone, and having fitted it into a recovered Soviet economic and political system, his most important goal seems to have been reached. He was prepared to dabble in others' troubled waters, and certainly had no reason to welcome the reemergence of a strong and prosperous Western Europe, especially if it included a new Germany and was connected in any meaningful way with the power of the United States.

Perhaps in his ultimate fantasy world he dreamed of going to Paris like Tsar Alexander, and he had his own hope against hope that with a bit of prodding, and many threats, a destitute and divided Western Europe might fall into his hands like ripe fruit. But when this dream was destroyed by Marshall's offer of reconstruction aid, not only did the Soviet Union not take any rash immediate countermeasures, Molotov got in the Paris queue to see if the U.S.A. might be willing to give the USSR anything on the cheap. Only when that hope proved vain did the USSR stamp down harder on the satellites, pull out all the stops in political abuse and disruption, and after a western Germany definitely appeared to be in the making, tried to upset matters by means of the relatively limited counterstroke of the Berlin blockade.

Thus throughout the early postwar period, Stalinist Russia faithfully followed the example of New York's Senator Plunkett, who allegedly once remarked, "I seen my opportunities and I took 'em." When the postwar opportunities disappeared, so did the takings, for Stalin, like Plunkett, was in essence a deeply conservative man who only liked to bet on sure things. Although he played rough, he was not a plunger, but a man who stuck to "honest graft." Above all, whatever he acquired, and no matter how much he disturbed the West, he consolidated Stalinist Russia as a superpower without playing the game that the world's greatest power had wanted him to play. This most suspicious and craftiest of men had led his highly nationalistic and deeply inward-looking nation to acquire a large slice of world power, and he had done it while thumbing his nose at those who said that a wounded USSR needed the outside world in order to recover. In its own way, Soviet Russia, like America, made maximum use of its fundamental disregard for the rest of the world, and its potential for near self-sufficiency, to turn itself into a superpower which left old-fashioned states behind, and then took its place near the top of the first division.

7

A Casualty of War:

CHINA, 1945–1949

The sudden arrival of V-J Day in August 1945 took all groups and factions in China by surprise. The Japanese armies, nearly two million strong, and further strengthened by Chinese collaborationist units numbering an additional one million, had not been adequately alerted by Tokyo to the imminence of collapse, and the order to lay down arms came as a great shock to the units in the field. The abrupt capitulation by the Tokyo government on 14 August was equally unexpected, and nearly as disturbing, to Chiang Kai-shek and his aides, for they had assumed that the Japanese would only be worn down gradually, that landings in China by large United States forces would inevitably occur, and that the armies of the Kuomintang (KMT) would be able to occupy the coastal regions of China as armed companions of a powerful American military machine. Up until the sudden surrender ceremony on the battleship *Missouri,* even the Communist leaders in China seem to have assumed that for the Allies to win the war against Japan, the Americans would ultimately be compelled to move into China in great force, and Mao and his colleagues would simply have to do what they could to make the best of that situation.

But the combination of American conventional air and naval power, the use of the atomic bomb, and the Soviet declaration of war upon Japan upset this scenario. On 14 August, the fighting in China simply stopped, only token United States forces were landed to facilitate capitulation and withdrawal of Japanese forces as well as provide limited assistance to the recovery efforts of the Kuomintang government, and the Soviet invading armies did not have time to penetrate beyond Manchuria and Korea. What no one in China had foreseen as possible suddenly became the dominant reality—the armed forces of the KMT and the Communist party confronted each other in the immediate postwar period in a China where none of the great powers were present in overwhelming force.

The KMT, which held the west at war's end, managed through American transport to move its armed forces and administration into the southern and central areas of east China soon after V-J Day. The military forces with which Chiang held the region up to the Yellow River by late 1945 were made up of approximately 3.7 million men, armed with six thousand pieces of artillery and supported by a respectable American-trained air force. Large supply dumps which the Americans had built up in China during the war were turned over to Chiang after V-J Day, and additional American military and relief assistance was sent in by sea. But aside from the units which had been trained and equipped for the Burma campaigns planned by General Stilwell, Chiang's troops were of poor fighting quality, with little experience of modern warfare, and their morale was weakened by the years spent in passive defense against the Japanese. The KMT generals, who were frequently chosen for political reliability rather than military skill, tended to prize cities, railroads, and a static defense. The military efficiency of the KMT was further limited by political and psychological factors. The bulk of the men in Chiang's armies continued to be peasants who had been shanghaied into service and were held there by brute force. When they had the opportunity, these men tended to treat civilians with the same exploitive ferocity which their officers used on them. Since the KMT officer corps was frequently as corrupt as it was brutal, and the regime was only too glad to enroll large numbers of for-

mer Japanese collaborators into its ranks, it was difficult for anyone to believe that the establishment of Nationalist civil and
military administration could constitute anything resembling democracy or the triumph of high morality.

Although the military forces which he had at his command
were much smaller and less well equipped than those of Chiang,
Mao's military, political, and economic situation coincided more
closely with the general condition of China in 1945. His nine-
hundred-thousand-man army was concentrated in northwest
China, with isolated pockets of strength scattered through areas
nominally controlled by the KMT. The Communist military units
were not made up of men forced into service against their will,
but were largely composed of volunteers who had been welded
into an effective fighting machine by years of hard training, successful guerrilla warfare tactics, and the conviction, hammered
home by continuous political "education," that they were the
cutting edge of a great popular revolution which would save
China. This military organization, fittingly named the "People's
Liberation Army," was the first large Chinese army that rigor-
ously abstained from assaulting or looting the civilian population.

Mao's creation and use of a revolutionary peasant army in the
postwar period was, of course, not merely an opportunistic tactical move. Ever since the KMT attack on the Communists in
1927, Mao had left the urban struggle to others (including Zhou
Enlai until the early 1930s), and put his maximum effort into
building up a peasant revolutionary armed force, first in Honan,
then in the "revolutionary bases" of Jiangxi, and after the Long
March of 1934–1935, in the remote north central area around
Yanan. His success in saving a nucleus of Communist influence
and power during the prewar period rested on four fundamental
principles: the rising national consciousness of the whole Chinese population, the revolutionary potential of the Chinese peasantry, the need to build up rural Communist military bases, and
the general effectiveness of guerrilla warfare. Although the development of these principles and their first successful application
occurred during the nine-year struggle with the KMT, as early

as 1936, Mao had set forth a plan for waging a guerrilla war against the Japanese, and openly advocated creation of a united front to oppose further encroachments by Japan. Following the Xi'an deal with the KMT in 1936, Mao temporarily agreed to put down the hatchet of civil war, but neither he nor Chiang had the slightest intention of actually burying it. In the nine years following 1936, the Chinese Communist party (CCP) and the KMT waged largely independent wars against Japan, eyed each other with great suspicion, occasionally clashed along the border of their respective zones of operations, and each one went on "dreaming his own dreams while sleeping in the same bed."

Since the Communists were unable to secure significant aid from either the KMT or outside governments to assist them in their war against Japan, they were compelled to make maximum use of the few assets they possessed. To raise food production, Mao introduced some central planning and sent the army into the fields, with soldiers working side by side with civilian peasants to serve as examples, and to increase output. This not only helped to weld together the army and the people, it produced such dramatic increases in output that by 1942–1943 the Communist army was better nourished than it had been in 1939. The standard of living of the whole peasant population in Communist areas was at least as high in 1945 as it had been in 1937, and the Communist land reform programs were popular, for during the war with Japan Mao prudently limited himself to compulsory reduction of land rents and rates of interest, while making no move to seize the land or punish the landlords. Thus by 1945, most of the 100 million people who were living in Communist-controlled areas had little economic or political reason to complain, and enjoyed the great psychological bonus of having been part of a system which had fought a long, aggressive, and successful guerrilla campaign against the Japanese.

Mao's long-term policy of staking his case on rural areas and the peasants' revolutionary potential coincided with postwar conditions, not only because there were ultimately more peasants than city people in China, but because the economic foundation of the rural economy was in better shape than the urban one in 1945. The simple, largely self-sufficient village had not been basically harmed by wartime shortages, and not even eight years of bombing and shelling had done much long-term damage to the essential productive assets of rural China, namely land and human labor. The amount of rice acreage cultivated throughout China in 1948 equalled the prewar figure, while per-acre output was 10 percent higher, and the amount of acreage in wheat, barley, and oats had risen as well. Therefore, although there was great misery in the rural areas beyond Communist control, this arose chiefly from the system of confiscatory rents, interest charges, and taxes which had run riot in China, especially since the warlord era of the 1920s. But, as Mao understood, in a serious political conflict, these were merely diseases of the skin, because a peasant-based movement that had the support of the bulk of the rural population would be able to find sufficient productive capacity in the rural areas to fuel a successful long-term struggle against any regime which was based primarily on the rural landlords and China's fragile urban economic centers.

Mao had picked up the right end of the stick by stressing that this was a genuine Chinese revolution which sought to end all foreign exploitation of China. Since the USSR was the only outside power likely to look on the Communist party with any touch of favor, circumstances made it easy for Mao to portray himself as both an anti-imperialist and a supernationalist. The Soviet Union was too economically weak, and too embroiled in postwar difficulties in Europe, to send any significant quantity of assistance to the Chinese Communist party. Stalin was hostile to Mao's rural revolutionary emphasis and, as always, was highly suspicious of any "foreign" Communist revolutionary movement that was not under the absolute control of Moscow. The Soviet leader consequently continued to recognize the Kuomintang government throughout the period 1945–1949, and generally tried to cooperate with Chiang, while urging Mao to go slow, because an open bid for power was premature.

This Soviet aloofness left behind resentments within the CCP which contributed to the Sino-Soviet split of the 1960s. But in the short run, Stalin's unwillingness to throw Soviet influence behind Mao in his late-1940s confrontation with Chiang Kai-shek actually made the Chinese Communist leader a more popular and attractive figure within China. World War II had broken the hold of Western control and superiority in Asia, for despite all the evils that Japan had perpetrated, it had at least demonstrated that the traditional imperial powers could be beaten by Asians. This lesson was learned in every corner of the continent, and nowhere more graphically than in China. Despite the continued dabbling of the "new imperialists," America and Soviet Russia, the traditional pattern of outside control had been broken by the war. Old "China hands" returning to the country between 1945 and 1947 noted with surprise how quickly the end of territoriality had turned even Shanghai into a real "Chinese" city. The *pax Britannia* was finished; though Britain made an effort to "liberate" Hong Kong with British troops *after* Japan had surrendered, the day in which such hoaxes could produce much effect were over in China. The clearest sign of the times was that in January 1946, Chinese roads were changed from the British system to right-hand drive, a trick which the Americans never managed to accomplish in Japan despite five years of tightly controlled occupation. Britain still had an investment of 400 million pounds sterling (worth around $1.5 billion in 1985 currency) in China as late as 1948, but the British were unable to exert the kind of foreign control which had traditionally accompanied such investment. In fact it could not even play its customary trading role effectively, because the economic difficulties at home compelled the London government actually to discourage exports to China in 1947 since British goods had to be sold in hard-currency areas such as the United States and the Commonwealth.

Many Chinese people met this great change with their customary good sense and courtesy. A Chinese acquaintance remarked to a British missionary in 1947 that the war had finally brought the fate of the old exploiter and the exploited into line, for "we both belong to countries where we have to wear old clothes and where we are having a bitter struggle." But the importance of the changes which had turned the once all-powerful Britain into "a squalid imitation" were not lost upon the mass of the Chinese people. Without an organized campaign being necessary, all parties and factions grasped that in the minds of the people, the period of the white man's domination in China had come to an end. In January 1946, when the minister of information of the Japanese puppet administration was put on trial for treason by the KMT, he declared to the court that he had done what he thought was best for China, but understood that he must die because something had to be done to appease "the white man" who was trying to prop up the Kuomintang. At this remark, the audience in the courtroom gave him a great round of applause, indicating that whatever had happened during the war, or would occur in the civil conflict, no successful Chinese government could henceforth even appear to yield to foreign pressure. Indeed, democratically inclined members of the KMT confided to Westerners as late as April 1947, that even though Mao and his associates were Communists, the leaders of the CCP would never accept Russian domination.

By combining both communism and nationalism in his revolutionary movement, Mao greatly enhanced its popular appeal and its ability to expand rapidly when opportunity offered. In the first two weeks after V-J Day, for example, the number of Communist-controlled counties jumped from 116 to 175, and by October 1945 had risen to 313. Such demonstrations of the movement's vitality, when coupled with the apparent reasonableness of the Communist leadership and the fact that it was nationalistic, and in some respects not truly Stalinist, led many Western observers to conclude that it was not really a Communist movement. The tendency of many American liberals to portray the CCP as merely a band of agrarian reformers is notorious, but even such hardheaded and determined anti-Communists as Ernest Bevin failed to get a firm grasp on the nature of communism in China. In January 1946, during an off-the-record survey of world conditions for British diplomatic correspondents, Foreign

Secretary Bevin said of the CCP: "I don't think they are communists as we understand the term at all," by which he apparently meant that because they were not directly under Moscow's control, they were not a determined revolutionary force.

Such misapprehensions about the movement led by Mao Zedong were relatively easy to make for people who were halfway around the world, but in China there was no ground for believing that the CCP was anything but a full-blown revolutionary movement. It was not even necessary for foreigners in China to be clever, or use their detective abilities, to get the story straight, for the Communist leaders went out of their way to proclaim their radicalism and dedication to dramatic, and even violent change. In the very month that Bevin concluded that they were not "communists as we understand the term at all" (January 1946), Zhou Enlai called a group of Westerners together in Nanjing to inform them that he was sick and tired of having the CCP referred to as a band of agrarian reformers. "You must realize that we are not that," Zhou emphasized, "we are communists and Marxists with all that means now, and for the future."

Most Westerners still did not grasp that what Zhou was telling them was that though it was not a tool of Moscow, the CCP was actually an extraordinarily radical revolutionary force. For all his blind spots and troubles, Chiang Kai-shek at least got that right. He understood that Mao was a Communist who could not be fobbed off with paper concessions, but after using all the arts of maneuver and deception, would sooner or later simply settle down to the grim business of fighting his way to power. As stubborn as Mao, but lacking the Communist leader's grasp of social-economic processes, Chiang was determined to destroy the Communist movement by armed force at the earliest opportunity. Therefore, as soon as he overcame the shock of the sudden arrival of V-J Day, and the absence of the long-promised large American military forces in China, he pushed the KMT forces forward as fast as he could.

But Chiang's effort to defeat the Communists and seize China by armed might was doomed from the beginning. The KMT leader emerged from the war with great prestige as the man who had led China to final victory over Japan, but he was not even master in his own political house. The KMT was a faction-riddled organization, increasingly dominated by its reactionary wing, and the KMT army was so feeble that its units needed masses of equipment and a three-to-one advantage in numbers to stand any chance of defeating the People's Liberation Army. More basically, Chiang's primary base of power lay with the landlords and among the commercial classes of the east coast cities. Once back in these cities in late 1945 and early 1946, the KMT could draw some financial and political benefits therefrom. It actually managed to get a portion of the productive and transportation system, especially the railroads, working rather quickly, and gained benefits from the improvements which the Japanese occupation authorities had instituted in the coastal regions. But since world trade was badly depressed in the immediate postwar period, the cities could not progress by keying on overseas markets, and since the KMT could not secure control of much of the countryside, the amount of internal trade was sharply limited, and Chiang's landlord constituents in many provinces were unable to provide him with any significant economic or political assistance.

The KMT leader therefore sought to secure from the United States the bulk of the military and economic resources which he needed to fight the CCP. By stressing that he represented the "legitimate" government and was fighting communism, he hoped to persuade Washington to bankroll his regime and his massive military campaign against Mao's party. Indeed, for those who were not very clear-sighted, the rising mood of anticommunism in Washington, which accompanied postwar Soviet-American troubles, offered promise that Chiang could continue to bend United States officials to his purposes until he secured gigantic subsidies and perhaps even massive American intervention. It seemed that if he cried loud and long that the Communist bear was at the door, "the Americans would . . . play in the end," for if Chiang "let them get a little more frightened [of Reds] . . . they would pay up, reforms, or no reforms."

Indeed, in 1945 the Americans did hand over large quantities of surplus military supplies to Chiang; they also poured in UNRRA aid, airlifted his troops into the north, and dispatched fifty thousand marines to China in an effort to stabilize the situation. They continued supporting the KMT on a reduced scale in 1946, and even sent in the most prestigious living American official, George C. Marshall, in an effort to work out a compromise that would preserve the KMT and avoid a protracted civil war. But the corruption and incompetence of the KMT when coupled with Chiang's deviousness soon alienated Marshall, angered Byrnes, and so "depressed" President Truman that by the end of 1946 the Marshall mission was withdrawn and American assistance substantially reduced.

The American pullback alarmed hotheads in both Nanjing and Washington, and while KMT hard-liners dreamed of an imminent start of World War III as the only thing which could save them, some American officials in 1947 weighed the possibility of sending General MacArthur in to impose the same kind of American proconsular rule in China that he had set up in Japan. But such dangerous dreams had no possibility of realization. Mao would not have been any more inclined to yield to MacArthur than he had been to Marshall, for he was the leader of a successful, and advancing, revolutionary force. Nor was there the slightest possibility that the American government of 1947–1948 would have been willing, or able, to put the kind of military power into China that would have been required to impose a solution. With a total complement of one million men, the American army in 1947 was only the sixth biggest in the world. The armies of the USSR, Britain, India-Pakistan, and *both* Chinese armies were larger. Furthermore, the public opinion polls showed that the American people were ill informed and apathetic about China, and Washington already had more than it could easily handle trying to impose containment in Europe and the Middle East.

In any event, it was not the lack of American aid which doomed Chiang. The assistance which the Americans did provide was actually an important element in the vicious circle that helped to step up the tempo of Chiang's collapse. American aid marked out Chiang as the tool of foreign, white, imperialist forces, and the more troops and officials Washington sent to China in the hope of bolstering up Chiang (and lessening the corruption and waste), the more obvious it seemed that the KMT was a puppet of the West, and that the only hope for "real" Chinese control lay with the People's Liberation Army (PLA).

Chiang was actually hopelessly trapped. His opponent would not give up, outside aid to the KMT was counterproductive, and the regime was incapable of fighting a protracted civil war on its own without undermining the system it represented. From 1945 until the demise of the KMT on the mainland in 1949, the regime's civil budget remained roughly in balance, but there was no tax revenue to cover the military cost, and the necessary confidence was lacking at home and abroad for the government to cover the deficit by selling bonds. In consequence, it printed money to pay for the war, thereby setting off another galloping inflation which quickly undermined the economic and political system and destroyed any hope for the survival of "Nationalist China."

Immediately following V-J Day, before the serious clashes with the Communists had begun, inflation actually declined because the public and businessmen hoped that there might be real peace. The wholesale price index fell from 1,754 to 1,184 yuan between midsummer and the fall of 1945. But Chiang, whose economic views have been aptly characterized as a belief in "confucian feudalism," failed to grasp that this improvement depended on an end to hostilities. With no concern for either public opinion or the economic and military consequences, the KMT leader attempted to push his troops into every inch of Chinese territory being evacuated by the Japanese. This failed to inflict any serious damage on the Communists, who merely consolidated their positions in their northwest heartland, but it badly overextended the army of the KMT, and even more importantly, drastically increased military expenditure. Inflation immediately resumed, with the wholesale price index rising over 2,000 percent between 1945 and early 1947, thereby forcing the government to put its chief economic effort into raising the number and denomination of the bank notes. The British pound which had been valued at eighteen prewar Chinese dollars (yuan), netted forty-eight thousand in May 1947, and ten million in June 1948. With the inflation outrunning the ability of Chiang's government even to print money, a confiscatory re-evaluation was carried out in 1948 that was so extreme that it left a Szechwan missionary with only nineteen cents in the bank. But even the introduction of this so-called Gold Yuan failed to stem the tide, and the government was compelled to continue increasing the number and size of the bank notes.

The swift advance of the last phase of the inflation can be charted in the amount which an Englishman, resident in China, had to pay to send a letter home to his family in the United Kingdom. In May 1947, the cost of postage already stood at 3,000 yuan. It then rose to 24,000 by October, 59,000 in March 1948, 90,000 in April, and 170,000 by June. Soon thereafter the Gold Yuan was introduced and the postage fell to under 10; but by January 1949 it was up to 40, a month later stood at 300, and it then raced out of sight as the regime tottered toward collapse.

The economic chaos generated by the inflation hit Chiang's urban constituents especially hard. By March 1947, people in interior cities found that not even two million yuan could buy a can of kerosene, and a year later coal was priced at eleven thousand yuan per *pound*. By 1948, the urban areas were filled with desperate cries that "nobody dare keep any money," and "nobody wants a check; they all want ready cash." Such attitudes not only reduced business to a crawl, they created an ever-expanding mood of pessimism. A KMT banker declared in June 1948 that public suspicion and pessimism would nullify any government fiscal changes, and even silver coinage would fail, because it would merely "be hoarded or smuggled from the country." There was nothing to do but stand by and wait, the banker told a friend, because inevitably "things will get worse and worse until the smash comes."

As the urban sector disintegrated, and the money supply became ever more chaotic, the peasants chose to hoard their rice and refused to sell to the cities. Government efforts to prompt sales at fixed prices, or control the black market, invariably failed, and urban people soon began secretly to raise swine even inside their houses. By late 1948, rich agricultural provinces like Szechwan showed such a shortage of urban food supplies that the government was compelled to adopt emergency measures to secure and distribute a minimum ration of rice. Writing home to England in September 1948, a missionary in Chengdu described a scene that typified the effects of the food shortage: "People have to wait in queues for a long time, only usually they do not wait in a queue but in a crowd or mob outside the shop which puts up its shutters and leaves only a small crack through which people can pass their baskets." The anxieties and pressures of such "mobs" called forth ever more repressive measures. In the case described by the missionary, the police, who were armed with "long bamboo switches," continuously moved around the waiting shoppers, using the switches "to keep the people in order."

Of course the KMT had always been authoritarian, and especially harsh to the common people. An American official in Nanking noted in April 1946 that after discovering that a coolie's work permit was not in order, a policeman simply seized the offender and hung him up by his thumbs right on the spot. Like every previous regime in China, that was the way the KMT had always dealt with social problems and poor malefactors. But the postwar struggle against the Communists increased the repressive character of the regime. The KMT took no effective action against the corruption within its own ranks, but employed all the weapons of the police state against a populace worried to the point of desperation by the social-economic disintegration in the urban areas. The right wing of the KMT had only one policy, and that was to wage a war to the death against the Communists and to suppress all discontent or opposition in the areas occupied by Chiang's armies. Elections were shams, with the content of the ballot rigged, and the ballot boxes stuffed. On the eve of the November 1947 "national elections," one observer noted that his relatively prosperous neighbor had been routinely presented with ten ballots.

The tenderhearted, or those who had sought a "liberal middle way," were killed, jailed, or forced into silence. As a Western former KMT sympathizer put it in early 1948, the Kuomintang had "once had a spark of liberalism within it," but the postwar crisis had caused it to lose "its power of natural leadership," and it had "become more and more reactionary." It became in fact a siege society in which everything had to be settled on the battle-field, and as the public soon sensed, it would not take long before the crucial question turned from "if the change comes" to "when the change comes."

After moving his troops into every remote area to which his navy, the railroads, and the American air force could carry them in 1946, Chiang attempted a series of overland offensives against what he considered strategically important northern cities. Brushing aside General Marshall's efforts to mediate, as well as his military advice to limit the advance and consolidate what the KMT already held, Chiang plunged on, finally taking Zhang-jiakou on the edge of Inner Mongolia during October 1946. But in the same period he also lost two vital quiet struggles which meant that all his northern conquests rested on sand. He was unable to open a rail route to Manchuria via Tianjin, and his forces in the far north were thereby made into isolated garrisons, largely supplied by air, and highly vulnerable to the Communists' guerrilla tactics. The immobility of his forces in Manchuria, and the effectiveness of Mao's guerrillas, were also partly responsible for Chiang's second great reversal, the failure of the KMT to beat the Communists to the caches of arms that the Japanese had left in Manchuria. Of course the Soviet Red Army had a hand in the PLA's success in reaching the Japanese weapons dumps first, but considering that the Soviets took for themselves virtually everything else of value in Manchuria, and also cooperated with the KMT on many matters, Chiang had no special grounds for complaint. If the KMT leader had been a tenth as successful in utilizing the mountain of aid he secured from America as Mao was in making use of this single instance of grudging support from the USSR, the future of China might have been very different.

As it was, by the end of 1946, the final result of the civil war had virtually been decided, and only questions of tempo and sequence remained. Marshall left China at the end of the year. American aid, though sharply reduced, was never eliminated, so Chiang kept the imperialist liability on his back. If he had been successful in his secret efforts of October 1946, he would have been saddled with two such liabilities, for only joint action by Bevin and Byrnes blocked the KMT leader's attempt to secure weapons from Britain as well as the United States.

But no such interference by outside government leaders could limit the adverse effects of Chiang's military follies. Having lost the initiative and dispersed his forces, the KMT leader faced a dynamic and increasingly well-armed opponent, who could easily recognize the military weakness and social decomposition present on the other side, for along with the problems of finance, corruption, and repression, the KMT was faced with a wholesale loss of weapons through capture and defection. Between July 1946 and June 1948, the PLA captured sixty-four thousand machine guns and fourteen thousand pieces of artillery, which amounted to over twice the total armament which the KMT had possessed in 1945!

Being the "learned, resolute, experienced, ruthless and sensitive" man that he was, Mao Zedong clearly grasped that he was on the road to military victory although even he underestimated its imminence. He also understood that a great peasant revolution was spreading over China at least as rapidly as were his armies. Therefore, the Communist party made its rural land policy overtly more radical in 1947, ordering the confiscation of the property of rich landlords while protecting small and medium peasant holdings, and for the time being leaving urban private business property alone. The open declaration of this policy in 1947 showed that rural traditionalism had become a serious political liability, and that the People's Liberation Army could move forward on the back of a massive rural revolutionary force. This was the foundation for Mao's decision in the summer of 1948 to turn away from guerrilla warfare far enough to mount large-unit offensives in Henan and Shandung. As always, the change caught the KMT leadership by surprise, but these offensives were actually merely a coup de grâce, because although the KMT's army still had the advantage in numbers (2.1 million to 1.5 million men), the Communists actually had more artillery. Guerrilla warfare triumphs, corruption, and defection had reversed the relative armed might of the two sides, for as a banker confided to a foreigner on the eve of Mao's Henan-Shandung offensive, "American help to China means arms and munitions for the Communists—they either capture it or it is sold to them and those who sell, send their private gains back to the States for security."

Here then, was the ultimate legacy of the Second World War in China. The traditional, and fragile, KMT had been unable to fight a modern economic and technological war in a modern way, and its attempt to thwart the Japanese by a policy of retreat and delay had accelerated the mortally dangerous triple forces of corruption, inflation, and factionalism, which drained the vitality from the regime. The KMT had become merely a paper dragon without either a strong infrastructure or an effective cause to counterbalance the efficient and dynamic movement led by Mao, which genuinely embodied the peasant craving for social-economic change, and the whole country's longing for national status and power which had been building up rapidly since the mid-1930s.

In such circumstances, the end approached with blinding speed, for even much of the urban middle class had come to believe that nothing could be worse for China "than the present state of affairs." Aided by general KMT defeatism, the regular

PLA units quickly swept through most of Henan and Shandung, and under the double pressure of regular and guerrilla attack, the last of Chiang's isolated centers of resistance in Manchuria fell in October 1948. By this time the KMT had little left north of the Yangtse except large pockets around Wuhan and Beijing, and quick campaigns begun against these two areas in November 1948 gave Mao control of all north, and most of central, China by January 1949. Thereafter nothing remained for total victory except a virtually unopposed crossing of the Yangtse, and a triumphal advance through south China. Chiang, the bulk of the political, economic, and military elite of the KMT, and a few crack army units as well as the air force and navy, fled to Formosa in the summer of 1949, and the People's Liberation Army spent the remainder of 1949 and early 1950 mopping up isolated pockets of resistance, and taking possession of the remote regions of west China. But long before this process was finally wound up, Mao and the Communist leadership had their supreme moment of vindication and triumph with the proclamation on October 1, 1949, in Beijing, of the birth of the People's Republic of China.

It cannot be said that any Western leaders actually welcomed the appearance of the new China, although some officials, such as George Kennan, accepted that the United States had lost its halfhearted effort to "become the arbiter of change" in Asia, and that it was best to assume the position of having no policy regarding the internal affairs of a country like China. For the vast majority of Westerners, however, the speed and completeness of Mao's triumph unleashed a wave of erroneous estimates about how and why this had happened. For the China Lobby, American hawks, and many military strategists worried about their position in Japan, as well as that portion of the American public already possessed by the danger of an alleged monolithic communism controlled by Moscow, Mao's victory was a product of deceit and treachery, and heralded a wave of Sino-Soviet expansion in Asia. Under great pressure from a Congress whose anticommunism had been in large measure whipped up by the

"Red peril" propaganda which the Truman administration itself had used to gain support for such foreign assistance programs as the Truman Doctrine and the Marshall Plan in 1947–1948, Secretary of State Acheson had decided as early as September 1949 to take a hard line on Mao, who he believed was in Stalin's pocket. Three months later, ignoring British doubts and Nehru's warnings, Acheson closed the door on American recognition of Beijing, or its membership in the United Nations, and prepared to send aid to the French in Indochina, in part because he had persuaded himself that in order to take the "Chinese public's mind off Manchuria" and other northern areas where the Soviets might demand concessions, Mao would be compelled to launch a massive southern expansion campaign.

While Washington blundered off in one direction because of its mistaken assessment of the nature and dynamics of the Chinese revolution, Stalin pursued an equally counterproductive policy of his own toward the new China. He seems to have expected Mao to let bygones be bygones, forgive the Soviet Union's failure to grant assistance when it was really needed, accept the permanent loss of the territory and bases that the Soviet leader had squeezed out of Chiang, and willingly act as the advance man for the furthering of Soviet security interests in the Pacific. But Stalin's policy was as far off base as was that of the Americans. There had been a nationalist as well as Communist revolution in China, and though when pressed, Mao was forced to give some ground, neither he nor anyone else in the new Chinese leadership would ever permanently acquiesce in the loss of an inch of Chinese territory. As Mao was to tell Khrushchev in 1959, when the Chinese leader's position was rather stronger than it had been a decade earlier, "We're not ever going to let anyone use our land for their purposes again." That meant that although Mao had said that he would "lean to one side" in the cold war, he was unwilling to do the Soviets' dirty work for them, or put any other country's security needs ahead of his own.

The new China actually lacked the means to pursue the kind of expansionist campaign that the Americans feared, and that

Stalin apparently dreamed of harnessing to his purposes. China had an enormous population, a massive (if only moderately well-equipped army), and a glowing pride in its revolution and its national consciousness. But it was a poor, underdeveloped country, which desperately required industrialization and general modernization if it was going to hold its own. Therefore, as a number of Communist leaders realized even before their final victory, China's best interest lay in keeping on sufficiently good terms with both East and West to allow Beijing time to get the situation at home under control and at least begin the process of modernization. As early as June 1949, and then again a month later, Zhou Enlai tried via Australian and British intermediaries to alert Western leaders to the fact that he led a strong faction within the Communist party that sought to normalize relations with the West. Zhou, along with a number of other prominent leaders including Yeh Jianying and Lin Biao understood that if their country was diplomatically isolated, Stalin would take advantage of the situation. Soviet incursions in Manchuria, in part to secure uranium, had already aroused Zhou's opposition, and Lin Biao—although his views would later be radically different—was then so hostile to the USSR that he allegedly declared that the "Russians were foreigners as much as anyone else," "that one imperialist was as bad as any other," and that he "would therefore resist Russian imperialism as he would any other."

Zhou stressed that he wanted good relations primarily because the "economic difficulties which the New China is experiencing show the need for peace and normal relations with the west." He admitted that there were strong factions in the Chinese Communist party opposed to Western ties, and that Mao himself had not yet made up his mind which was the best course to follow. In any event, Zhou emphasized, good Sino-Western relations would only be possible if the outside world really understood that "the Chinese Communist Party have won the greatest victory in Chinese history," and the West treated the Beijing regime accordingly.

Given the host of divisive factors ranging from the Maoist revolutionary temper to the great Red scare which prevailed in America, Zhou's 1949 attempt at moderation stood no chance of success. The Washington government was determined to view Beijing as a dangerously expansive satellite of the USSR, while the Soviet leader clung to the hope that he could make Mao over into a victim or a stooge. However, the most basic factor in the situation was that the People's Republic of China did not owe its existence to the East, the West, or the tensions between them. In the years 1945 to 1949, China and the rest of the Third World were merely marginal "problem areas," for at that time the superpowers had their eyes occasionally focused on the Middle East, frequently fixed on Europe, and always riveted on each other.

Both the People's Republic of China and the East-West cold war led by the United States and the USSR sprang directly from the effects of World War II. But they were parallel developments, which operated with a minimum of interaction between them. Only with the outbreak of the Korean War in June 1950 was Mao's China pulled into a more significant, and more dangerous, position in East-West relations. But that was part of a new phase of expansion and solidification of East-West tensions, and until that moment the Chinese Communist party had largely gone its own way, working out the destiny of disruption, liberation, and anguish which the Second World War had given to the Third World.

8

The Permanently Disabled:

GREAT BRITAIN, 1945–1950

> *Having fought two wars and spent all this money and pawned our assets and done all those kinds of things, they seem to think we are down and out.*
>
> Foreign Secretary Ernest Bevin to the National Union of Mine Workers, July 1947

Throughout Great Britain the spring and early summer of 1945 was a time of great satisfaction, pride, and hope for the future. The final victory over Nazi Germany was, to most Britons, a highly personal triumph, in which their own grit and endurance played a key part in bringing down Nazism. They celebrated that May victory with the special enthusiasm of those who have shared in a good job well done, and look toward the next task with a mixture of relief and expectant optimism. The dominant mood in the United Kingdom was not a longing to return to the good old days, but a great desire to go forward from the victory to the creation of a new, happier, more just, and more modern Britain. Except for a bitterly disappointed Winston Churchill, and a band of Tory diehards who thought the Bolshies had got-

211

ten through the gates, the overwhelming Labour party success in the parliamentary elections, which came two months after V-E Day, was recognized by nearly everyone as a simple clarion call by the British people that they had had enough of austerity, international humiliations, working-class misery, "great depressions," and general backwardness. They wanted a "radical" Labour government to turn the country around and quickly build a new Britain that would fulfill the age-old promises of justice and plenty through social democracy and, at the same time, restore the country's international power.

What neither the new government nor the British public accurately foresaw in 1945 was that even radical reforms would be insufficient to give Britons the kind of new society which they desired. The economic difficulties which faced the United Kingdom turned out to be so serious, and so deeply intertwined with the country's imperial and international political problems, that no purely domestic changes could solve them. On the other hand, without a sharp economic turnabout, British dreams of hanging on as one of the Allied Big Three, while reforming and democratizing the empire and Commonwealth to a point where they could provide enough power to allow the United Kingdom truly to merit a position equal to that of the USSR and the U.S.A., were doomed to failure.

The immediate postwar history of Britain was therefore essentially a chronicle of frustration and disappointment. The economic and international failures bumped together and intertwined with each other until they gradually destroyed any prospect of a great leap forward and dumped Britain into a permanent second-class international position by 1950.

The first and most obvious feature of this multifaceted British postwar disaster was the need immediately to pick up the bill for three-quarters of a century of industrial decline and mismanagement. From the late nineteenth century on, British industry had fallen steadily behind the newly developing countries both in gross output and in modern production methods. By the turn of the century British commodity exports no longer covered the cost of imports, and to make up the difference and attain a balance of payments, Britain had fallen into dependence on "invisibles." The appearance of Germany and the United States on the world's economic stage threatened to overwhelm Britain even before World War I, but it was that conflict which loaded the British with an international debt burden and forced them to try to hold on in a postwar trading environment encumbered by economic dislocation, political and ideological divisions, and the Great Depression of the 1930s. Although in the course of the 1930s the United States quietly wrote off the remaining British debts left over from the First World War, at the time Britain entered the second great world conflict in 1939 no significant headway had been made in altering the long-term trend of relative economic decline, or the injuries which the Great War and the depression had inflicted upon the British economy.

Confronting an extremely powerful Nazi Reich, and surrounded by Allies who were even more feeble than she was, Britain was compelled to pay for the first portion of her Second World War effort through scrimping and an international campaign of beg and borrow. Between 1939 and 1945 the British government spent 16.9 billion pounds abroad. This expenditure was in part offset by 6.9 billion pounds' worth of exports and the sale of overseas investments valued at 1.2 billion pounds. A further 5.4 billion pounds' worth of credits came in the form of free gifts from Canada, the rest of the Commonwealth, and the lend-lease assistance from the United States, which began in the spring of 1941. But there remained a wartime deficit of 3.3 billion pounds, much of which had been caused by purchases in America, Argentina, and the Commonwealth during the first eighteen months of the war when Britain was receiving no significant American financial aid.

If the wartime British balance-of-payments deficit of 3.3 billion pounds had been spread out over the whole war period, it would have meant that in each year of the conflict the United Kingdom's total of private and government overseas expenditure exceeded its income by 13 percent. Put another way, the 3.3

billion pounds' worth of wartime international debts which the British government piled up after 1939 amounted to the equivalent of 70 percent of the country's total national income in 1938, the last prewar year of peace.

Given the magnitude of this debt, and the monumental problems it posed, British leaders found it comforting to argue that it had been caused solely by the early period of the war, when Britain had "stood alone" and shouldered the rest of the world's anti-Nazi obligations. As Hugh Dalton, the chancellor of the exchequer, put that case in October 1945:

Our financial difficulties began when we had to make those huge cash payments for munitions and food from the United States [1939–1941] and despite Lend Lease and the substantial but temporary income from American troops, we have never been able to recover from this initial burden.

Stating the argument thus put Britain's case in its best possible form and also coincided with the intense feeling of the overwhelmingly majority of Britons that they should not have to bear this burden alone because, again in Dalton's words, the debts "arose directly from the shape and width of our war effort[,] and we owe them also to those with whom and for whom we fought."

Though as accurate in its own way as the contention of Yugoslavia, Poland, the USSR, and China that they deserved special postwar consideration because of their great wartime loss of life and property, Britain's hope of international help in bearing its debt burden had little chance of a completely just reward. The only countries even theoretically capable of rendering assistance in 1945–1946 were the United States, Argentina, and some members of the Commonwealth, and all of those countries believed, rightly or wrongly, that they had already distinguished themselves by their wartime assistance to the United Kingdom. There was a strong feeling, especially in Washington but present in other creditor countries as well, that much of Britain's financial difficulty had been caused by decades of overblown foreign policy ambition coupled with a reluctance to modernize economically or make necessary domestic reforms. Since Britain had not been able to achieve a balance of trade for decades, most international economic observers concluded that extreme pressure would be required before the United Kingdom would bring order to its international economic house.

Indeed, despite various forms of outside assistance and stringent domestic austerity programs, the pattern of overimportation proved painfully resistant to change. In 1945, the value of imports into the United Kingdom exceeded that of exports by two and a half to one. By 1947 the ratio had been narrowed to four to three, and by 1950 it was down to five to four. But in regard to the trade deficit with the U.S.A., which was simultaneously the world's greatest producer, consumer, and banker—as well as being the United Kingdom's crucial creditor—the results of Britain's herculean efforts were much less encouraging. In 1937 the imbalance of trade between the two countries stood at three and a half to one in America's favor. By 1946 with the volume of trade much larger, this ratio had leapt to six to one, and three years later it still stood at nearly four to one. Since 80 percent of Britain's tobacco came from the United States, in 1947 the total value of British exports to America barely equalled the cost of Britain's tobacco imports.

In order to help contain the adverse effects of this imbalance, British overseas investments were sold off at an accelerated rate. Between 1945 and 1947, 1.6 billion pounds' worth of foreign securities were sold, nearly half a billion more than had been disposed of during the war years. Not until 1948–1949 was it possible to stop this wholesale sell-off, and by that time Britain's yearly income from foreign investments had been sharply reduced; from 175 million pounds per year in 1938 to 73 million by 1946. Since reduction of this "invisible" income was paralleled by similar losses due to the decrease in the size and importance of the merchant marine and New York's success in wresting much of the world's financial business away from London, there was far less "invisible" income available than in the prewar period to help neutralize the problem of excess imports.

In consequence, as Foreign Secretary Ernest Bevin once remarked, the government was caught "in difficulties every day"
and did "not know which way to turn because of the balance of
payments position."

Forced to slide along with a minimum of dollar and gold reserves—around two billion dollars' worth in most years—the
Labour government was caught in a situation which would have
seemed like a nightmare to any political authority. But the cabinet that had taken office in July 1945 did not consider itself to
be simply one more political agglomeration in Whitehall. The
Labour party was of course a parliamentary party, and it was as
torn by diverse interests and political, as well as personality, conflicts, as were the Tories and the Liberals. In the person of
Clement Attlee, Labour had found a prime minister so quiet and
soft-spoken that outsiders were inclined to write him off as a
timid nonentity. Churchill and other partisan critics had endless
fun with such quips as the one alleging that the mild-mannered
Attlee did not dare attend a summit meeting abroad for fear that
"when the mouse is away the cats will play."

This made for amusing politics, but under the usually calm
and gray surface of the Labour government there burned a genuine determination to turn Britain around. "We are the masters at
the moment," Hartley Shawcross cried in the House during an
April 1946 debate with the Tories, and between 1945 and 1950
the government did its best to use this mastery to pass measures
which would fundamentally improve the economic and social
foundations of British life. Nationalization was the most dramatic aspect of this policy, with the Bank of England being taken
over in October 1945, coal in July 1946, the railroads and
canals between 1946 and 1948, and steel in 1949–1950. In addition, the government made permanent much of the centralized
direction of the economy, which had been begun by the war
cabinet in the years 1939–1945. With strong support from large
numbers of Tories, Keynesian economics was institutionalized in
Whitehall with a generous measure of economic planning and

a basic commitment to full employment and a policy of encouraging high wages.

Given the dire condition of the British postwar economy, substantial planning would have been virtually inevitable whatever government had been in office, and though it would be difficult to maintain that nationalization produced short-term production wonders, it is equally implausible to contend that it was a drag on recovery. As had been true before the war, British output rose very slowly in the postwar years, with the GNP measured in constant prices rising only 1.5 percent per annum between 1946 and 1948. Growth in heavy industry, which was essential if exports were to increase, remained painfully slow. Coal production was lower in 1946 than 1943, and though it rose sharply, output in 1949 was still 16.5 million metric tons less than it had been in 1939. Gross steel production was likewise lower in 1946 than in 1943, but then like coal, it made a sharp rise surpassing the 1939 output by 1.7 million tons in 1949.

These output figures constituted a substantial achievement if one considers the multitude of problems fettering British heavy industry. Plant and equipment, long outmoded and undercapitalized, had been seriously run down by the extremely heavy utilization and low maintenance required in the wartime emergency. The skilled labor force was not only underpaid and overworked, but decades of low wages had so turned the workers against employment in the basic industries that they bent every effort "to educate their children so that they could leave the mines" and mills. The Conservative government's near-fatal 1939 error of initially taking essential miners and steelworkers into military service, when combined with the general social mobility available in wartime, opened the floodgates, and much of heavy industry's skilled labor force left, never to return.

The postwar government was therefore compelled to try to make up for the deficiency in skilled workers and lack of modern means of production, by throwing in excessive numbers of unskilled workers. Although this condition automatically—if paradoxically—fulfilled the Labour party's pledge to maintain full employment, it left the government facing chronic labor shortages. British women who had entered the work force during the wartime emergency tended to continue working longer than their American counterparts, and at a time when the United States was trying to clamp down on the entry of foreign laborers, Britain was recruiting workers from Ireland and making extensive use of German POWs. There were over four hundred thousand German prisoners of war in Britain in 1946, and their labor was considered so important for British economic recovery that Foreign Secretary Bevin—supported by the leaders of the Low Countries, the USSR, and other former Nazi-occupied countries—categorically rejected George Marshall's April 1947 suggestion that all German prisoners of war still in Allied hands should be repatriated.

Although a large portion of the unskilled labor force that the government gathered from hither and yon poured into essential manufacturing, British postwar agriculture also needed large inputs of unskilled labor. Food shortages and a high level of imports were an important element of the "economic morass" in which Britain found itself, and high domestic farm output was therefore essential. As during wartime, little regard could be paid to British agriculture's "natural" specializations, because maximum production of basic necessities was indispensable. A November 1945 public opinion poll showed the gravity of the problem, for when the respondents were asked if they were getting enough food to work efficiently 47 percent said yes, and 50 percent replied no, while a mere 3 percent voiced no opinion on what had become a vital issue in nearly everyone's life.

By using masses of unskilled labor and plowing up nearly every piece of potentially arable land, including a high percentage of the 240,000 acres which had been used as airfields during the war, the output of essential crops was kept high. Cereals production, which had stood at 4.6 billion metric tons in 1938, and had been raised to 7.8 billion in 1943 by the nearly superhuman exertions of wartime, reached 7.07 billion metric tons again in

1949, following a brief slump to 5.6 billion in the drought year 1947. The yield of potatoes followed a similar pattern. The pre-war crop of 4.4 billion metric tons had soared to 8.6 in 1943, and continued to hover around the wartime level with a 7.72 billion-ton crop in 1949. These large potato and cereal yields were necessary to provide the public with even minimal food supplies, but the use of large blocks of acreage for this purpose reduced the amount of land available for livestock. British meat production, which had declined during the war, stayed down in the postwar period, with the 1938 output of 1.4 billion metric tons declining to 934 million in 1945 and remaining at 952 million in 1949.

This system of emergency, basic, cultivation left the public with a dull, drab diet and far less protein than before, or even during, the war. In early 1946, the combination of a world-wide grain shortage and Britain's balance-of-payments problems forced the government to reduce the level of the general food ration. In April, the size of loaves of bread was decreased, and three months later (July 1946), bread was rationed for the first time, with each person granted a weekly maximum of three and a half pounds of what the Ministry of Food called "bread units."

Then came the dreadful winter of 1946–1947, the worst of the century, with freezing temperatures, snowdrifts, and power cuts, followed by spring floods and a summer drought. For two months in midwinter, the country nearly ground to a halt with road and rail lines clogged by snow, and many plants forced to shut due to lack of fuel. BBC-TV and Radio Three went off the air, and the inability to produce, or move, goods immediately brought back mass unemployment, with 15.5 percent of the work force out in the worst part of the winter. Stringent controls on home heating inflicted additional suffering, especially on the poor and the elderly. Amid the general shortages and the fall of manufacturing and agricultural output, the government was com-pelled to stop all imports except the most essential. To help meet this new balance-of-payments crisis, the general ration was re-duced again, and by October 1947 British subjects were forbidden to leave the country except for official travel or for visits within the sterling area. The public lost all hope of acquiring luxuries, and when asked by a *Daily Mirror* poll which imports from America they would be willing to sacrifice, the respondents indicated that they would be happy to give up movies, fruit, and even tobacco, if only they could hold on to the existing meager levels of such necessities as dried milk, cheese, meat, and grain. But even that could not be, and by 1948 the average adult Briton found that the weekly ration included only microscopic bits of protein, such as one and a half ounces of cheese, thirteen ounces of meat, two pints of milk, one ounce of cooking oil, and one egg. This marked the rationing nadir of the postwar age of austerity, although when, in 1949, a slight recession in the United States decreased the volume of exports to that country and produced yet another balance-of-payments crisis which saw the value of the pound cut from $4.03 to $2.80, the public fearfully expected still more decreases in the basic ration.

No British government would have found it easy to inflict such sacrifices as these on its own people, if for no other reason than that it was both inhumane and bad politics. But the international situation intruded here as well. As Hugh Dalton observed two months after V-J Day, if a harsh austerity policy had to be followed, no one could "fail to note the contrast between the kind of life which our people, after all their sacrifices, [would] have to face for some years, and that which the people of the United States can immediately enjoy."

The first years of the postwar era showed the developed world divided between those countries which had prospered during the war and looked to become even more prosperous thereafter, such as Canada, Australia, and especially the United States, and those countries which had been defeated, occupied, or exhausted by the conflict, and whose people seemed doomed to an interminable fate of austerity and deprivation, such as Germany, France and Britain. That Britain should have found her daily life comparable to that of the other also-rans, lacking even the hope of repeating a recent developmental achievement, such as that which inspired the Soviets, inevitably raised serious doubt about the ability of Britain, and the Labour government, to deliver on the great hopes of 1945.

But the pain which the imposition of austerity measures inflicted on Labour ministers went well beyond considerations of traditional morality, party politics, or worries about Britain's long-term international prospects. All the senior members of the Attlee government were sincere idealists who had entered public life with a mission to carry out social reform. Whether members of the professional middle class such as Attlee, Dalton, and Cripps, or genuine working-class spokesmen like the ex-Durham miner, Aneurin (Nye) Bevan and the former general secretary of the Transport and General Workers Union, Ernest Bevin, the whole Labour party leadership was united in a commitment to lift the burden of suffering and injustice from the backs of the working people of Britain. This sense of mission drove the government on to finally establish the kind of social protections for the population of the United Kingdom that had been commonplace on the Continent for generations, and even existed to some degree in the U.S.A. Between 1946 and 1948, a national system of old-age assistance and unemployment relief was set up, and due above all to the energy and determination of Nye Bevan, the National Health Service came into being.

Whatever differences existed on other matters—and there were plenty—cabinet near-unanimity prevailed on the importance of establishing and defending the welfare state. As Foreign Secretary Bevin—who had at least his share of disagreements with Nye Bevan—once declared to the executive of the National Union of Miners with pardonable exaggeration, "As we have a Socialist Government returned to this country and want to carry things out on the basis of a socialist democracy . . . when anybody [abroad] has mentioned to me the socialist policy in Britain and nationalization and all the rest of it, I have told them to mind their own business." Even after the government had been buffeted by every possible adverse economic wind, Bevin still continued to give extended expression to the depth of his commitment. In a private letter to Walter Reuther, written late in the life of the Labour government, he declared:

With regard to what is called the welfare state, we are determined to look after the health of the people. I am sure that it will pay handsome dividends and while it is very costly at the beginning it would have been fatal to have neglected it. . . . We were under no illusion when we took office as to how difficult the job would be [*sic*]. We have been mobilized one day in three in the last 30 years. That means 10 years of war, and to pull a country round after such a waste of slaughter and destruction has been no easy task. However, the Labour Government decided to ride whatever storms might blow up and take the decisions whether they were popular or unpopular on the basis of what was right for the people in the long run. We have not stopped to count up the cost of these decisions in votes, we have determined to go on, believing that what we were doing was right.

Many people in Britain understood that the Labour government had a commitment to the common people's welfare that went well beyond the ordinary, and such measures as establishment of the National Health Service were highly popular. A 1949 poll showed that when people were asked to select the Labour actions of which they most approved, the National Health Service received as many votes as all other items combined.

Where the government had the most trouble, of course, was at those points where its social democratic inclinations conflicted most sharply with the postwar economic realities. The Labour party could proclaim that it stood for the principle of high wages, but with little in the shops, and the overriding importance of keeping the price of British exports down, the government had to put inflation control first. Although it confronted far more serious inflationary pressure than did the Truman administration in the United States, the Attlee government actually kept a tighter lid on prices and wages, holding inflation to an average of 5 percent per annum between 1945 and 1950.

Such "successes" often looked less than impressive to the millions of men and women who had voted for Labour in hope of realizing a rise in real wages only to receive austerity and a policy of holding the line instead. The situation was almost as troubling to an old trade union leader like Bevin, and in 1948 he even wrote a "Dear Clem" letter to the prime minister deploring that "all the standard rates of the country . . . are very much on the low side," and contending that aside from the fact that "there is not the risk of unemployment," the laboring "people are if anything worse off now than they were in 1938."

But the iron laws of the imbalance of payments and austerity inevitably won all the arguments, the government held to its hard-line policy, and ministers turned repeatedly to the Trade Union Congress begging for cooperation although they had nothing to offer in return except equality and hope for a better future. As Bevin put it when appealing for higher output without an increase in wages to a closed-door meeting of the miners' leadership, all were agreed that "no request should be made to one branch of the community and not to another." The economic crisis was so severe, however, that special interests would have to come second even on the matter of wages, and to Bevin's mind, the situation did at least offer opportunity for an important spiritual triumph:

We have got to put our heads together, and I do not regard this as the Labour Government's problem. I think it is the Labour Movement's problem, because I feel that if we now ride the storm and find a way with common action, together, it will be such a victory for the Labour Movement [hear, hear] that it will be a triumph for generations to come in this country. If we do not we may get a wretched, lousy period of reaction again.

Such earthy idealism led most union leaders to go along with unpleasant government policies, and because many of the men who imposed the sacrifices required by austerity had themselves endured hard physical toil, and had the interests of the working class at heart, there was at least a special tolerance in much of the population. The Labour government looked and sounded as if it had arisen out of the life of the common people, and that made hard times easier to bear. It was not so much that "the Red Flag" was sung on the floor of the House for the first time soon after the Labour party electoral triumph, or that two-shilling dinners were actually introduced into the traditionally elitist Commons dining room, but that the regular ways of many of the leaders were truly democratic for the first time in British history. The foreign secretary and some other ministers had authentic working-class accents, a minimum of formal education, and, on occasion, serious difficulties with the written language. Bevin frequently insisted on inviting his chauffeur and detective in for a drink, even on formal occasions such as an award ceremony at Eton, and he protested vigorously when rumor reached him that dinner jackets would be required on the newly built *Queen Elizabeth,* for he found such a "snobbish rule" highly offensive. Most of all, he was genuinely tormented by the distress and discomfort which the austerity policies were imposing on the common people. In what must surely be the only incidence of its kind in the history of the world, the foreign secretary took time out from his busy schedule at a major international conference (the Paris peace conference for the minor Axis countries) to write a private letter to the prime minister putting forth his special worries:

I cannot believe that it is not possible to do more than we are doing to make things easier this coming winter for our people . . . I see from the newspapers that we are now getting plentiful supplies of rubber. Why must we still perpetuate the system of not being able to get [elastic] for belts, corsets etc. . . . and why must women still have to go to the trouble of producing doctor's certificates for a corset? I find these irksome restrictions are continuing . . . which our women folk gladly bore during the war. But I earnestly beg you to make a more human approach to this problem at the earliest date.

. . . Cannot we ease the situation for sheets and pillow-slips? This problem is driving our women to distraction.

Such genuine concern and kindness really helped, as did the fact that despite discomfort, and much grumbling, the ration never slipped to a level that undermined public health. The nation's death rate actually continued to decline, dropping nearly 20 percent between 1940 and 1948. Furthermore, by the end of the decade, there were clear signs of increased upward mobility; savings continued to rise, and even without a British "G.I. Bill" to aid the education of veterans, university enrollments were up 66 percent over the prewar period. Even continuing austerity was not completely able to darken the brightness and glitter which would ultimately characterize the postwar era. While the British film industry first blazed forth, only to flicker out rather quickly, television made an astonishingly rapid advance in a country as destitute as postwar Britain. In 1947 the number of TV licenses* issued in the United Kingdom appears to have stood at under 14,000, but within four years the number of television license payers had risen to over 750,000.

Although the government tended to see such improvements as evidence that its belt-tightening policies had paid off, it is likely that the glittering world opening up to the people through films and TV, as well as the new opportunities to rise in the world, actually made the burden of shortages and government controls even less bearable. The opinion polls indicate that the public, which had welcomed the "morning of socialism" in July 1945, was already showing serious doubts one year later. A poll of August 1946 found that only one-fourth of the respondents felt that they were better off than they had been before the war, while half believed that their situation had become worse and another quarter thought that they had stayed the same. Even among La-

---

* BBC had a monopoly on television transmissions until the establishment of ITV in the mid-1950s, hence the use of a TV license, then and now, to finance the BBC.

bour party supporters, the division between those who believed they had risen and those who thought they had fallen was fifty-fifty, while only a tiny majority of the overall sample believed that the Labour government had performed well.

The great winter crisis of 1946–1947 inevitably produced another slump in the government's popularity, and though the majority of the public did not think the government had caused the crisis, it did feel that it lacked a firm grip and was muddling about. The Tory party, reformed and revitalized, made effective use of the opportunity, and by November 1947 had taken a slight lead in the public opinion polls. In the same month, Labour lost 652 seats in the municipal elections.

It is probable, as some observers have concluded, that in 1945 many voters had chosen Labour because they believed that with its concern for the little man it would find the quickest way out of scarcity, but largely due to reasons beyond its control the Attlee government was unable to provide relief quickly enough or in the right quantities. In January 1946 when the public had been polled on the most important problem facing the country, 61 percent of the respondents chose the housing shortage. In the summer of 1950 when another survey asked if the government had made satisfactory progress in dealing with the housing problem, 61 percent replied no. The symmetry of percentages is too perfect, but it tells the main tale, for Attlee and his colleagues had been guilty of the greatest crime in partisan politics when faced with rising expectations; they had delivered too little and too late. Forced to hold a general election in February 1950, with two of the strongmen of the cabinet—Bevin and Cripps—seriously ill, and many foods still on ration, Labour was left with a razor-thin Commons majority of seventeen. The government managed to hang on for an additional eighteen months, but lacking a solid working majority, torn by internal strife, and losing Bevan, Cripps, and Bevin through resignation and death, the Attlee government had become a shadow of its former self, and it was driven from office by the Tories in October 1951.

✣   ✣   ✣

Surely the Labour government had won its great victory of 1945 primarily on the basis of its promise to make significant domestic reforms, and it lost its mandate chiefly because it was unable to lift enough of the burden of shortage and austerity from the backs of the British people. But there had also been many important international dimensions to Labour's electoral triumph, as well as its ultimate political defeat, for virtually all of the international aspects of Britain's political experience between 1945 and 1950 were ultimately entered in the debit column. These, in turn, weakened the economy, the Labour government, and Britain's international status, which meant that through its domestic and international failures in the immediate postwar period, Britain stumbled toward the sidelines, and thereby gradually left the world to be polarized between the new, and erratic, superpowers. Thus Britain, by her own fall from power, played a highly significant role in producing the bipolarity which would be the foundation stone of the cold war.

Balance-of-payments and export troubles were the most obvious and pressing of international problems that intruded into British everyday life, but the public had also come out of the war with a pair of deeply felt, but not very consistent, desires regarding foreign relations, which were also very important. On the one hand, as part of its wartime conversion to "home-grown socialism," the bulk of the British public, like people everywhere, had come to believe that a new international order had to be created to prevent recurrence of disasters such as the one which had overtaken the world between 1939 and 1945. Devotion to a new system based on a powerful United Nations was especially strong in the United Kingdom, and it carried with it a corollary belief that every effort had to be made to prevent splits or conflicts between the victorious Allied powers. Especially within the Labour party, but among Tories and Liberals as well in the fall of 1945, there was heartfelt opposition to anything which smacked of an Anglo-American lineup against the USSR. Such a course was vehemently rejected because it would have been a remake of the failed *cordon sanitaire* policy of 1919 and seemed likely to lead to a general war. Formation of an anti-Soviet bloc was felt by most people to be especially unjust in light of Russia's great war-time sacrifices in the common cause, and farsighted observers believed that it was not in Britain's basic interest, because the London government's best hope for a bright future seemed to lie in a moderate, left-leaning position, somewhere between the two new superpowers. Therefore, a general settlement which preserved the equality and supremacy of the Big Three, and arranged for the resolution of serious future disputes within the United Nations, would be the best of all possible worlds for the United Kingdom, for it would simultaneously satisfy public opinion, establish favorable conditions for economic recovery, keep the peace, and allow Britain to masquerade as the equal of the United States and the Soviet Union.

Secondly, and in contrast to this enthusiasm for what might be called an idealistic—as well as opportunistic—internationalism, there was a stream of xenophobic resentment in British post-war public opinion, directed primarily against the superpowers that had taken away her position of world leadership, but with some spillover on other nationalities as well. The polls revealed a sharp fall in "friendly feelings" toward the U.S.A. within three month of V-J Day, and the British public's attitude toward the USSR took a comparable tumble during the subsequent six months. The polls further indicate that the British people wanted a stern, if humane, policy toward defeated Germany, and repeatedly voiced their support for a long period of military occupation.

Considering their own miseries at home, Britons showed extraordinary generosity in sending help to the needy, not only to India, Africa, and the European Allied countries, but even to Italy and Germany when starvation threatened. However, the British people had little inclination to try to solve the human problems of the war on their own shores. A poll of June 1946 revealed that two-thirds of those questioned were opposed to allowing even the Polish troops who had fought under British command to remain in the United Kingdom.

The primary target of most of the initial British nationalistic resentment was, quite naturally, the fat and contented cousin across the Atlantic. In the opinion of most officials in the Treasury, the Foreign Office, and other sections of Whitehall, the United States government and its people were unreliable, erratic, and in the words of Ernest Bevin, lacking "in all the experience that this stupid old country has got." Americans seemed too ready to don an attitude of remote and unconcerned superiority while protecting their own interests and telling others what to do.

But unfortunately for Britain, American support was required at many levels, and the need to lean on the U.S.A. immediately undercut the hope of establishing the United Kingdom as a nation that belonged in the front rank of great powers. American supplies and military transport were especially important in winding down the "post hostilities" phase of World War II, and since the Combined Chiefs of Staff still operated, this meant continued routine Anglo-American cooperation up through 1947 in many areas of the globe, but especially in Italy, and to some degree, in Germany. The British government also sought additional American diplomatic support in those areas of dispute which Whitehall considered vital, such as Greece, the Straits of the Bosporus, and Turkey. Beyond all these specific matters, London desperately needed a firm commitment that America would not repeat the international disappearing act which she had performed in 1919. For only if the United States continued to maintain a strong worldwide diplomatic, economic, and perhaps military presence, capable of balancing off that of the USSR, was there any chance that the United Kingdom could act as an independent, left-leaning, great power.

Yet none of these political matters, significant though they were, touched on the most basic feature of British postwar dependence on the United States, for America could offer important assistance in dealing with all the serious economic problems which were immediately threatening the British government. The flow of vital goods to Britain, the opening up of profitable markets for British exports, and especially the necessary credits to tide the United Kingdom over its most pressing difficulties, could only be provided in sufficient quantities by the United States. Although the British public was ignorant of the intricacies of balance-of-payment troubles, the majority seem to have realized the importance of American aid, for in a January 1946 poll, three out of five declared that austerity alone would not be enough to surmount the economic crises, and that an American loan was essential.

The cabinet had obviously come to the same conclusion, and after the dashing of its dream that the Americans might simply give a large grant as a reward for Britain's wartime sacrifices, serious loan negotiations began in Washington in the late fall of 1945. Since the Americans held virtually all the high political and economic cards, British officials had little choice but to try to appeal to the Americans' sense of responsibility by piling up praise for their wealth, power, and magnanimity.

The wartime "special relationship" looked very threadbare in the Washington of late 1945 and early 1946, however. With first Roosevelt and then Churchill gone, most of the old personal intimacy had disappeared, and as Harry Truman's abrupt cutoff of lend-lease showed in September 1945, the new administration had little inclination to see Britain as a special case. Except for a handful of New Deal Anglophiles, led by Harry Hopkins, few of President Truman's associates had any great warmth of feeling for the United Kingdom. Even among the Anglophiles who did exist, although such men as Dean Acheson might develop real friendships with individual Labour party leaders—especially Ernest Bevin—they had little sympathy for the new social democratic programs, which tended to be scornfully dismissed as Britain's "social experiments."

The American loan negotiators were compelled to drive what would look like a good bargain at home, as the polls showed public opinion overwhelmingly opposed to new credits for Britain or anyone else. In addition, the Republican contingent in the Seventy-ninth Congress, generally overrepresenting localism and the small-town business outlook, was solidly opposed to foreign aid, low-tariff policies, and reciprocal trade agreements. Washington officials therefore sought to secure "sweeteners" from the British, such as the grant of Pacific bases, which could be used to show Congress and public that Uncle Sam had not been taken by another group of smooth talkers from across the seas.

Despite such tactical thinking, in the first phase following the end of the war Washington officials actually underestimated the extent of their country's economic dominance almost as much as the public did. They were nearly obsessed with the desire to make use of the loan negotiations to peel away impediments to world trade such as imperial preference and blocked sterling accounts, not merely because, as many Britons thought, they were greedy children, but because they failed to grasp the extent of their power and had no clear long-term idea as how best to preserve and expand the great American economic balloon.

With the Americans pushing hard, and the British cabinet, as Bevin said later, anxious to avoid any appearance that it was "going to become a sort of financial colony of somebody else" because "one cannot have that without one begins to be told what to do," there were bound to be disappointments, misunderstandings, and bruised feelings. Especially was this so because although desire to put Britain on her feet to act as a barrier to the USSR appears to have played no part in the actual negotiations, it was trotted out in the spring of 1946 to help persuade a reluctant Congress to ratify the loan agreement.

Accusations of power politics and unconscionable greed therefore filled the British press, while comparable complaints about Britain's manipulative begging appeared regularly in American newspapers. Actually Britain secured five billion dollars in credit from the U.S.A. and Canada in July 1946 at what now seems a laughably low true interest rate of 1.63 percent, and procedures were even included to waive these interest charges during periods when the United Kingdom faced serious balance-of-payments difficulties. The only serious string in the arrangement consisted of a requirement that sterling had to be made convertible by July 1947, which meant that countries which had amassed huge sterling credits during the war, such as Argentina and the Commonwealth nations, would then be able to convert into dollars and would no longer be compelled to discharge the credits by purchasing British goods.

When the terms of the agreement became known, something analogous to an anti-American fever swept through Britain, and the cabinet had long impassioned debates before sullenly deciding to accept the loan as the only possibility available. As the chief British negotiator, John Maynard Keynes, had cabled home as early as October 1945, not to have done so would have meant:

. . . that we should decline for the time being to the position of a second rate power abroad[,] and we should not only have to postpone for at least five years any improvement in the standard of living at home[,] but would have to ask the public to accept greater sacrifices than at any time during the war.

Even though London reluctantly accepted the loan agreement in the end, the bleak picture painted by Keynes still became reality. Britain's basic economic difficulties, the unsettled state of the world, and the winter crisis of 1946–1947 actually landed Britain in a more serious plight than anyone on either side of the Atlantic had imagined possible in 1945–1946. But even when that finally became obvious to all, and the existence of the loan should have made it clear that Britain had slipped permanently into America's shadow, Labour government leaders and much of the British public continued to deny that the hope of a revival of British power was lost. As Bevin declared to the miners executive in July 1947:

I do not think we are down and out . . . I think that with the resources we have got in the Commonwealth and the co-operation and skill at home, brought into proper co-operation with a tremendous drive in the next two years, Britain will be in as good a position as she ever has been in her history, with this advantage: it will be a Commonwealth built on a decent standard of living instead of upon extreme wealth and extreme poverty, as there was all through the nineteenth century . . .

it will be a win for Labour and for the world, giving us a chance to make a better deal with the rest of the world for everybody when the time comes.

The idea that after 1945 Britain could have retained her great power and imperial position abroad, and that when these were linked to a revitalized social democratic system at home they would constitute a boon for all mankind, may seem far-fetched today, but it had real popular force in the United Kingdom during the late 1940s. It even allowed Bevin to give the classic provincial reply to a trade union critic from southeast England in November 1946 that the primary goal of his foreign policy was "to build a sound peace in order to save the people of Kent and the world from being again the victims of attacks."

None of the senior government ministers, and only a few individuals across the broad reaches of the general public, gave serious thought to the possibility of simply throwing in the hand and becoming an island version of Luxembourg. Britain would hold the line abroad, gradually cutting back her imperial commitments and yielding as little as possible to the two superpowers. Such a policy was highly popular with the majority of the British people, for they wanted social democracy to revitalize Great Britain, not abolish it. "Labour foreign policy" was also acceptable to most of the opposition, and despite all differences of class and social outlook, received the steady support of the shadow foreign secretary, Anthony Eden, since there seemed to be few viable alternatives, and in its general outlines the policy coincided with the traditional aims and methods of Whitehall.

Specifically because the Attlee government's policy did not make a clear break with the past, it received sharp criticism from a sizable bloc of backbench Labour MPs. The left-wing group wanted the government to chart a new course which would reassure the Soviet Union, distance British policy from that of the capitalist American colossus, and, if possible, lead to the creation of a European social democratic grouping which would fulfill the dreams of those who had made the great wartime "swing to the Left." Although the members of Labour's left wing produced considerable alarm in conservative circles in both Britain and America, they were unable to exert any significant influence on foreign policy. Primarily this was true because even if one disregarded the rising cold war pressures, the scenario of the Left hardly coincided with the postwar facts. The moderate Left had not won control of the government in any important West European country except Britain, and the economic weakness and general disorganization of the whole region made impossible any idea of simply snubbing America, the only country in the world which had the means to keep the fragile postwar structures upright and to facilitate recovery.

The Labour Left's influence on policy was further limited by the formidable personage in charge of Britain's postwar foreign relations. Attlee's selection of Ernest Bevin to head the Foregin Office, and his decision to give the foreign secretary nearly complete autonomy in directing international affairs, effectively slammed the door on ideologues of both the Left and the extreme Right. Bevin was a tough old trade unionist who, although not especially popular with the parliamentary party and not a strong member of the House, had broad support from the union movement and was soon recognized by the public as the government's strong man. As early as the spring of 1946, polls indicated that if circumstances had forced Attlee to step down, Bevin would have been far and away the most popular replacement from either political party, for in personal popularity he led even Churchill by better than two to one.

Bevin had a reasonable measure of international experience from his years as an official of the Trade Union Congress and the Transport and General Workers Union, and his service as minister of labour in Churchill's war cabinet had taught him what he needed to know about the ways of Whitehall. He was an extremely hard worker, and a strong negotiator, so little overawed by the pretentious world of diplomacy that he once remarked to a group of senior Foreign Office officials that when faced by the "plain truth," professional diplomats were "absolutely mystified by it." He certainly did not give up his class biases, on one occasion advising an aide to disregard cries of alarm from Clare Boothe Luce and Lord Beaverbrook, since "wealthy people are always in a state of jitters." But he won the affection and support of virtually every regular official in the Foreign Office through his intelligence, conscientiousness, and a genuine trade unionist's concern for his subordinates' welfare, regardless of the social class from which they came. Not even the most cynical and elitist noble could stand aloof from the charm of a foreign secretary who could write to a young diplomat guilty of a serious indiscretion, "Do not worry too much; when you get into a tangle like this, we old ones have to get you young ones out of trouble."

Inside his new house, Bevin quickly clipped the wings of those officials inclined to be too hostile to the U.S.A., or too enamored with the USSR, and drove nearly everyone into the moderate centrist position that he favored. By 1946, career Foreign Office officials were routinely making policies, and preparing minutes, as if they had been lifelong members of the Trade Union Congress and had always thought that social democracy was the best answer for the whole human race.

The Labour foreign secretary brought the major newspapers into line with equal speed, and where necessary used a heavy hand. While disregarding extremes and refusing "to worry about the 'Daily Mail' or the 'Daily Worker,' " Bevin made use of confidential off-the-record press conferences to get his views across to the diplomatic correspondents. If this did not have the desired effect, however, he did not hesitate to apply additional pressure. Even the editor of the *Times,* Barrington Ward, received a stern and successful personal lecture from the foreign secretary on his paper's "jellyfish" attitude in not enthusiastically supporting the government's anti-Communist policy in Greece and its aggressive assertion of Britain's traditional interests throughout the eastern Mediterranean.

However, aside from the Labour Left, the postwar policies pursued by Bevin and the Foreign Office only ran into repeated public difficulties with one prominent Briton, Winston Churchill. The opposition leader accepted the basic tenets of the postwar policy, and he respected, and had great affection for, Bevin, with whom he had teamed up in the war cabinet. But the former prime minister's restless energy made it difficult for him to keep a steady course or maintain a slender silhouette.

Churchill's public advocacy at Fulton, Missouri, of a strong Anglo-American alliance to confront the Soviets' "Iron Curtain" unleashed a storm of press protest in the United States in the spring of 1946, with many influential newspapers denouncing the speech as provocative and a threat to world peace. The Fulton speech also brought some embarrassment to the British government, for it was seen by many suspicious American liberals and moderates as the overture to a campaign by Whitehall to isolate the USSR and use American power to protect British colonies and zones of influence around the world. Churchill's later dramatic advocacy of a United States of Europe, which would include Germany, produced more problems for Whitehall, because most countries in Europe, and many of the British people, had no inclination to let bygones be bygones with Germany.

But it was primarily the former prime minister's erraticism and unpredictable pixielike character which kept his supporters, as well as those in the Labour government, constantly on edge. Viewing him at close range, Harold Nicholson found the Churchill of the late 1940s simultaneously "difficult and foolish," as well as "somewhat daft but very sharp." By mid-1946, a number of his closest colleagues, including apparently Field Marshal Smuts, seem to have concluded that it was time for the old Tory to step down. But Churchill would have none of it and continued to dabble in sensitive international matters. In September 1946, he suddenly turned up in Paris during the time of the foreign secretaries meeting, determined to talk with the American secretary of state, James Byrnes. Alarmed that if news of such a meeting leaked out the public might conclude that Churchill was calling the tune for Britain's policy, the ambassador, Alfred Duff

Cooper, slipped Byrnes into the British embassy through the garden. After exchanging a few pleasantries with the former prime minister, Byrnes was sneaked out again, and in the words of Duff Cooper, "having possibly endangered international relations and having certainly caused immense inconvenience to a large number of people," Churchill "seemed thoroughly to enjoy himself, was with difficulty induced to go to bed soon after midnight[,] and left at 10 a.m. the following morning for London in high spirits."

Such spectacles imposed a serious nervous strain on Foreign Office personnel, but a far more significant threat to Britain's postwar foreign policy was posed by holes in the country's security screen. Bevin was very security-minded, but as everyone knew, there were numerous press leaks, "off-the-record" conversations with leading Americans and West Europeans, and "leaky" allies, especially in Paris and Washington. What was not known until the 1951 defections to Moscow, which mercifully occurred two months after Bevin's death, was that two of the three most important Soviet spies in postwar Britain had been working in the Foreign Office. Up to February 1947, Guy Burgess had been secretary and personal assistant to the minister of state, Hector McNeil, and Donald Maclean, after serving as the number three in the British embassy in Washington, returned to head the North American section of the Foreign Office. The position of minister of state in the Foreign Office was to some degree ceremonial, but McNeil was a trusted protégé of Bevin's, and certainly some significant policy papers had to have passed Guy Burgess's way. Maclean's posts were even more important, and in his case it is possible to prove that he was privy to a large number of critical matters, because he was a member of such highly confidential committees as the one created in 1946 by the British and Americans to arrange for control of overseas military bases, the "uranium committee," and the highly secret 1948 committee that laid the foundations for the creation of NATO.

But even though the Soviet government unquestionably acquired from the Cambridge spies full information on the policy attitudes prevailing in Whitehall, and was thereby able to negate any element of surprise that Bevin hoped to achieve, one should be cautious in attributing too much of Britain's postwar international difficulty to Soviet espionage. The secret information passed on to Moscow certainly provided the Soviets with ample evidence to feed their suspicions that at least some Anglo-American leaders were taking political, economic, and military measures to offset Soviet power and impose limits to Soviet expansion. But that suspicion would have been there in any case, and the crucial factors in the ultimate failure of Bevin's policy of holding on until Britain could establish herself in a left-leaning centrist great power position were not caused by treason or espionage. Britain needed a quick worldwide economic recovery and a general international settlement, but Stalin certainly did not need Donald Maclean or Guy Burgess to tell him that. In a disordered world, time was on Stalin's side, not Bevin's, and every passing day which left the world in limbo after August 1945 weakened Bevin's position and undercut his hopes for an independent policy.

Even during the first eighteen months, the Labour government was compelled to hold on by its teeth without a penny to spend on foreign economic development. London therefore engaged in a great military holding action abroad, despite the fact that in early 1946 the military authorities had erected their long-range plans on the assumption that there would be no war for ten years. The polls indicate that the majority of the public was willing to make some sacrifices to sustain the British worldwide military presence, for strong majorities favored retention of the draft. But the overall economic strain, and especially the balance-of-payments problem soon brought the government up against a stone wall. Of Britain's six-hundred-million-pound balance-of-payments deficit in 1947, a full third was due to military expenditure in Europe and overseas, and when the disastrous 1946–1947 winter struck Britain, no choice remained except to carry out rapid pruning of overseas commitments.

In March 1947 Attlee announced that the British government

would allow no more time for negotiation or transitional arrangements, and would leave the Indian subcontinent by June 1948 at the latest. Britain's precipitate withdrawal from India, which was completed by December 1947, left behind the independent states of Pakistan and India, and a great wave of disorder and rioting. Indian liberation was quickly followed by that of Burma in January, and Ceylon in February 1948. Within six months London had lost over half a billion of its subjects, and due in part to British mediation efforts, the Dutch also gave up their East Indian colonies in the course of 1948, and British "peacekeeping" forces were able to withdraw from the whole area. Aside from Malaya and Hong Kong, Britain had cut her East Asian commitments to the bone, leaving the French to carry on a hopeless colonial war in Indochina and handing on to the Americans the main responsibility for the West's traditional "watchman" duties in Asia and the Pacific.

Further westward, the harsh winter of 1947 prompted a major reduction in Britain's commitments in the eastern Mediterranean. As early as February–March 1946, Attlee had suggested such a reduction, perhaps extending to complete abandonment of the traditional Middle East zone of influence. The Ministry of Defence and the Foreign Office had managed to prevent such a withdrawal in 1946, but by the time the 1947 crisis came around, events in Palestine had made at least some retreat necessary.

Following V-E Day, Jewish Holocaust survivors had streamed toward Palestine in hopes of establishing a Jewish state, which would finally provide them with peace and security. Most Western opinion, especially that in the left wing of the Labour party and throughout the United States, strongly supported unlimited Jewish immigration to Palestine and creation of an Israeli state there. But the Arab population opposed any substantial increased Jewish entry, fearing that large numbers of Jews would create the basis for a Zionist state that would be able to end Arab settlement and influence in Palestine.

The British authorities in Palestine, holding mandate rights from the old League of Nations, found themselves in a very difficult situation. Although the Balfour Declaration of November 1917 had proclaimed British support for creation of a "Jewish homeland" in the region, throughout the quarter century of the Palestine mandate the London government had generally sided with Arab fears and limited Jewish immigration.

Faced with the massive postwar Jewish immigrant pressure as well as the threat of an Arab rising that might threaten Britain's position throughout the Middle East, the London government chose to use its modest military power to try to close the door on the Jews. This set off a murderous round of terrorist acts and military reprisals. A worldwide press campaign then accused the British authorities in Palestine of being similar to the Nazis in Germany, and the government soon found itself the object of allegations that it was anti-Semitic and insensitive to human suffering. Such charges came not merely from the sensational press, but also from within the Labour party and were even made on the floor of the House. The government's attempts to defend its policy by arguing that it had to protect the interests of Arabs as well as Jews carried little weight with the critics, who could in any event quite rightly point to cases where British authorities had operated against Jews with a heavy and awkward hand. Not even the wave of indignation which swept over Britain in the wake of the slaughter of British soldiers in the King David Hotel massacre engineered by Menachem Begin in July 1946 could alter the fact that the government was caught in a no-win situation in Palestine. In February 1947 Bevin announced that Britain would turn the whole problem back to the United Nations, and the cabinet formalized the decision to withdraw in December of the same year.

But not even the withdrawals from southern Asia and Palestine were enough to bring the British out of the woods. Evacuation from these areas helped to give Britain the appearance of the special devotion to justice which the government and most of the public wanted, but the pullback also produced the impression of defeat and decline, which nearly everyone in the United Kingdom had sought to avoid. Furthermore, these reductions were not in themselves sufficient to lift austerity-plagued Britain out of its balance-of-payments crisis, yet once these areas were gone, nothing of importance remained that Britain had exclusive power to give up. Every other area of commitment which imposed a heavy burden on the exchequer, including the Middle East, Greece, Italy, and the occupation forces in Germany, lay immediately adjacent to areas of Soviet occupation, and therefore touched important interests of the superpowers as well as those of the United Kingdom.

Until early 1947, the British government had tried to be patient, while it made economic reforms and waited for the disordered world to right itself, and for the two slow-moving and reluctant giants to take the lead in producing a world settlement which would decrease tensions and lessen Britain's military expenditure. During the first eighteen months following V-J Day, London had scrimped and made cutbacks, and though siding more frequently with Washington than Moscow and trying to gain as much American economic and diplomatic support as possible, had urged the United States to adopt forthright and well-reasoned long-term policies. Throughout that period, Bevin had tried to act like the spokesman of a great power and had sought to retain as independent a policy position for Britain as possible, while constantly cautioning against precipitous action or resort to policies of confrontation.

But now a cornered Britain could no longer merely wait and hope. The combined pressure of economic difficulties and excessive overseas commitments, which had been building up for half a century and had been greatly intensified by World War II, finally pushed the country over the brink during the terrible winter of 1946–1947. Moderate retrenchment was no longer enough; Britain had to make further, and more radical, reductions in its international commitments, and since the political power of France, Germany, and Italy had already been nullified by the war, when Britain stepped aside in the eastern Mediterranean and central Europe during 1947, the United States and the Soviet Union were left as the only significant political factors in the western half of the Eurasian landmass. For the first time in its modern history, Europe had been reduced to a condition of two-power confrontation. Bipolarity thereby came into being, and with its existence, the essential prerequisite for a Soviet-American cold war had been established.

9

The Beginning of the Cold War in Two Acts:

1945–1946 AND 1947–1949

From the long perspective provided by a half century of historical experience, it seems obvious that the most basic causes of Britain's back step in 1947, and the subsequent Soviet-American confrontation, were the broad sociopolitical forces which had been released in the three countries by the Second World War. But at the time it was difficult to see this clearly, and the pressures of day-to-day circumstance, and the need to cope with the detailed problems left over by the war, had to occupy most of the attention of the leaders of the major countries in 1945–1946.

During the eighteen months following V-J Day, the USSR, the U.S.A., and the United Kingdom therefore moved hesitantly in the direction of a general worldwide settlement, which most people assumed would be a new Treaty of Paris analogous to that of 1919. But each of tne Big Three also held tightly to the territories it held in military occupation, or for which it had secured recognized title during the war.

Anglo-American military forces occupied Italy, the western portions of Germany and Austria, and were spread across wide areas of France and the Low Countries. Additional British units

243

were stationed in Greece, across the Middle East and in Egypt, with a garrison in southern Iran until late 1945. Britain's forces had also reoccupied the colonial territories that had fallen to the Japanese, and her peacekeeping units were sent into Indochina for a short period immediately after the end of the Pacific war, and into the East Indies for somewhat longer.

American units retained their hold on the territories acquired by late nineteenth- and early twentieth-century imperialism: the Panama Canal, Samoa, Wake, Guam, Midway, and the Philippine Islands. They retained the central Pacific islands that had been captured from the Japanese as well as the Japanese home islands. In addition, as part of last-minute wartime agreements, and to shield the United States position in Japan, small American forces were stationed in southern Korea, and other contingents were sprinkled across northern and eastern China.

The Soviet Red Army remained in extreme north China until early 1946, kept units in northern Korea for three additional years, and maintained regular garrisons in the Kuriles, on Sakhalin Island, and at Port Arthur. Soviet units also stayed in northern Iran for a year after the end of the European war, and took up permanent positions in those portions of Europe which lay behind the "Iron Curtain" line stretching, as Churchill would say, "from Stettin on the Baltic to Trieste on the Adriatic."

While holding these positions, which appeared to indicate the enormous strength of the victorious powers, the Big Three governments held four special meetings in the first year and a half of peace in a cautious attempt to move toward a general settlement. The council of Big Three foreign ministers (sometimes supplemented by French and other representatives) met in London in September–October 1945, and again in Moscow during December of the same year. They came together once more in London during the January 1946 opening session of the United Nations General Assembly, and finally gathered for the peripatetic "Paris" peace conference for the "minor Axis states"—Rumania, Bulgaria, Hungary, Italy, and Finland. The latter conference began in Paris in April 1946, reassembled in the French capital in June and early July, and met there again from late July to October. These negotiations then continued during the end-of-the-year United Nations meeting in New York, and were finally concluded in Paris in January–February 1947.

The negotiations regarding the "minor Axis states" were actually the major focal point of high-level East-West meetings in the immediate postwar period. Although they seemed endlessly long to most Western officials, they were actually not much more protracted than the previous great Paris Conference of 1919. The Big Three foreign ministers did not attempt to deal directly with the German problem or issues lying beyond Eastern Europe or the Mediterranean; their brief was nonetheless dauntingly complicated. Some of the difficulties which loomed largest then, such as Soviet claims to a portion of the Italian colonies, or the bitter Italo-Yugoslavian struggle over control of Venezia Guilia, have now been largely forgotten, since no government any longer finds it expedient to mention colonies, and Tito's exit from the Soviet bloc in 1948 took most of the sting out of the Venezia Guilia problem. The bitterness of the troubles over boundaries and reparations may be difficult to appreciate adequately forty years after the event, but in light of the savagery of the war, and the wretched conditions which continued into the postwar period, contemporaries took them very seriously. Aroused public opinion and the need for funds not only compelled such Soviet satellites as Yugoslavia and Czechoslovakia to demand redress; the USSR had itself suffered grievous harm from Hitler's Balkan allies, France had endured losses at the hands of the Italians, and Greece had been abused by nearly every Axis country.

The effort to do something for the Greeks had a special dimension, because although Stalin and Churchill had agreed in 1944 that it should remain in the British sphere, and British troops were stationed there, a bitter civil war was raging between the conservative British-supported government and Communist guerrilla bands, which were being aided by the Soviets' Yugoslav and Bulgarian associates. London considered the maintenance of its position in Greece as vital to the protection of the Straits of the Bosporus and its lifeline to India, and throughout the whole immediate postwar period tended to see Greece, in the words of Bevin's private secretary, Piers Dixon, as "our most difficult satellite."

The "Little Axis" negotiations were deeply concerned with two of the Soviets' principle satellites as well, Rumania and Bulgaria. Not only had the USSR imposed the harshest and most repressive Communist regimes on these two countries, but unlike Poland, Czechoslovakia, Albania, and Yugoslavia, which had been on the Allied side, Rumania and Bulgaria had fought for Hitler, and their fate was a proper subject for consideration by a conference making peace with "Axis countries." Of course one might have said the same thing about Hungary, but during 1946, the Budapest regime was notably milder than that which had been installed in Sofia and Bucharest, and the Western powers seemed to walk more softly in the case of Hungary.

The British criticized the Rumanian and Bulgarian governments, as well as their Soviet creators, for pursuing policies of repression, and limiting Western access, which the London government felt violated wartime inter-Allied agreements as well as general human rights. Britain was concerned by these governments' confiscation of private businesses, for there had been considerable British investment in the area, especially in the Rumanian oil fields. Bevin and his aides called for compensation, a freer policy on trade and press contacts, and a general liberalizing of the regimes, but they were careful not to push too hard, recognizing that the Soviets held all the high cards in the region, and perhaps hoping, as Bevin suggested in early 1946, that the Soviet Union might ultimately opt for Finnish-type balanced governments in Bucharest and Sofia.

The United States authorities, however, although they had much less economic stake in the region, and could entertain little realistic hope that such a backward and underdeveloped area would ever play an important role in the economic life of the American colossus, bitterly attacked the USSR for its repressive role in Bulgaria and Rumania. The American government lodged frequent and impassioned protests, and even threw in attacks on the systems existing in Yugoslavia and Albania, although these matters were clearly beyond the purview of the Paris conference.

Despite the failure of the aggressive American protests, and the frequent Soviet resort to vilification and "bad manners," the Paris talks—as well as the other East-West meetings in late 1945 and throughout 1946—were real negotiations. Maneuver and bluff were punctuated by theatrically overstated demands, and off-the-record sessions, in which each side took the measure of the other. In November 1946, Molotov probed Bevin to see how long the Labour government was likely to last, and how the congressional elections would affect the American negotiating position. Although usually stubborn in the public sessions, the Soviet foreign minister made a number of confidential offers to trade concessions, especially on difficult points related to Yugoslavia and Greece.

After ten months of complicated, frustrating, and often abusive dealings, the "minor Axis" peace treaties were finally signed by all the powers, and formal relations were thereby restored for all states except Germany and Japan by early 1947. Looking back over a distance of nearly four decades during which East and West have been unable to make few additional agreements of any significance, the achievements of 1946 seem highly impressive. But they did not strike contemporaries that way, in part because there were so many other sources of disorder and dispute left over from World War II that a new general settlement looked unobtainable if every problem had to pass through a bitter, divisive, and dilatory process such as that which had taken place in the "Little Axis" conference.

Difficulties such as the conflict in Palestine and the British troubles in India were not made the subject of negotiation in any international meeting of the Big Three, nor was the problem of the atomic bomb dealt with on any serious basis during the eighteen months following the destruction of Hiroshima and Nagasaki. After a brief period of indecision, the Truman administration decided to bar even its wartime partners, Britain and

Canada, from its nuclear bomb program, and presented the Soviets with proposals for international control that would have required Stalin to allow foreign observers to wander freely through Soviet military establishments, a concession which the Soviet dictator had resolutely refused to make even during the wartime period of great Russian need, and East-West cordiality. Regarding the occupation program for Japan, the U.S.A. was just as intransigent as over the atom bomb, conceding to none of its allies anything more than token participation in powerless advisory councils, while the Americans kept all real authority in their own hands. Some United States officials, apparently including Averell Harriman, inclined toward the view in late 1945 that this was a mistake, and that a sharing of power in Tokyo might possibly be traded off for a lowering of the Eastern European Iron Curtain. But the top Washington leadership, remorselessly driven on by General MacArthur, refused to give an inch, even during November 1945, when an "uncommonly nervous and jumpy" Harriman sought to try for a deal because he felt "it would be better to curb the General than to break with the Russians."

So Japan too failed to become the subject of serious negotiations, and the U.S.A. was able to go on alone remodeling the country and gradually, after 1947, turning it into an economic, and later a military, asset in the cold war. The future of Germany and the occupation policies to be followed there were the subject of endless talk and bickering in the Allied Control Council, but surprisingly little high-level discussion of this most significant of matters took place during 1946. The big powers made a number of attempts to find a common formula for the future of the German miniproblem, the Austrian Republic, but they were ultimately unsuccessful. In fact, aside from the matters considered at Paris, the only important controversial matter that was seriously dealt with, and fortunately ultimately resolved, was the extended Soviet occupation of northern Iran. Direct talks between the Western foreign ministers and Stalin, when supplemented by traditional diplomacy, a whiff of military pressure in the form of a Mediterranean cruise by the United States Navy, and the blaze of unfavorable publicity in the United Nations, were ultimately sufficient to make the Soviets back down, and the Red Army withdrew from Iran in May 1946.

But the amount of effort which had been required to resolve this relatively modest dispute, when combined with the lack of progress on the much more vital issues of Germany, Japan, the A-bomb, and the interminable "minor Axis" negotiations, inclined the public nearly everywhere to the view that something had gone badly wrong. Their hope that victory over the Axis would produce a better and happier world seemed to have lost all chance of realization. Each of the big powers was quick to point fingers at the others and claim that the difficulties had arisen solely from the stubbornness of everyone but themselves, with London and Washington attributing most of the responsibility to Moscow, and the Soviets pouring the blame, and their bile, on the West.

Behind this discouraging spectacle of division and name-calling lay basic and significant reasons why a rapid reconstruction of the world order proved impossible to establish, and the most important of them had nothing to do with either ideology or malice. The United States already had its prosperity, and the nucleus of a postwar high-tech military machine, while Stalin, in possession of his security zone and the Red Army, had decided that the USSR could get back on its feet by its own efforts with minimal dependence on the outside world. Neither of the superpowers needed a postwar world recovery so badly that they felt compelled to make an all-out, sustained attempt to get one. Britain did want a world settlement more than either the U.S.A. or the USSR, but London was in no position to push the two giants into rapid motion. The superpowers thought it was better to delay rather than get a general settlement that was not exactly to their liking. They thought they could afford to wait, and they did.

In addition, although the superpowers were sufficiently content with their own situations at home to incline them to go slow abroad, their effective power actually decreased very quickly.

During the war, the governments of the Big Three had grown accustomed to getting their way, and their publics had come to take it for granted that Moscow, Washington, and London could have whatever they wanted. But after August 1945, the operative military might of the "Giants" was actually severely limited. The Red Army steadily declined until it reached a size comparable to that of Britain's wartime army, and since the USSR's military supply system still depended largely on horse power, it was hardly the all-powerful machine of popular myth. American army demobilization was more rapid and more far-reaching than that of the Soviet Union, and even the much-vaunted United States atomic arsenal actually contained only a handful of nuclear weapons.

Paralleling the postwar fall in superpower military muscle came a decrease in the volume of money and resources that the governments of the Big Three were able to commit to foreign economic and political matters, as the wartime sense of total emergency and ideological passion gradually dissipated. None of the Allied great powers had actually gone to war against the Axis states and Japan chiefly because of ideological hostility to fascism. They had primarily done it because either they, or a state which they saw as a vital ally, had actually been attacked. Therefore, during much of the conflict images of self-defense and national protection had remained uppermost in the public mind. Thwarting Hitler and remembering Pearl Harbor were the ideas which produced the most sonorous echoes among the British and American publics, while in the Soviet Union, traditional Russian nationalistic beliefs and symbols had anchored much of the public support for the war. But the Allied governments, along with private "opinion makers" in the Western countries, had not been content to leave their wartime publics alone with their patchwork of desires for self-defense and personified hatreds of Hitler, Mussolini, and Tojo. In every land, the authorities attempted to raise the consciousness of the people so that they would see all the enemy belligerents as part of a single evil and dangerous, right-wing "Fascist" threat. Through ideology, each government systematized and strengthened the public's commitment to the wartime cause, and in this way the various peoples acquired a greater willingness to share the total war burdens.

Only under total-war conditions, reinforced by ideology, had the Big Three secured sufficient manpower, money and public support to push their way into the wide range of territories in which they found themselves in August 1945. But once the immediate security and ideological threat posed by the Axis powers and Japan evaporated, the governments were unable to wring sufficient means out of their peoples to enforce their will in all the devastated corners of the world in which they found themselves. Whatever their pretensions in 1945–1946, all of the Big Three were actually overextended.

Their problems were compounded because when faced with the chaos of the world's economic, political, and social structure, not one of the three great Allied "isms" acted the way ideological determinists, and many subsequent cold war theorists, thought they should have. As the classic, traditional imperialist power, Great Britain ought to have dashed forward, seizing vulnerable territory and converted it into colonies or portions of a zone of influence. Many Americans, from free-trade business spokesmen to liberal leaders like Henry Wallace, expected and feared that Britain would launch off on a postwar spree of expanding its zones of influence. The Soviet authorities also initially aimed most of their postwar anti-Western propaganda barrages against British imperialism rather than American "capitalism," presumably because at least in part what Moscow saw as Britain's imperial assertiveness appeared to be the most pressing threat to Soviet interests in southeast Europe and the Middle East during the postwar era. But despite the Labour government's efforts to use reforms to put some bite back into Britain's imperial bark, the United Kingdom proved too weak to play the role which much of the world's opinion had assigned to her.

The Soviet Union also failed to play its assigned part and did not launch a centrally directed and aggressive global revolutionary campaign. The USSR was too poor and badly hurt, while

Stalin continued to be highly suspicious of foreign Communist parties and remained wedded to traditional ideas of balance-of-power politics and protective security zones. The Soviet government and the Communist parties played at propaganda and espionage, but nothing approaching a broad campaign of Moscow-led social revolution occurred.

Even the performance of the American capitalists was disappointing, for they did not seize the opportunity offered by world dislocation and bankruptcy. Instead of leaping in and buying up the destitute world's assets for a song, American business stayed home in 1945–1946, too entranced with its domestic economic bubble to invest more than a bit of loose change abroad.

If any one of the great "isms" had acted assertively, it might well have prompted a sufficient counterreaction to force real moves toward a settlement. But in the absence of such an initiative, and with the two strongest of the major governments simultaneously feeling underpowered and lacking in a sense of urgency, the world was caught in a limbo of wretchedness, delay, and disappointment. In that environment, dangerous feelings of apprehension and suspicion then began to grow.

In Washington, when what was seen as Soviet intransigence combined with the rapid demobilization of the armed forces and low postwar military budgets, many military leaders were seized by genuine alarm. They called for larger military appropriations, attempted to draw Canada and the rest of the Western Hemisphere into a defensive system dominated by Washington, and sought to acquire military bases from the British stretching as far as India. These developments in turn tended to feed the American political leaders' desire and ability to take strong stands abroad, and inevitably increased the anxieties of other governments.

Comparable, if modest, developments in the direction of military security measures can be seen in the case of Britain, and though documentary evidence is not available from the USSR, it is reasonable to assume that a parallel pattern of diplomatic clashes followed by rising military alarm led to a stiffening of

Soviet diplomatic postures. Certainly, as soon as the Western powers and the USSR began to feel threatened, analogies between the diplomatic clashes of 1945–1946 and those of the 1930s immediately appeared. For the Soviets, images of encirclement, the creation of a hostile capitalistic bloc, and the threat of possible attack quickly led to accusations that men like Winston Churchill were warmongers comparable to Hitler. Throughout the West, the analogy between Stalin and Hitler made rapid headway, with Foreign Office officials soon routinely referring to Communist parties as Stalin's "Fifth Column" and Washington bureaucrats absorbed by the threatening characteristics of generic "totalitarianism" and something called "Red Fascism."

When in late 1945, following the defection of Igor Gouzenko from the Soviet embassy in Ottawa, great publicity was given to the resulting breakup of Soviet espionage rings in the United States and Canada, American public anxiety increased. At the same time, the steady flow of anti-Communist scare stories, which the FBI provided to congressional leaders and selected newspaper editors, as well as the inner circle of the Truman administration, helped to enmesh Washington as well as the rest of the country in a significant Red scare.

The promptings of alarm were perhaps not as overt in other countries as in the United States, but the first three months of 1946 did witness four separate appeals for hardening the difficulties between East and West. During January 1946, in what passed for an election speech, Stalin gave one of his rare, and in this case very harsh, public orations. The Soviet leader's prediction of a "violent disturbance," a new capitalist war, and the necessity for the USSR to have three more five-year plans was widely interpreted in the West as a call for an end to the wartime honeymoon and the start of a ruthless struggle between Communist and capitalist. A month later, the "Long Telegram" of the Soviet specialist at the American embassy in Moscow, George Kennan, arrived in Washington. Tracing Soviet intransigence to the system's Marxist-Leninist ideological roots, predicting unlimited and never-ending expansionist pressure, and calling for a policy of what would soon be called Western "containment," the Long Telegram went through official Washington like a forest fire. In March, Winston Churchill delivered his famous "Iron Curtain" speech at Fulton, Missouri, plumping for a new Anglo-American alliance to check the advancing Red Tide. Although there was much public opposition to the former prime minister's views on both sides of the Atlantic, with most American press reaction ranging from cool to overtly hostile toward the speech, Harry Truman had not only been in the audience, he had read and approved the speech beforehand. Other Western leaders also gave Churchill's views a sympathetic ear, Canadian Prime Minister Mackenzie King confidentially informing Attlee that he felt "it was the most courageous utterance I have ever heard by any public man[,] and one that has been made none too soon." While the Labour government publicly tried to distance itself both from such opinions and from the Fulton speech itself, it had not been without prior knowledge of its contents, and within a month the Foreign Office had produced its own basic policy paper, authored by C. F. A. Warner, which, like Kennan's Long Telegram, called for Anglo-American containment of the USSR.

Opinion polls suggest, however, that the Western public was much slower than its leaders to make the jump from being anti-Nazi to anti-Communist, although disillusionment with the USSR was rife in both Britain and the U.S.A. by mid-1946. From the scattered evidence available it seems that the Soviet public was also slow to make the swing to hate and suspicion of the West. Soviet citizens' confidential assurances to Westerners that they genuinely wanted peace and an understanding with the West frequently had the ring of sincerity, but in the USSR, what the people at the time actually thought was even less significant than it was in the West.

The worried national leaders were the only ones in a position to set the course, but they could not come up with any plausible plans for action. Overcommitted, lacking any significant assistance from imperialism, capitalism, or Soviet-led revolution, each of the Big Three fell back on the most tired of clichés, deciding to do little except sit, wait, and hope that time was on its side. The Soviet leaders clutched their belief that dislocations generated by the war would sooner or later produce a Western economic collapse, and the resulting social discontent would ultimately force London and Washington to deal on terms favorable to the USSR.

The American government initially tried a planned "experiment," seeking a quick deal with Stalin during the December 1945 Foreign Ministers Conference in Moscow, but when that failed, Truman and his aides concluded that a firm policy of "standing up to the Russians" on such matters as Iran, Turkey, Germany, and Austria would have to be followed to make Stalin see reason. However, the Americans tended to have a short fuse, and the isolationism and Anglophobia which lingered in the country, when coupled with the old feelings of moral and ideological superiority, produced currents moving in the direction of withdrawal that ran counter to the anti-Communist impulse urging the government and public to take more active stands. There was genuine American unwillingness to be involved in new international crises so soon after the great victory of 1945. Even George Marshall privately admitted at the time he was made secretary of state that although he had great respect for active work, by the end of 1946 he had come to feel "I would like to confine mine to my own vine and fig tree." The president himself had no basic interest in most remote regions of the world. Ernest Bevin was unable to strike the slightest spark of concern in Mr. Truman in late 1946 by describing the difficulties existing in Egypt and the Dutch East Indies, and later on in the same conversation, the president stated flatly that he was in no particular hurry to arrange peace settlements for Germany or Japan. Even when the American government did express an interest in a particular problem, that did not necessarily mean Washington would make any serious effort to assist in its resolution. As Sir Francis Fox wrote in November 1946 regarding the difficulties in Palestine, "Some of our American friends (charming people as they are) have a liking to be in a 'poker party' without putting any chips on the table." But such reluctant activists as Harry Truman and George Marshall looked like impassioned internationalists compared with much of the public and the majority of those elected to the ultraconservative Eightieth Congress in November 1946.

Britain, the weakest of the three powers, was most threatened by drift in a chaotic world, but the lack of realistic alternatives and the belief that reform, austerity, and the American loan would give Britain five years of grace, inclined London to move cautiously. From the beginning Bevin feared that "the three imperialisms" (Britain, the USSR, and the U.S.A.) would create "Three Monroes" (i.e., three zones of influence analogous to that which the Monroe Doctrine had proclaimed for the United States in the Western Hemisphere), thereby dividing the world into closed economic and security zones, which would block a general settlement and inhibit world trade. But the only way the foreign secretary could see to help prevent such a development was to try to dampen down the "war of nerves," and preach calmness and the importance of economic recovery, while trying to persuade the Americans not to run out on their responsibilities in Europe and Asia. He did not believe it possible to deal successfully "with the Russians if you lie down and let them walk over you," for "it's patience you want in this sort of thing." As he said in January 1946, the chief dangers arose where the interests of the three great powers touched, such as Germany and the Balkans, and it was therefore essential to "keep the ball-bearings" of negotiation "set and properly greased," while waiting for favorable circumstances for discussion.

By the summer of 1946, Bevin's patience, like that of his American colleagues in the "minor Axis" negotiations, was wearing thin, and he admitted to a friend that he had lost all hope in Molotov and focused his aspirations on the possibility that the next turn of the Soviet policy wheel might get rid of old "iron pants" and bring back someone more moderate such as Litvinov or Maisky. Many officials in the Foreign Office were even readier than the foreign secretary to give up on the policy of waiting patiently, and by mid-1946 there was strong support for a program of East-West confrontation. But Bevin continued to extoll the virtues of calm restraint as late as May 1947, when in a speech to the Labour Party Conference he claimed that he had "cultivated for the first time in my life, as all my colleagues will agree, [such] a quite remarkable patience [that] I must have been born again." However, not even such apparent interventions by divine providence were sufficient to permit Britain to stay the course after the arrival of the terrible winter of 1946–1947. That economic catastrophe made the United Kingdom more dependent on American trade and aid, and required the British to push more of the cost and responsibility for Western firmness onto the United States. Inevitably, as Britain was compelled to step back, the two superpowers, though still not controlling as much effective power as they wished, and surrounded by a destitute and broken world, were steadily pushed toward a position in which they were left alone to confront each other face to face.

The first significant move into this second, and more active, phase of the cold war came right in the middle of the great British winter crisis. In December 1946, Britain was compelled to throw in her independent hand in the occupation of Germany, and succeeded in persuading the Americans to create a "Bizone" fusion of the two countries' areas of occupation. Bevin had long clung to the hope that a cooperative four-power occupation of Germany, carried out jointly by the French, British, Americans, and Russians, might provide the setting for a closer general understanding and contribute to the ultimate raising of the Iron Curtain. But the centripetal forces had been too strong. Not only had the Soviets looted their zone and tried to extract the maximum in reparations, other Eastern and Western countries, led by the Czechs, Poles, French, and Belgians, had dismantled and removed much of Germany's industrial plant, collected extra reparations, and refused to pay for German exports. Between 1945 and 1947, 75 percent of Germany's "exports" were actually hidden reparations, because such "buyers" as the French and Poles failed to pay. To make matters in Germany even worse, France, whose ego was badly bruised and its economy seriously disrupted, insisted that the Saar, Ruhr, and Rhineland be separated from the rest of Germany to provide the French with greater security. Paris refused to participate in any joint Allied occupation efforts unless France was at least permitted to annex the Saar and convert the Rhine and the Ruhr into a French puppet state.

As a result of Soviet and French hard-line policies, and the general impoverishment in Germany, the British and American occupation authorities were placed in an impossible position. The Foreign Office and the State Department tended to put the main responsibility for the trouble on the Soviets, while despite the fact that the American army commander in Germany, General Clay, cut off reparations payments from the American zone to the USSR in May 1946, both the general and the American War Department believed that the chief source of their difficulties lay in Paris rather than Moscow. In any event, the British War Office and the American War Department were compelled to subsidize the economies of their zones to the tune of millions of dollars annually, merely to keep the population from starvation. By the winter of 1946–1947 the dreadful condition of the German population, the lack of any prospects for basic improvement, and the scale of the Anglo-American subsidies had produced sharp criticism and calls for immediate change in both the British parliament and the American Congress.

Therefore, when the great winter crisis struck Britain in 1946–1947 the exchequer demanded that the situation be immediately set right, for as Dalton was to write to Bevin, Britain had been compelled to spend a large portion of the American loan merely trying to keep "the wretched Germans" alive. All the foreign secretary's hopes of putting the Ruhr coal industry into public ownership, and persuading his allies to internationalize the region, therefore had to be abandoned.

The creation of the Bizone in December 1946 somewhat lessened Britain's financial burdens, and by intertwining the interests of the two powers in Germany, it became more difficult for the Americans to throw in their hand and flee from Europe. The fusion agreement also gave the United States government the means to block Labour's nationalization program in the Ruhr, and helped extinguish the last flicker of hope for an effective four-power administration of Germany. By the time the foreign ministers of the USSR, Britain, and America met in Moscow in March 1947, no form of German deal was even theoretically possible because the British could not pay the costs of reparations and support of the German population, and the Americans would not pay them, so the only question given serious consideration by both the Eastern and Western sides was how to throw the blame for the conference failure upon the other.

The second major instance of a British pullback in Europe prompted by the winter of 1946–1947 was the February 1947 cutoff of economic and military aid to Greece and Turkey. Here again, under British prompting, the Americans moved into the breach, and in so doing extended the line of two-power confrontation across the face of Europe. But in the Greek case, far more than in that of the Bizone agreement, Washington might have been seen by the American public as merely stepping in to take the place of a faltering Britain, and such a crass shouldering of Britain's "imperial burden" was highly unpopular in America. In 1945–1946, the United States had provided eleven billion dollars' worth of economic assistance to Europe via the United Nations relief agencies, much of which had actually gone to the USSR and its Eastern European satellites. But by early 1947, in order to substitute a mere four hundred million dollars of American aid for that which had previously been supplied by Britain, President Truman felt it advisable to capitalize on the country's anticommunism and defend the move by using provocative ideological language. In presenting the Greek and Turkish aid bill to Congress, the president, although not mentioning the USSR by name, declared that this was the first step in a "Truman Doctrine," which would commit the United States to "support free peoples who are resisting attempted subjugation by armed minorities or outside aggression."

The Bizone agreement and the Truman Doctrine brought to

an end the period of postwar drift and decay, replacing it with an American effort to shore up Western Europe. This in itself marked a major turning point. But, especially in regard to the Truman Doctrine, the administration consciously chose to obtain the money by trying "to scare hell out of Congress," and it fanned the flames of domestic anticommunism in order to ground its more assertive, and more expensive, foreign policy in some form of anti-Soviet crusade. The Washington government did not push its ideological campaign to extremes, but as many historians have persuasively argued, by using anticommunism to justify an active foreign policy, it paved the way for the kind of Red scare that was soon driven forward by Senator McCarthy.

The Truman Doctrine began to move the United States into a condition of partial ideological mobilization. This was not sufficient to give the administration the kind of unlimited public support and money which had existed during total war, but henceforth Washington had the means to exert greater influence abroad, even as it had to contend with more volatile public, and especially congressional, pressure at home.

One of the first manifestations of the new situation was a reorganization, and modernization, of the American military and foreign relations machinery. In July 1947 the National Security Act was passed, which gave birth to a unified Department of Defense, created the CIA, and established a foreign policy command center in the form of the National Security Council. President Truman was still not ready to authorize the scale of expenditure which would have made possible a massive increase of American military power, but when, in April 1947, he was finally told that the U.S.A. actually only held a dozen or so atomic bombs, he ordered a production increase which was sufficient to put fifty bombs in the atomic arsenal by the spring of 1948.

London was quick to grasp the significance of the changed situation in Washington, and sought to take advantage of it to improve its own shaky position. In the early summer of 1947, Bevin ordered that an inventory of strategic materials available in the British Empire be made so that he could use it as a bargaining counter in his dealings with security-conscious American officials, and in the fall of 1947, the London Government went on to score an even bigger success. British and American delegations secretly met in Washington in November–December 1947, and wrote up separate, but identical, recommendations to their home governments regarding basic policy in the Middle East. Both recommendations declared that "free world" control of the Middle East was essential, and that the United States government would support the British position there, because it had decided that its security "would be jeopardised if the Soviet Union should succeed in its efforts to obtain control of any one of the following countries: Italy, Greece, Turkey or Iran." This was another major step forward in shoring up Britain, and substituting American power for that of the United Kingdom, even though, as Bevin and Marshall agreed in a most highly secret discussion on 4 December, "there was no agreement[,] nor even an understanding between the two Governments on the questions which had been discussed at Washington; it had merely happened that each of the Governments had been presented by their officials with recommendations which substantially coincided," and had then accepted them.

But if the extent of these American cold war political and military initiatives during 1947 were not obvious to all, the major international economic move of the United States was made openly, and in a full blaze of publicity. During late 1946 and early 1947, State Department planners and those in the American military occupation organization in Germany had become increasingly concerned about the negative effect which impoverished western Germany was having on the economic recovery and political stability of Western Europe. Numerous vague sketches for some kind of American economic recovery scheme for Western Europe therefore floated about the War and State departments in early 1947, and with some justice it might just be argued that the final proposal should have been named after Under Secretary of State Acheson or the United States commander in Germany, General Lucius Clay. But it was the June 1947 call for a European Recovery Plan made at Harvard by the secretary of state which caught the public's imagination, and America's main postwar political-economic initiative for Europe therefore went forward as "the Marshall Plan."

The proposal called for Europe to produce a broad economic recovery plan, which would then be subsidized in part by the United States. The program did not in principle ban Soviet participation, but it was clearly intended to hang the Soviet leaders on the horns of a serious dilemma. Together with their satellites they could either join the plan on American terms, which would have opened the USSR's economy to Western inspection and partial supervision to guarantee conformity with the plan's terms, or follow the more likely course and stand apart watching while Western Europe became stronger, more closely tied to America, and less vulnerable to Soviet pressure.

The plan was therefore simultaneously a proposal to get Western Europe on its feet so it would become a real trading partner and not a permanent ward of the American taxpayer, and a political weapon aimed directly at the USSR.

Believing that Europe faced a choice of being either partially Americanized or so pauperized that it would ultimately slip under Soviet control, Bevin immediately took the lead in moving toward a European development plan that would pull in substantial recovery assistance from the U.S.A. Following an exploratory mission by Molotov to the European Marshall Plan preparatory conference in Paris during June 1947, the Soviets did what most American officials wanted them to do, and concluded that any plan which had a real chance of being effective was incompatible with their basic policy of holding their own zone in isolation while leaving the rest of Europe weak and divided. Communist propaganda denouncing the Marshall Plan soon flooded over Western Europe, and this made the tasks of the participating governments much more onerous, while further increasing the polarization of the two halves of the continent. The Soviet pressure compelled Poland and Czechoslovakia to withdraw their initial requests to participate, and the hostility of the Western

Communist parties to the plan, especially in France and Italy, kept many leaders highly jittery while they struggled to come up with proposals acceptable to the United States.

The foreign ministers of the Western European countries were inclined to feel that the Americans had left them in a highly exposed position, despite a French public opinion poll of September 1947 that revealed that even with the country's large Communist party membership and the heavy anti–Marshall Plan propaganda, 64 percent of the respondents favored French participation in the plan, while only 8 percent were definitely opposed. In September, simply inverting much of what most Americans thought of Europeans, Count Sforza of Italy and Ernest Bevin agreed that the Americans were undependable, "isolationist," inclined to do "too little and too late," "niggardly," desirous of Western cooperation while keeping the Monroe Doctrine in place "to get a monopoly of trade," and frequently blinded by the specter of Communism, which was their "greatest fear." Three months later, Bevin and French Foreign Minister Bidault fantasized about the possibility that Britain and France might somehow merge their poverty, and by exploiting their African colonies, turn Europe into a third force between the two superpowers. But such momentary heresies did not prevent the Western European governments, after considerable American pushing and shoving, from finally agreeing to a fairly realistic development plan, and then doing everything possible to assist the American administration in its effort to get the appropriation bills through Congress.

Since most of the Western European leaders were not only terrified of the Soviets, but were long-term anti-Communists in their own right, they frequently found it convenient to fan the very American fears of communism which they privately ridiculed. Bidault had based much of his political career on anti-Communism, Bevin prided himself on his thirty years of struggle against Communist influence in the trade union movement, and Attlee was, if anything, more inclined to a hard-line on the USSR than his foreign secretary. When responding to Bevin's request for guidance on what he could do to assist passage of the Marshall Plan, the British ambassador in Washington, Sir Oliver Franks, replied in November 1947 that one of the best things would be "reiterating again now and then your detestation of communism." Bevin not only fullfilled this assignment, he tried to scare the Americans with stories of new Communist dangers. In a conversation with the United States Ambassador on 24 November he managed twice to announce his belief that the Soviets were smuggling Jews who were "indoctrinated communists" into Palestine, and a week later he confided to Secretary of State Marshall the odd notion that the Soviets were enaged in a disruptive campaign in Palestine and the rest of the Middle East with the intention of opening the way for their own seizure of Iraq.

Amid much anti-Communist rhetoric the Marshall Plan interim aid bill passed through Congress in late December 1947, and the general proposal was signed by the president in April 1948. But just as American money began to flow into Western Europe and the confidence of the region started to revive, the Soviet countereffort to further tighten the screws in the East produced new Western worries. In February 1948, the most Western-oriented of the Soviet satellite governments—the Beneš-Masaryk regime in Czechoslovakia—was suddenly toppled by a Communist coup. Western leaders, who had strong sympathy for Beneš, and some twangs of conscience about the shabby part which the West had played during the previous rape of Czechoslovakia at Munich in 1938, were truly and deeply shocked. Bevin decried the "ruthlessness of communism" which the coup had displayed, and the British ambassador in Prague rose to a pitch of indignation that would later have been much admired by Senator McCarthy and the John Birch Society, declaring in a letter to the foreign secretary that if he were actually religious he would now "believe that Lenin is Anti-Christ," for he had witnessed "all the values of civilized man, patiently evolved over thousands of years since the days of Hammurabi and Solon [and Jesus?], being overthrown and replaced by evil."

Both sides had locked themselves into position and were tightening down the screws. What had begun as political-economic jockeying for advantage was increasingly being defined in ideological terms as a necessary element in a face-off between hostile systems. In such an apocalyptic atmosphere there was little complacency and very few European snide remarks about America's alleged anti-Communist "obsessions." When Bevin and Bidault met in March 1948, they launched a covert attack on Communist "infiltration" into Western countries, with combined Anglo-French intelligence and police operations. In the same month, the British government took a number of public and "covert" steps to strengthen moderate parties in Italy on the eve of the elections, and on 6 March the British foreign secretary suggested to the American ambassador that the two governments should study what countermeasures to employ—including armed intervention—"to prevent any coup d'état in Italy similar to that which had just taken place in Czechoslovakia."

The overall effect of the Marshall Plan, as had been at least partially intended from the beginning, was therefore to build up the western portion of Europe as a partial counterweight to Soviet power in the East. Beneath this political surface of increasing opposition to what was perceived as a real Communist threat, Marshall Plan money, and the European Recovery Plan itself, gradually transformed the western half of the continent. Although the Americans exercised considerable restraint, they did insist that to secure grants from Washington Western Europe had to move toward economic integration and concentrate on the development of export industries. The American government's main economic obsession was to raise European output, especially of export goods, which could be exchanged for essential imports from the United States, and thus gradually decrease the need for American subsidies. These policies extended little sympathy to what Washington saw as "leftist social experiments," or attempts to shield economic sectors from competition in order to protect high levels of employment. Competition was the American motto even though high United States tariff policies were hardly a model for an international system of free trade.

Despite much talk about the wonders of free enterprise, the Marshall Plan was not simply a weapon of crusading capitalism. It was a United States government program, paid for by the public—which had learned to pay high income taxes during World War II and had been partially reactivated by the Red scare—and administered by Washington bureaucrats. American private capitalists showed little more eagerness to invest in Europe during the Marshall Plan era than they had previously, and the bureaucrats were therefore able to do what they felt capitalists should have done if they had only possessed the necessary brains and courage. Consequently, centralized planning was not necessarily anathema to Marshall Plan officials, who frequently favored left-leaning governments rather than those made up of old-fashioned conservatives, because the latter tended to resist change, favor protective tariffs, and oppose broad economic projects. The only social democratic government with which the American Marshall Plan authorities frequently locked horns over economic policy was that of Britain, for in order to maintain Commonwealth ties and its "special relationship" with the United States, as well as to protect its inefficient industries from foreign competition, Britain did everything in its power to hold back European economic integration and the development of what was to become known as the Common Market.

Although Bevin had played a major part in putting the Marshall Plan into motion, the British government soon showed itself much more interested in matters of Western defense than in creating effective economic projects that would benefit all of Western Europe. As early as February 1948, London had succeeded in concluding the Brussels Pact, which bound France, the Benelux, and Britain into a mutual defense system that they hoped would draw in enough American support so that in the event of a Soviet attack, the American military would intervene "from the first day," and "we should not have to wait for another Pearl Harbour." The Brussels Pact had been warmly welcomed by the United States government, and Washington had promised that military assistance would soon be sent, but the driving force behind the pact had been Bevin, not Bidault, Spaak, Marshall, or Truman. Throughout 1947 and the first half of 1948, the Americans continued to put their primary emphasis on European economic development. During the whole period 1946–1952, for every dollar's worth of American military assistance which went abroad, nine dollars in economic aid was sent.

In early 1948 there were signs of panic in Washington when the usually cautious General Clay cabled from Germany that for the first time he had gained the impression that the Soviets might actually be gearing up to launch a general war. The more prudent of American officials had some difficulty controlling the alarmist reaction produced in some parts of Washington by Clay's cable, and the British Foreign Office moved quickly to pour oil on the troubled American waters, and to reassure those British cabinet members, including Cripps, who feared that Washington was about to make the jump into general war.

In London too, some of the more exuberant political and military figures were in a highly agitated state about the USSR in early 1948. Churchill felt that the immediate future looked very uncertain, and Field Marshal Montgomery, then chief of the Imperial General Staff, prepared a staff paper at the end of January 1948 which carried the straightforward title: "The Problem of Future War and the Strategy of War with Russia." Montgomery had decided that even if the Western European states should be forced to go it alone with a minimum of help from the United States, a defense line needed immediately to be built along the Rhine. In mid-March, the field marshal wrote to his old wartime colleague General Omar Bradley, in 1948 chairman of the American Joint Chiefs of Staff, to see if he agreed with Montgomery's view "that the time had come to marshal the forces of the West against the menace from the East." He called on Bradley to help him reconstruct a global system of Anglo-American joint commands and asked that the Americans "should agree that the main bombing effort against Russia comes from them."

In March 1948, Bevin moved quickly to get Montgomery's foray into Anglo-American relations under control, scrawling across a copy of the field marshal's letter to Bradley, "I must see the Minister of Defence." Restraint seemed especially necessary then, because Montgomery's colleagues on the Chiefs of Staff Committee had already concluded that without American participation in a general European defense system, and a steady buildup of American forces, the field marshal's idea of a defense on the Rhine was nonsense.

By June, however, what had seemed like alarmist fantasizing just three months earlier had taken on the appearance of a rising reality. With the Marshall Plan beginning to produce serious economic recovery in western Germany, and the first Western moves pointing toward ultimate creation of a west German state, the USSR struck back by cutting off the surface transport through the Soviet zone of Germany, which was the main means that had been used to supply the Western occupation zone within the former German capital. The Soviet's Berlin blockade was soon matched by the famous airlift, which flew in enough supplies to keep alive the Allied troops and the West Berliners, but there was a rising apprehension, especially in Western Europe, that general war might be imminent. In the first week of July, the British chiefs of staff and the Ministry of Defence concluded that although they thought the USSR would not "deliberately provoke a war," it was the Soviets' "long term task to hasten the elimination of capitalism," and they therefore might make a "miscalculation."

The Foreign Office was also gravely worried, and its July 1948 general situation estimate was markedly pessimistic. Completely dismissing Tito's recent expulsion from the Soviet bloc as nothing but "a family quarrel," the Foreign Office already viewed the situation in a manner similar to that of the later "domino theory." From their "secure entrenchments" in Eastern Europe, the Soviets were seen to be "probing along the Western line," seeking to find "a weak spot" through which they could "infiltrate" and "cause the whole line to collapse."

Both the Foreign Office and the Ministry of Defence believed that the only hope in this threatening situation was constant vigilance, and a speeding up of efforts to commit the Americans to a large-scale defense of Western Europe. Of course such moves toward a steady buildup were not enough for the real enthusiasts. Field Marshal Montgomery had persuaded himself that "the religion of communism[,] operated from Moscow[,] was drawing the world toward great dangers," and that the West would not be able to hang on in Berlin indefinitely in defiance of the Soviets. During a tour of his proposed western front in July 1948, the field marshal explained what he thought was required. Dismissing the need to await American aid as "utter and complete nonsense [which] Ministers must stamp on . . . at once," Montgomery declared:

There are in France plenty of rifles, light machine guns, pistols and carving knives. These are sufficient for immediate needs. The philosophy must be that the fighting men of France will line up on the Rhine with these weapons, however inadequate they may seem, and will fight to the death. Every man must be imbued with the spirit that if he cannot stay on the Rhine alive, he will stay there dead; each man must be determined that, if he has to die, he will take at least two of the enemy with him: either to Heaven or to Hell.

Furthermore, the philosophy must be clear that any enemy soldiers from the East who pass the Rhine and enter France will be dealt with by the Resistance movements. Those enemy who escape the men will be strangled by the women.

Although not going to as ludicrous lengths as Montgomery, Secretary of State Marshall also had convinced himself of the truth of a dangerous military fallacy by the autumn of 1948. Speaking confidentially to a group of Western leaders on 4 October, Marshall declared that "he was convinced the greatest anxiety of the Soviet Government was the atom bomb[,] which they now for the first time thought might really be used against them." To be in a position to exploit the supposed Soviet fear of the bomb politically, Marshall advocated a crash program of arms shipments to Europe, which, by rapidly equipping thirty

French divisions, would supplement the atomic bomb and put the West in the driver's seat.

Given the adventuresome inclinations of these two influential voices from the Second World War, it was probably best that the calm, if rather unimaginative, course favored by the bureaucrats was pursued instead. Representatives of the Western governments began to meet in Washington in July 1948 to work out a system of Western European, and ultimately, North Atlantic defense. The meetings continued intermittently throughout the summer, fall, and winter of 1948, and on into early 1949, culminating in the preparation and signing of the NATO agreement in April, and its ratification by the United States Senate three months later. Since Donald Maclean was a charter member of the planning group, not only were all the Western governments aware of the limited strength and nervous defensiveness of NATO, but the Soviet Union was equally well informed, and therefore had no reason to overreact.

During the eleven months of the Berlin blockade and airlift— June 1948 to May 1949—as the Marshall Plan began to produce its European *Wirtschaftswunder* and Western confidence revived—a draft constitution for West Germany was also completed. Although the French managed to block ambitious American plans for the immediate arming of West Germany, the general level of Western European armament was improved, more American ground units arrived, and heavy bomber groups of the United States Air Force were stationed in Britain.

Shortly after the Soviets called off the blockade in May 1949, the foreign ministers of the wartime Big Four from the European war (which included France) held their last formal meeting in Paris, tacitly recognizing that the era of four-power joint control over Germany was at an end, and so was the Grand Alliance. The two blocks had become sharply divided, but Western Europe was no longer economically disintegrating, nor as militarily vulnerable. A new European balance had been created by American economic support, topped with a sprinkling of weapons and collective security agreements, for the first time since the end of

World War II. Although as had been true throughout modern history, Western Europe was again becoming much richer than the Soviet zone of Eastern European satellites, the actual military-economic power possessed by the major East-West contenders in that region coincided fairly well with their claims and pretentions. As such, a new plateau had been built, more realistic and therefore more favorable to stability and prevention of the kind of conflict which could result from miscalculation or an excess of zeal.

There were certainly serious drawbacks and dangerous elements within the new balance created in 1949. The success of the Berlin airlift had increased the inclination of Washington's new national security elite to seek political confrontations that bordered on what John Foster Dulles would later call "brinkmanship." The incoming American secretary of state, Dean Acheson, subsequently claimed that the whole idea behind the creation of NATO had been to raise the stakes for Stalin, in the hope that he would be left with no choice except "to start World War III or abandon his aggression." The Soviet explosion of an atomic bomb in Siberia during September 1949 heightened the enthusiasm of many in the American military to concentrate on a strategy of atomic blitz. This then led on to the inauguration of a crash development program for the hydrogen bomb once the military chiefs had come to believe in February–March 1950 that the USSR might be ahead of them in H-bomb development.

Some basis was thereby laid for a high-tech arms race, but President Truman's upset victory in the November 1948 elections strengthened his ability to continue holding military spending in check. Throughout early 1950 the president resisted heavy military urging that the United States drastically expand its military forces in order to counter what the National Security Council had persuaded itself was a global Soviet military threat to American interests.

But even while President Truman managed to hold the line on the military budget, that pressure tended to distract Washington's attention from the great successes it had achieved by economic programs rather than arms buildups. The shift from an economic to a military outlook undoubtedly played a part in Washington's slowness in nursing Tito's independent course with economic aid, even though the Yugoslavian leader openly sought Western assistance, and the idea had come to be supported by the British Government and influential sections of the American press.

The increase of American military and security awareness heighted concern about what symptomatically soon came to be called in Washington "critical" rather than "strategic," materials. For example, by 1949, the Pentagon had ranked the Congo and South Africa as the two most important future sources of uranium, and this trend inevitably increased the political importance of these areas. Averell Harriman, the special ambassador designated to deal with Marshall Plan matters, had already pressured the British government to use its influence to guarantee that such critical materials were sold to Washington as part of America's emergency stockpiling program. By January 1950, the South Africans had begun to grasp that this situation gave them increased political as well as economic bargaining power, and they demanded that London arrange for the Pretoria government to be taken into the "inner circle" of states concerned with atomic policy on a level at least equal to that of Canada.

As a result of the "critical materials" chase, officials in London and Washington began to fret about possible Communist dangers in Britain's African colonies, and the "security" of yet another continent began to take its place in the cold war drama. But none of the new developments accompanying the pursuit of "critical" materials was more significant than the financial pressures it released. Increased demand inevitably produced shortages, and just as inevitably raised commodity prices. This trend, when coupled with government encouragement and the slowdown of the domestic economic boom, inclined more American capital to go abroad. A new and unpredictable piece was thereby placed upon the board that had not been present to any sizable degree outside the Western Hemisphere during the first three postwar years. The accelerating export of American capital would produce a series of global economic and political complications which neither the government of the United States, nor that of any other nation, would find easy to control.

Although some countries, especially France, were initially cautious about permitting large American private investments, a number of West European governments including that of Britain welcomed private capital from the United States. Western Europe's economic position was still very shaky and Britain was especially vulnerable. Despite her slump in effective power and the fact that she had withdrawn from some of her large colonial holdings, the United Kingdom continued to cling to a large number of colonial liabilities and was highly sensitive about her great power status. She not only distanced herself from the European integration movement, but on more than one occasion scolded the United States for interference in Britain's internal affairs, claiming that despite all her troubles she should still be treated like a great power and her officials left "to do our own business in our own way."

But the slight 1949 downturn in the American economy quickly proved the hollowness of such British pretentions. As exports from Britain to the U.S.A. declined, the balance-of-crisis returned. In February 1949, British officials in Washington were forbidden to speak publicly about the condition of Britain's economy, and by June the foreign secretary was appealing to the United States government to do something to increase its imports from Europe in order to prevent jeopardizing West European recovery, the development of NATO, and "our progress in the cold war." In the following month Bevin remarked to M. Schuman that under such circumstances it was not possible "to take an anti-American line . . . and then go and get dollars," and by November 1949 the foreign secretary himself was developing detailed plans to help rescue Britain from bankruptcy by such mundane campaigns as one to attract American student tourists.

In addition to its continuing economic vulnerabilities, Western Europe also had grounds for nervousness because NATO was

much weaker in conventional ground forces than were the Soviets, and the explosive question of rearming West Germany continued to agitate the whole continent. Across the Atlantic, Americans were prey to fits of excited apprehension. In September
1949 the leaders of the American Communist party were convicted under the Smith Act of conspiring to overthrow the
United States government by force. Two months later (November 1949), Alger Hiss, the former high State Department official who had been accused of having passed official documents
to the Russians in the 1930s, was found guilty of perjury, and
in the following month (December 1949) Klaus Fuchs, a British
nuclear scientist who had worked at Los Alamos, was arrested
and charged with spying for the Soviet Union.

These cases, when combined with the general rise of ideological tensions associated with the Soviet-American confrontation
and the administration's use of the Communist danger to whip
up support for its containment foreign policy, were enough to
bring the Red scare to a white heat. By late 1949 Senator Joseph
McCarthy had seized this opportunity, and his accusations of
treachery and treason made the American public even more worried and apprehensive.

Nor did all the uncertainties and possible threats to the new
balance of power that had succeeded the Berlin airlift lie in
America and Western Europe. If Moscow chose not to accept it,
lacked sufficient restraint, or decided to unleash military attacks
or massive revolutionary pressure, the new balance was obviously doomed. Surely Stalin was always an ominous question
mark, and there must have been some expansive individuals
within the Kremlin who were actually tempted to take big gam-
bles. However, in retrospect it seems unlikely that Stalin's Russia
would have been capable of knowingly staking everything on a
single card, or striking out so boldly that the only possible result
would have been either total victory or complete defeat. That
cautious and lumbering system never acted in the manner of a
high roller, and since it had just acquired and consolidated its

Eastern European and northern Asian security zones, there was still less reason to take big risks.

Even allowing for the existence of the broad range of destabilizing factors, the cold war balance formed by 1949 was a substantial accomplishment, which offered some prospects for the future. Neither East nor West had wanted to accept anything short of success, yet both had stopped short of immediate war or the fanning of the ideological flames to the point where they could outfit themselves with enough military power to fight a general war. World War II's legacy of anarchic drift had been arrested, Europe's dangerously low standard of living had risen, the new balance rested on realistic power foundations, and the East-West hostilities were of such recent origin that a miracle might not have been necessary to lessen them gradually. With most of the world's power in the hands of the two countries that continued to be both unusually inward-looking and self-absorbed, there were reasons to hope that they would eschew the temptation to become universal meddlers, and allow a little warmth gradually to work its way back into the cold war.

What was most required to allow that to happen was a combination of caution and deft statesmanship, and it was these which were notably lacking on both sides. Stalin seems to have approved, if he did not orchestrate, the North Korean invasion of the south in June 1950, and this set off a chain reaction, and a series of counterreactions, which destroyed the recently created post–World War II equilibrium. Throughout late 1949 and the first half of 1950, President Truman had been under intense pressure from the military security lobby to drastically expand American armed might so that worldwide lines of confrontation could be created with the USSR and its satellites. Many American political and military officials, emboldened by their success over Berlin, had come to welcome opportunities to score additional confrontation triumphs over matters which were *not* vital to the interests of the United States. Led by Secretary of State Acheson and the joint chiefs, Washington had leapt at the chance to send military assistance to the French in Indochina in late 1949, and then when the North Koreans crossed the thirty-eighth parallel, they rushed forward to meet what they perceived as an overt instance of Stalinist military aggression in Korea. In conjunction with the latter action, the United States assumed a protectorate over Chiang's regime in Formosa, and in the course of the war, disregarding Beijing's warnings, invaded North Korea and soon found itself engaged in a bitter, if geographically limited, war with China.

Whoever was most to blame for the series of escalations, the three years of armed conflict in Korea undermined the stabilizing developments of the years 1948–1949, and radically altered the nature of the cold war. Although the Korean conflict was a limited war, or "police action," in the words of President Truman, the commitment of American forces to serious combat so soon after the end of the Second World War inevitably awakened echoes of the total-war experience which the country had just passed through. Fifty-four thousand American troops died in Korea, many of the men who fought there were veterans of the Second World War, and much of the equipment was the same as that which had been used in 1945. Since this was the first real television war, parallels with World War II could not help but reverberate even through the public's visual memory. The military, economic, and psychic mobilization of the country at this time, even if it was supposed to be done on a limited scale and for restricted purposes, was highly dangerous. Expectations of total triumph, with V-E and V-J days to be supplemented by V-Korea and V-Soviet Russia days, inevitably appeared, and it soon became extremely difficult to satisfy the public with half measures or moderate successes. Surely it was no accident that the period of the Korean War saw the full flowering of Senator McCarthy's crusade, and a substantial jump of militant anti-Soviet sentiment in the public opinion polls.

The Korean emergency gave the government, for the first time since World War II, something approaching carte blanche to acquire money, material, and men. The initial effect was the doubling of the draft quota and a 450 percent increase in the military budget within two years. Since Washington perceived the Korean War as merely a Kremlin political stroke—a kind of bloody Berlin blockade—it believed the appropriate response was the rapid global buildup of American military power. In addition to sending armed forces to protect Chiang in Formosa, the Korean crisis led to a massive increase of arms and American manpower for NATO, the entry of West German soldiers into that organization, and the trebling of the American air force in Britain. By the time of the Korean truce in mid-1953, the United States government had also made a long-term defense agreement with Japan, which granted permanent base rights there to the American military.

Inevitably the conflict in Korea drove Moscow and Beijing closer together because once the People's Republic entered the conflict, it became more dependent on the USSR for diplomatic support, economic aid, and sophisticated military equipment. This went a long way in the direction of creating the very kind of Moscow-controlled far-flung Communist social revolutionary movement that enthusiasts in Washington had believed already existed.

At the very moment when Beijing, with its stress on peasant revolutionary action, was forced by the Korean War into the arms of Moscow, the same conflict sent the American government and American business off on a new, and even more frantic, pursuit of "critical" materials. This chase after resources produced new international economic strains, serious problems in the Third World, and provided inviting opportunities for Sino-Soviet–supported national liberation movements. Since America's attempt to gather in the world's natural resources was paralleled by the imposition of more stringent bans on Western export of "strategic" commodities to the People's Republic as well as to the USSR, there were a multitude of practical reasons for the Sino-Soviet bloc to make life in the underdeveloped world as difficult as possible for the Americans.

But it was undoubtedly the American military expansion related to the Korean conflict which produced the most serious consequences. The rising military consciousness in Washington, when coupled with what seemed in other Western capitals to be American rashness, opened up serious fissures in the Western alliance. With more and more American money going to armaments, there was less available for economic aid, and indeed in the seven years following the Korean truce, the assistance programs slumped from a ratio of nine to one in favor of economic aid to a point where one dollar of arms went abroad for every dollar's worth of economic assistance. Washington threw away the technique of government economic aid which had proven so effective and relatively safe between 1945 and 1950 in favor of a unilateral arms buildup that gravely worried many of America's closest allies.

The militarization of American policy, and the sharp increase in armed might and overseas deployment by the United States, inevitably led the USSR to launch a new armaments program of its own. This produced the first significant strengthening and modernization of the Red Army since the Second World War, and began the series of arms races, with their rising peril for everyone, which have continued to the present day. As the Soviet and American authorities rushed about the earth deploying every possible man, gun, ship, plane, and then missile, they assumed such enormous commitments that their peacetime political and economic structures were soon unable effectively to carry the burden. Moscow and Washington were therefore compelled to operate on the basis of permanent semimobilization, which meant that they were overextended, and the whole world, as well as East-West relations, again was made to rest on very unstable foundations.

This was indeed a watershed. Until the United States and the Soviet Union launched their global military balancing act, they had functioned within an era mainly colored by the efforts of the four great victorious Allied powers to tidy up the mess and cope with the great shadows that had been cast by the Second World War. The cold war that evolved between 1945 and 1949 had been primarily a balancing act performed in a devastated Europe by two rather reluctant giants who had fallen into a situation in which political pressure and economic and military assistance projects, as well as ideological propaganda, had become the chief tools of superpower competition. Feelings of vulnerability together with ideological passion and the combined effect of Soviet tanks, American bombers, and atomic weapons had certainly added dangerous imponderables to that cold war balance. But until 1950, limit and restraint had been basic watchwords on both sides, for neither one had been ready to initiate another general conflict or even to stoke the home fires of ideology to a point where either of them acquired the means to wage an all-out, global, war.

But the Korean conflict changed much of that. Henceforth, although the label of "cold war" would continue to be employed by all, rather than grappling with the aftereffects of the Second World War, the giants of East and West devoted themselves to a general arms race and a global competition to see which of them could acquire the most influence and control in remote corners of the Third World. In this new era of limitless armed confrontation, the long shadow which had been cast by the Second World War finally receded, and such matters as the Battle of Britain, lend-lease, and the defense of Stalingrad ceased to set the tone for all mankind.

Two decades after the Japanese had first occupied Manchuria, events in neighboring Korea had moved the world into a new era, and finally allowed the Second World War to slip into the past, and thus, presumably, into history.

Conclusion

Although World War II and the early cold war should by now have been resting contentedly in the hands of historians for nearly a third of a century, the era of the 1940s has proven unusually resistant to the soothing arts of historical study. Countless books have been written about the war, and a sizable number on the origins of the cold war as well, but the 1940s have not taken on the kind of coherent and composed historical persona which has come to the decade of the Great Depression, the Roaring Twenties, or the era of the first great war. The forties have tended to remain more segmented, more controversial, and more intertwined with present events and current political controversies than most other recent historical epochs, even though they are now as remote in chronological time from us as the turn of the century was from the generation which fought the Second World War.

Usually, by keeping the idea clearly in view that "then" is not "now," and that developments in a particular place, as well as in a particular time, have a special quality of their own, professional historians are able to see developments within a balanced perspective. To do their work effectively, however, they not only require a zone of time between themselves and the events which they are examining, above all their subject needs to be insulated from the passions and disputes of the present. But when this is not the case—as has certainly been true of the Second World War as well as the early cold war—and the consequences of a past era continue to reverberate loudly into the present, historical distancing becomes very difficult to achieve. When governments and the media then compound the problem by continually using

skewed interpretations of such past events to justify current public policies, the historian is repeatedly forced to return to basics
in order to acquire perspectives on past eras that have stayed
overactive and been overexploited.

When we make the extra effort to stand back and look at the
1940s with a detached view, the most obvious and fundamental
feature of that era seems to have been the cataclysmic impact of
the Second World War, whose most basic dynamic was the mass
mobilization of countries in nearly every sector of the globe. As
everyone has long recognized, the scale and intensity of that
mobilization brought shattering consequences to the war's losers
(especially Germany, Italy, and Japan), smashing their economies, destroying their governments, and abolishing their status as
great powers. But as we have just seen, the process of total wartime mobilization had consequences for the major victorious
powers that were almost as far-reaching.

The weak and overextended Kuomintang regime in China was
pushed over the brink into economic, social, and political disintegration by its effort to fight a war of endurance against
Japan. The decomposition of the Kuomintang then opened the
way for a quick leap to power by Mao's Communist forces,
which had developed effective guerrilla warfare methods while
fighting the Japanese, and whose demand for radical political-
economic change coincided with the peasants' cry for drastic
reform and the rise in national consciousness and desire for
modernization which had gripped China's entire population.
These developments, which spanned the period 1937–1949,
turned Chinese attention almost completely inward, and built a
wall of special experience between China and the rest of the
world during the early postwar era.

The traditional political-economic system of Great Britain
was also seriously weakened by the strain of attempting to wage
a prolonged war of endurance, but in the case of the United
Kingdom, the result was a slump in relative power and a cry for
reform rather than a recourse to social revolution and civil war.
Britain survived the war by austerity, but as her relative power

fell, her people's eagerness for a sharp improvement in the postwar domestic system and international standing of their country actually rose. By 1945, though she was comparatively much weaker than before the war, Britain was determined to try to hold on, and attempted to play an international role out of all proportion to her actual power.

The Soviet Union, which was the third of the major powers to join the Allied cause during the conflict, actually suffered more casualties and more destruction than any other combatant, but instead of lessening her relative power and influence, the war actually increased it. The defeat of Germany and Japan eliminated her most threatening immediate neighbors, and the great heroism of her population, when coupled with the productive and innovative achievements of both the people and the Soviet Government, greatly enhanced her worldwide reputation. The Soviet armed forces bore the heaviest share of the burden of defeating Nazi Germany, and at war's end Soviet military power, and the fact that the Red Army had advanced far beyond her prewar borders in both Europe and Asia, made her an object of fear as well as awe. She was militarily triumphant, while economically devastated, and it seems that her people most craved an era of security and peace in which they could turn inward to rebuild and develop their country. But how the Soviet Union made use of its wartime heritage in the postwar period ultimately depended almost completely on the perspective and decisions of Joseph Stalin, who had come through the war with enormous power and prestige at home and a proven ability at least to hold his own in international relations. For Stalin, even more than for the Soviet people, the need for security, and a desire to draw a line between the USSR and the rest of the world, would have top priority in the late 1940s, and that fact, along with the superpower status which the war had brought to the USSR, would constitute the greatest impact which wartime Russia would exert on the early postwar world.

The last of the Allied Big Four, the United States of America, experienced a Second World War which was sharply different

from that of any other belligerent. Although the U.S.A. quickly
built up an enormous military machine, and in fact was the only
large power to vigorously fight wars in both the Pacific and
Europe, it was her wartime economic mobilization which had
the most important long-range effects. The American productive
miracle, which was financed in large part by generalizing the income tax, gave the U.S.A. top position in agricultural output
and nearly 50 percent of the world's manufacturing production
in 1945. This provided the United States with a degree of world
military and economic supremacy unrivaled by any other power
before or since, and also gave the American people over full-
employment, enormous sums of personal savings, high expectations of a postwar consumer boom, and a nearly universal determination to retain and increase this unprecedented prosperity
after the war. Like the people and leader of the Soviet Union,
most Americans emerged from the war with a heightened desire
for national security as well as a sense of their own power and an
inclination to look inward during the postwar period. But the
people of the United States were unique in their degree of contentment and self-satisfaction in 1945, as well as their predilec-
tion to believe that they could continue their economic extrava-
ganza with a minimum regard for the needs and desires of the
rest of the world.

Due to the destructive impact of the war and the divergent experiences of the four major countries that had won it, the years
immediately following V-E and V-J Day were marked by political drift, and little progress was made in putting the economy of
the world into anything resembling good working order. China
immediately set about her business of civil war and played no
part in determining the configuration which the rest of the world
would have in the early postwar years. Britain tried through a
Labour government simultaneously to carry out extensive domestic social-economic reforms and to continue holding on to
her colonies, maintaining her zones of influence, and performing
an equal role with that of the USSR and the U.S.A. on the post-

war global stage. Essentially, Britain was playing for time, hoping that her domestic reforms would strengthen her while the two superpowers helped to stabilize the postwar world quickly enough to create conditions in which Britain could reduce her military expenditure and expand her trade to avert the threat of bankruptcy and international impotence which was hanging over her.

But the two superpowers showed little readiness to act boldly in the world scene to stabilize economic conditions or establish a new comprehensive political settlement. The USSR settled down on top of its satellites, sealed off its borders, maintained a strong military force, poured abuse on the capitalist states, and dealt with every international issue by a mixture of hard bargaining, intimidation, and delay. Stalin had clearly decided to hold on to what he had, rebuild the USSR with a minimum of dependence on the outside world, and perhaps gather in any further territorial assets which might be there for the taking. Whether or not the USSR would actually expand further, it was definitely not prepared to take the lead in putting the world's pieces together again.

Although in a far more favorable economic position than any other country, the U.S.A. initially showed nearly as little concern about the consequences of global postwar economic and political drift, as did the USSR. America did not completely disarm nor go back into total isolation. She did join the United Nations, kept occupation forces in Europe and Asia, extended relief assistance worldwide, and participated in major conferences with the other powers. But despite their country's enormous power, the American people showed little inclination to take the lead in reordering the world. They were willing to give charity and pay taxes, they wanted to have a secure military screen, and to play their part in the United Nations. But they primarily wished to enjoy the great economic boom which the war had given them, and were not inclined to use the fruits of that boom to put the world on its feet or to organize it in such a way that American prosperity would rest on firm global foundations of direct political-military control by the United States and massive international investment.

Since neither the U.S.A. nor the USSR made a quick, decisive move, the world wafted along for nearly two years in a condition of ruin, hopeless disorder, and poverty, while fears, suspicions, and animosities increased on all sides. Then the dreadful winter of 1946–1947, which produced havoc throughout Europe, finally forced Britain to lay down many of her imperial and postwar military commitments. The United Kingdom surrendered the mandate in Palestine, while India, Pakistan, and Burma were given their independence. In Europe and the Mediterranean, Britain merged its occupation zone in Germany with that of the United States and handed over to the Americans the chief responsibility for stabilizing and protecting Greece and Turkey. As Britain withdrew from many of its advance commitments, the Americans lumbered forward to assume them, and the United States and the Soviet Union were left alone as the only effective great powers in Europe. A bipolar Europe was thereby born, and Washington and Moscow quickly fell into a stance of superpower confrontation.

For the United States this meant acquiring economic, and then military, means to revitalize and rearm the states of Western Europe and the eastern Mediterranean. For the USSR, superpower confrontation necessitated tightening control over the satellites, and maintenance of armament levels which were so high that they slowed the rate of the USSR's postwar economic recovery.

Through the Truman Doctrine, the Marshall Plan, NATO, and the creation of the west German state, the United States effectively used its economic and military assets to strengthen and solidify Western Europe, and thereby, as Washington saw it, America had succeeded in successfully "containing" Soviet expansionist pressure. The Soviet Union struck back at the American solidification efforts with more threats, the Berlin blockade, and disruptive agitation by the French and Italian Communist parties.

To secure the means to pay for these more assertive policies, and to rally their publics' support for them, both the U.S.A. and USSR began systematically cranking up the machinery of ideological fear and hate. Soviet and American society were dusted with propaganda declaring that the superpowers had to increase expenditure and expand their international commitments because an ideological struggle existed between the forces of communism and capitalism, with various versions of freedom and slavery being attributed to one side or the other.

Although both East and West initially tried to be cautious in the way they wielded ideological agitation, eschewing overt moves toward general war or a high-velocity arms race, the decision to use ideology to gain popular support for assertive international policies so soon after 1945 was nonetheless a highly dangerous game. The people of all the major countries had just passed through a wartime period in which every government had employed ideological agitation to whip up popular support. Such agitation had strengthened the populations' commitment to the wartime cause, and their willingness to sacrifice in order to assist the war effort. Ideological mobilization had contributed to the creation of each country's total war power, and especially in the two new superpowers, the public and government had come to accept that the kind of power which total-war mobilization had given them was a normal state of affairs and that when such ideological mobilization was utilized, decisive triumphs would soon follow.

Therefore once Washington and Moscow advanced into a position of containment via confrontation in 1947–1948, great restraint and care were necessary to keep the explosive potential of ideological mobilization under control. The two powers managed this trick, albeit with difficulty, until the summer of 1950, when the Korean conflict produced real casualties and activated vivid memories and expectations analogous to those of World

War II. Both East and West then dashed into a global arms race and a competition for influence and advantage in every hemisphere. Virtually all restraint ended in the use of ideology, as the USSR and the U.S.A. settled into a long-term struggle between the forces of light and those of darkness.

Soon after this full-blown apocalyptic ideological conflict had taken hold and been institutionalized, it was provided with the kind of legitimization that anthropologists characterize as an origins myth. Coupled with halfhearted efforts to trace the start of the conflict to the postrevolutionary skirmishes in Russia in 1918, or the diplomatic troubles of the 1930s when the later Allies failed to unite to stop Hitler, a popular and governmental consensus quickly formed placing the decisive beginnings of the apocalyptic cold war in the period immediately following V-E Day (with a backstep or two to gather in the Yalta Conference). The superpower protagonists of the early 1950s loudly proclaimed, and have been enthusiastically echoed ever since, that the early post–World War II expansionist pressure of Soviet communism and (or) the assertive advance of American capitalism had been the primary factors which caused the world to set off on a headlong rush into a cold war nightmare.

This back-dating of the Soviet-American expansionist confrontation to the 1945 era has helped drench the current cold war with both legitimacy and inevitability. Wherever one now turns seeking even a tiny opening that might point toward a decrease of tension or a side pathway from nuclear confrontation, a chorus of characters from Thomas Hardy immediately rise up chanting that the cold war both "had to be," and must remain, because ideology is our master and the course of events since 1945 has demonstrated that there was, and is, no alternative.

But not even endless repetition of the claim that the cold war is the unavoidable fate of the second half of the twentieth century can actually make time stand still. As the years roll by, different perspectives on the past inevitably appear, if for no other reason than that many important trends such as the rise of the mass media and high technology manifestly have little or nothing to do with cold war ideology. As such diverse aspects of the immediate past manifest themselves more and more clearly, historians start to come into their own, probing about among long-accepted truths, asking new questions, and suggesting new answers.

By shifting the analytic focus through such means as altering the scope of the time periods under study, or mixing together foreign and domestic matters, historians gradually produce significantly varied pictures of the way matters developed in the recent past. In so doing they not only give new intellectual life and interest to eras which had been lost to explanations marred by narrow traditionalism, they can help free the present by releasing the heavy hand of political orthodoxy from the way we view how we came to be the way we are.

Therefore by simply practicing their craft, historians in the near future may succeed in taking the early postwar era out of the hands of the politicians and ideologists, thereby perhaps doing more positive good for the future of the human race than all the world's missiles, and protest movements put together. That would be a strange development, to be sure, but possibly it is the kind of prosaically paradoxical step toward salvation that our times deserve.

Notes

Chapter 1: China's War

p. 23
"Manchus left the feast": Lu Xun, quoted in Spence, 279.

p. 25
"a kind of national warlord": Crozier, 173.

p. 26
"worst for opium": Sewell, report to Friends Committee [hereafter cited as report(s)], 5 November 1934.

p. 26
"squeeze" was back: Sewell, report, 27 April 1937.

p. 27
"Charging around Manchuria": Ienaga, 50.

p. 29
"beginning to find her feet" and "present national movements": Sewell, reports, 23 July and 30 October 1937.

p. 29
"very heavy defeats," "stand the first big shock," and "entirely on their side": Hugessen diary, 1/11, 20 August 1937.

p. 30
"good strategy is better than good arms": Sewell, diary scraps, December 1937.

p. 30
"China does not expect": Sewell, report, 8 February 1938.

p. 32
"as if overnight," "It *is* important," "little call upon them," "readiness of the best brains": Sewell, reports, 30 October 1937; 8 February and 25 July 1938.

p. 33
"until equipment is exhausted": Sewell, diary scrap, January 1938.

p. 34
"It is almost impossible" and "sheer force of numbers": Sewell, letter to his mother, 8 February 1941, and report, 25 July 1938.

291

pp. 34, 35
"Soldier class," "by the readiness of the elite" and "plenty of soldiers":
Sewell, reports, 18 September 1937 and 25 July 1938; diary scrap, 1937.

p. 36
"a principle at stake" and "were doubtless some of the most able":
Sewell, reports, 5 November 1934 and April 1936.

p. 36
"the Communists see the potentialities" and "special short courses":
Sewell, reports, 8 February and 20 December 1938.

p. 38
"more beggars and more prostitutes": Sewell, report, 10 December 1940.

p. 38
"exposed corpses": Barker, 42.

p. 41
"Kuomintang Government officials": Schaller, *The United States Crusade
in China,* 88.

p. 41
"the Japs seem to have started": Seymour, 9 December 1941, file 2/5.

p. 42
"very remarkable family": Seymour, 16 April 1942, file 2/6.

p. 43
"a short-term investment": Schaller, *The United States Crusade in China,*
163.

p. 44
"FBI type" training: Fairbank, 215–222.

p. 44
"would not be asked": Schaller, *The United States Crusade in China,* 243.

pp. 45, 46
"in a year or so" and "h.c. of l.": Seymour, 26 October 1942 and 3 December 1943, files 2/6 and 1/5.

p. 49
"It is going to be hard": Seymour, 1 November 1944, file 2/7.

p. 49
"While America was putting": Ienaga, 151.

p. 50
"essentially a Chinese response": Li, 188.

p. 51
"divided and desperate land": Djilas, 50.

Chapter 2: Great Britain at War

p. 52
"All the aid": Werth, xiv.

p. 53
"who gave their lives": memorial, Crouch End, London NW 6.

p. 64
"up west" to find shelter: Harrisson, 63.

p. 66
"terrible food": *Home Intelligence*, 11 March 1943, INF 1/293.

p. 68
"knows little and cares less": *Home Intelligence*, 22 April 1943, INF 1/282.

p. 68
"I have no feeling of elation": Nicholson, 29.

p. 69
"junior partner" to America: *Home Intelligence*, 4 June 1942, INF 1/293.

p. 69
"that we shall be dominated by the U.S.A.": *Home Intelligence*, 14 October 1943, INF 1/282.

p. 71
"prepared to make any sacrifice": *Home Intelligence*, 24 December 1941, INF 292/pt. 1.

p. 72
"should subordinate her interests": *Home Intelligence*, 29 April 1943, INF 1/292.

p. 72
"voicing of strong anti-Russian sentiments": *Home Intelligence*, 16–23 November 1943, INF 1/282.

p. 72
"Russo Polish relations etc.": *Home Intelligence*, 1–3 September 1944, HO 262/16.

p. 73
"a sort of intellectual deep shelter": Harrisson, 313–314.

p. 74
"a kind of home-made socialism": and following quotations from special report in *Home Intelligence*, 24 March 1942, INF/292/pt. 1.

p. 75
"for anything you can spare": Longmate, 186.

Chapter 3: The USSR in World War II

p. 76
"Some day soon": Ulam, 571.

p. 78
"I wonder how long": Seymour, 22 June 1941, 2/4.

p. 78
"if it is possible": Seymour, 24 July 1941, 2/4.

p. 81
"almost suicidal sincerity" and "engineering masterpieces": Clark, 166.

p. 81
"never in past history": N. Voznesensky, 131.

p. 82
"Privation": Elliott, 227.

p. 84
"anti-freeze": Ulam, 581.

p. 85
"The Eastern Front!": Clark, 225.

p. 86
"Even those of us who knew": Clark, 193.

p. 88
"slightly better" than Nazi Germany: *Public Opinion Quarterly,* Spring 1942.

p. 88
"help beat Hitler": *Public Opinion Quarterly,* Spring 1942.

p. 89
"Can the U.S.S.R. be trusted": *Public Opinion Quarterly,* Spring 1943.

p. 90
"For our Country, For Stalin, Forward!": Ulam, 540.

p. 90
"powers undreamed of": Ulam, 161.

p. 91
"objective" and "real" dangers: Ulam, 387.

p. 93
"stubborn, sharp, suspicious": Djilas, 119.

p. 93
"an extraordinarily devious man": McCagg, 215.

p. 93
"in this respect he stood out": quoted in Seaton, 199.

p. 94
"universal bias": McCagg, 160.

p. 95
"whoever occupies a territory": Djilas, 90.

p. 95
"gold": quoted in Seaton, 236.

p. 96
"played so masterful a part": Winston S. Churchill, *The Gathering Storm,* 289, cited in Medvedev.

p. 97
"during the war years": Medvedev, 455.

p. 97
"wring your necks like chickens": Talbott, *Khrushchev Remembers*, 392.

Chapter 4: The Great Arsenal of Democracy

p. 115
"made any real sacrifices": *Public Opinion Quarterly*, Winter 1943 and Spring 1945.

p. 117
"harmful" groups in the United States: *Public Opinion Quarterly*, Winter 1943.

p. 124
"believed it necessary": *Public Opinion Quarterly*, Summer 1944.

p. 126
"her military campaigns": *Public Opinion Quarterly*, Fall 1945.

p. 127
"police" the world: *Public Opinion Quarterly*, Winter 1943.

Chapter 5: Healthy, Wealthy, and Wise?

p. 144
"better break": *Public Opinion Quarterly*, Winter 1947–1948.

p. 145
"to keep this country": *Public Opinion Quarterly*, Winter 1948–1949. [Italics added.]

p. 146
"publishing the facts": Bevin, file 498.

p. 151
"unfriendly" to the United States: *Public Opinion Quarterly*, Fall 1947.

p. 152
"listless and waiting": Bevin, 16 August 1945, file 464.

p. 156
"to mold these two things together": Bevin, file 498.

p. 157
"ultimately it is this lot that counts": Bevin, file 513.

p. 157
"no easy job": Bevin, file 513.

p. 158
"short, simple and looks one straight in the face": Nicholson, 28.

p. 158
"self-possessed": Bevin, notes of private Bevin-Truman meeting, 8 December 1946, file 513.

p. 159
"American Legion Baroque": Donovan, 116.

p. 159
"licked," "shopworn," "Jewish blood": Bevin, report by General Gairdner, 26 December 1947, file 462.

p. 159
"jump in quick": Bevin, 20 December 1945 Harriman comment, file 501.

Chapter 6: The Walking Wounded

p. 170
"extremely dangerous": Rothwell, 19.

p. 170
"did not think anything could be done": Bevin, 24 March 1947, Bevin-Stalin talk, file 447.

p. 170
"isolationist": Bevin, 31 October 1945, file 461.

p. 171
"understood" that seventeen hundred towns: Bevin, 1 January 1946, file 498.

p. 174
"they were very busy here" and "The United States and England": Bevin, 15 April Marshall-Stalin talk, file 502.

p. 176
"if there was no drought": Bevin, 24 March 1947, Bevin-Stalin talk, file 447.

p. 177
on "the relations between Stalin and Molotov": Bevin, 1 January 1946, file 498.

p. 177
"the Marshals, Ministers (including Molotov and Vyshinsky)": Bevin, Montgomery-Stalin talk, 10 January 1947, file 502.

p. 178
"Frank Hague or Tom Pendergast": Messer, 82.

p. 179
"that the pan-Slav and world revolution elements": Nicholson, 49.

p. 179
"You bring me these presents": Bevin, file 502.

p. 180
"there was occasional sloppiness" and "possibly due to sloppiness": Bevin, file 502.

p. 180
"diversionary" activities: Bevin, 21 December 1945, Bevin-Stalin talks, file 507.

p. 180
"the British were not prepared": Bevin, 26 December 1945, Bevin-Stalin talks, file 489.

p. 181
"he had once said": Bevin, 24 March 1947, Bevin-Stalin talks, file 447.

p. 181
"success to Great Britain": Bevin, 25 March 1947, Bevin-Stalin talks, file 470.

p. 182
"He did not think the situation": Bevin, file 502.

p. 182
"there were those at the Kremlin": Bevin, 29 January 1946, file 501.

p. 183
"policy of reconnaissance in force": Medvedev, 479.

p. 183
"mentalities different from their own" and "a real opportunity of winning Europe": Nicholson, 93 and 219 (1 July 1947 and 1 April 1953).

p. 184
"certainly an odd man to deal with": Bevin, 8 December 1946, private Bevin-Truman meeting, file 513.

p. 184
"obvious pride": Bevin, 8 August 1945, file 461.

p. 184
"a modern robot": Djilas, 58.

p. 184
"Oh you must not take that seriously": Nicholson, 68.

p. 184
"ceaseless" Soviet propaganda attacks and "there were no attacks": Bevin, 6 December 1947, file 502.

p. 185
"Mr. Byrnes did not appreciate": Bevin, 25 November 1946, Byrnes-Bevin talk, file 522.

p. 187
"Perhaps even more than anyone": Bevin, 15 April 1947, Marshall-Stalin talks, file 502.

p. 188
"losing control of the instrument of German unity": Bevin, 15 April 1947, Marshall-Stalin talks, file 502.

p. 189
"an exercise in control": McCagg, 237.

Chapter 7: A Casualty of War: China 1945–1949

p. 194
"dreaming his own dreams": Ch'ên, 237.

pp. 196, 197
"we both belong to countries" and "a squalid imitation,": Sewell, report to

Friends Committee [hereafter cited as report(s)], 17 May 1947; letter of Ruth Sewell, 9 January, 1950.

p. 197
appease "the white man": Melby, 151–152.

p. 198
"I don't think they are communists": Bevin, 1 January 1946, file 498.

p. 198
"You must realize that we are not that": Melby, 76.

p. 199
"the Americans would play": Fitzgerald, *The Birth of Communist China,* 101.

p. 200
"depressed" President Truman: Bevin, 8 December 1946, private Bevin-Truman meeting, file 513.

p. 201
"confucian feudalism": Melby, 162.

pp. 202, 203
"nobody dare keep any money," "be hoarded or smuggled," "things will get worse and worse": Sewell, letters of Ruth Sewell, 14 March and 4 July 1948; report, 25 June 1948.

pp. 203, 204
"People have to wait" and "liberal middle way": Sewell, letter of Ruth Sewell, 12 September 1948; and report, 7 January 1948.

p. 204
"once had a spark of liberalism" and "if the change comes": Sewell, report, 25 June 1948.

p. 205
"learned, resolute, experienced": Ch'ên, 212–213.

p. 206
"American help to China" and "than the present state of affairs": Sewell, report, 25 June 1948.

p. 207
"become the arbiter of change": Schaller, *The United States Crusade in China,* 305.

p. 208
"Chinese public's mind off Manchuria": Bevin, Oliver Franks talk with Acheson, 17 December 1949, file 462.

p. 208
"we're not ever going to let": Talbott, *Khrushchev Remembers,* 473.

p. 209
"Russians were foreigners" and "economic difficulties": Bevin, report dated 10 August 1949, file 462. [Zhou's approach to the Americans has long been known, but there were interesting variations in this approach to the British.]

p. 209
"the Chinese Communist Party have won": Bevin, report dated 10 August 1949, file 462.

Chapter 8: The Permanently Disabled

p. 211
"Having fought two wars": Bevin, file 493.

p. 214
"Our financial difficulties began" and "arose directly from the shape": Bevin, 13 October 1945, file 512.

p. 216
"not know which way to turn": Bevin, 30 July 1947, file 493.

p. 216
"when the mouse is away": Nicholson, 76.

p. 216
"We are the masters at the moment": Sissons and French, 28. [Not "We are the masters now," as is often claimed.]

p. 217
"to educate their children": Bevin, Bevin to Attlee, 2 September 1946, file 494.

p. 218
"economic morass": Bevin, 30 July 1947, file 493.

p. 220
"fail to note the contrast": Bevin, 13 October 1945, memorandum by Hugh Dalton, file 512.

p. 221
"As we have a Socialist Government": Bevin, 30 July 1947, file 493.

p. 222
"With regard to what is called the welfare state": Bevin, file 495.

p. 223
"all the standard rates of the country": Bevin, 22 April 1948, file 494.

p. 223
"no request should be made" and "We have got to put our heads together": Bevin, 30 July 1947, file 493.

p. 224
"snobbish rule" and "I cannot believe that it is not possible": Bevin, 21 October 1946 and 19 August 1946, file 479.

p. 229
"in all the experience": Bevin, 1 January 1946, file 498.

p. 231
"going to become a sort of financial colony": Bevin, 30 July 1947, file 493.

p. 232
"that we should decline": Bevin, 4 October 1945, file 512.

p. 232
"I do not think we are down and out": Bevin, 30 July 1947, file 493.

p. 233
"to build a sound peace": Bevin, 26 November 1946, file 492.

pp. 234, 235
"plain truth" and "absolutely mystified by it": Bevin, 1 June 1949, file 471.

p. 235
"wealthy people" and "Do not worry too much": Bevin, 15 October 1947 and 26 February 1949, files 509 and 495.

p. 235
"worry about the 'Daily Mail' or the 'Daily Worker' " and "jellyfish" attitude: Bevin, 21 November 1949 and 21 January 1946, files 495 and 497.

p. 236
"difficult and foolish" and "somewhat daft but very sharp": Nicholson, 58, 175–76 (20 May 1946 and 9 March 1950).

p. 237
"having possibly endangered international relations": Bevin, 29 September 1946, file 464.

Chapter 9: The Beginning of the Cold War in Two Acts

p. 246
"our most difficult satellite": Rothwell, 361.

p. 248
"uncommonly nervous and jumpy" and "it would be better": Bevin, 14 November 1945, dispatch by Clark Kerr, file 461.

p. 253
Stalin's "Fifth Column": Rothwell, 269.

p. 254
"it was the most courageous utterance": Bevin, 5 March 1946, file 443.

p. 255
"experiment": Bevin, 20 December 1945, a comment by Harriman, file 501.

p. 255
"I would like to": Seymour, 30 January 1947, vol. 4/6.

p. 255
"Some of our American friends": Bevin, 14 November 1945, file 484.

p. 256
"three imperialisms," "Three Monroes," and "war of nerves": Bevin, 1 January 1946, file 498.

p. 256
"with the Russians" and "it's patience you want": Nicholson, 49, 69–70 (31 January and 6 September 1946).

p. 256
"keep the ball-bearings" "set and properly greased": Bevin, 1 January 1946, file 498.

p. 257
"cultivated . . . born again": Rothwell, 279.

p. 258
"wretched Germans": Bevin, 3 March 1947, file 514.

p. 261
"would be jeopardised": Bevin, 11 December 1947, message to prime minister, file 514.

p. 261
"there was no agreement": Bevin, 4 December 1947, file 476.

p. 263
"isolationist . . . greatest fear": Bevin, 22 September 1947, file 471.

p. 264
"reiterating again now and then" and "indoctrinated communists": Bevin, 4 November 1947 and 24 November 1947, files 514 and 487. [In latter file see as well Marshall-Bevin talk of 4 December 1947 regarding Palestine.]

p. 264
"ruthlessness of communism" "believe that . . . evil": Bevin, 22 and 29 April 1948, file 450.

p. 265
"to prevent any coup": Bevin, 6 March 1948, file 471.

p. 266
"from the first day . . . another Pearl Harbour": Bevin, 17 March 1948, file 460.

p. 267
"The Problem of Future War" and "that the time had come": Bevin (latter 8 March 1948), file 452.

pp. 267, 268
"should agree that the main bombing" and "I must see the Minister": Bevin, 8 March 1948, file 452.

p. 268
"deliberately provoke a war . . . miscalculation": Bevin, 2 July 1948, file 453.

p. 268
"a family quarrel . . . the whole line to collapse": Bevin, 28 July 1948, file 502.

p. 269
"the religion of communism" and "There are in France": Bevin, 19
August and mid-July 1948, files 453 and 456.

p. 269
"he was convinced": Bevin, 4 October 1948, file 460.

p. 271
"to start . . . or abandon his aggression": quoted in Donovan, 48–49.

p. 272
"critical" materials and "inner circle" of states: Bevin, 29 September
1948 [Harriman insisted on the word *critical*] and 16 January 1950, files
515 and 445.

p. 273
"to do our own business in our own way": Bevin, 21 July 1948, file 460.

p. 273
"our progress in the cold war" and "to take an anti-American line":
Bevin, 22 June and 4 July 1949, file 516.

Bibliography

The literature on the Second World War and the cold war is enormous, and no fully comprehensive bibliography could be included in a short book such as this. The materials listed below have been recently read, or reread, and have affected my thinking on the subject. The bibliographies of my other works, especially *The Shadow Warriors* (New York: 1983) and *The Road to Nuremberg* (New York: 1981) contain additional relevant references, and a helpful discussion of the recent literature for the second half of the period is John Lewis Gaddis, "An Emerging Post-Revisionist Synthesis on the Origins of the Cold War," *Diplomatic History* 7, no. 3 (Summer 1983): 171–190.

This volume is not primarily a work of original documentary research, and my reading debt to other scholars is great (especially to Professor Adam Ulam in chapter 3 and Professor Alan Bullock in chapter 9). But I have attempted to use many fresh quotations, especially from the Bevin papers, and therefore a short form is included in the bibliography for the four frequently cited manuscript collections.

Much material also comes from published statistical and public opinion sources, but since these should be largely self-evident to specialists, rather than clutter the volume with footnote numbers, I have included notes only for quotations, and the statistical and public opinion sources reside in a separate section of the bibliography. All other works have been grouped under the four individual countries, plus a category for general East-West diplomacy.

Manuscript Papers

BEVIN   Ernest Bevin, FO 800, Public Record Office, Kew Gardens, Surrey.

HOME INTELLIGENCE   *Home Intelligence Reports,* INF 1/282, 292, and 293; HO 262/16, Public Record Office.

HUGESSEN Sir Hugh Knatchbull Hugessen, Churchill College, Cambridge.

SEWELL   William G. Sewell, School of Oriental and African Studies, The University of London.

SEYMOUR   Sir Horace Seymour, Churchill College, Cambridge.

Statistics and Public Opinion Surveys

Baykou, Alexander, et al. *Bulletins on Soviet Economic Development, 1949–1950.* The University of Birmingham.

Clarke, Roger A. *Soviet Economic Facts, 1917–1970.* London: 1972.

Elliot, Gil. *Twentieth Century Book of the Dead.* London: 1972.

Goralski, Robert. *World War II Almanac.* New York and London: 1981.

Great Britain. *Annual Abstract of Statistics,* nrs. 84 and 88. London: 1948 and 1952.

———. *Statistical Digest of the War.* London: 1975.

Grove, Robert D., and Alice M. Hetzel. *Vital Statistics Rates in the United States, 1940–1960.* Washington: 1968.

Hero, Alfred O., Jr. *American Religious Groups View Foreign Policy: Trends in Rank and File Opinion 1937–1969.* Durham, North Carolina: 1973.

Levering, Ralph B. *American Opinion and the Russian Alliance 1939– 1945.* Chapel Hill, North Carolina: 1976.

Maxwell, Robert, ed. *Information USSR.* New York and London: 1962.

Mitchell, B. R. *European Historical Statistics 1750–1975.* 2d ed. London: 1981.

———. *International Historical Statistics, Africa and Asia.* London: 1982.

The Public Opinion Quarterly, 1940–1950.

Schmitz, Christopher. *World Non-ferrous Metal Production, 1700–1976.* London: 1979.

Shoup, Paul S. *The East European and Soviet Data Handbook.* New York: 1981.

Singer, J. David, and Melvin Small. *The Wages of War 1816–1965: A Statistical Handbook.* New York: 1972.

Urlanis, B. *Wars and Population.* Moscow: 1971.

U.S. Bureau of the Census. *Historical Abstracts.* Washington: 1939–1952.

———. *Historical Statistics of the United States.* Washington: 1975.

U.S. Department of the Army. *Army Battle Casualties. Final Report, 1941–1946.* n.p.: n.d.

China

Barker, Noel. *The Fall of Shanghai.* London: 1979.
Ch'ên, Jerome. *Mao and the Chinese Revolution.* London, Oxford: 1965.
Crozier, Brian. *The Man Who Lost China.* London: 1977.
Fairbank, John King. *Chinabound.* New York: 1982.
Fitzgerald, C. P. *The Birth of Communist China.* London: 1964.
————. *Mao Tse-Tung and China.* London: 1977.
Great Britain. *Chinese Industries.* Ministry of Information: 1944.
Ienaga, Saburo. *Japan's Last War.* Oxford: 1979.
Li, Lincoln. *The Japanese Army in North China, 1937–1941.* London, Oxford: 1975.
Melby, John F. *The Mandate of Heaven.* Garden City, New York: 1971.
Nagai, Yonosuke, and Akira Iriye, eds. *The Origins of the Cold War in Asia.* New York: 1977.
Schaller, Michael. *The United States Crusade in China, 1938–1945.* New York: 1979.
Sewell, William G. *I Stayed in China.* London: 1966.
Spence, Jonathan D. *The Gate of Heavenly Peace.* London: 1982.
Tuchman, Barbara W. *Stilwell and the American Experience in China 1911–1945.* New York: 1971.
White, Theodore H., and Annalee Jacoby. *Thunder Out of China.* New York and London: 1946.

Great Britain

Barker, Elisabeth. *The British between the Super Powers, 1945–1950.* London: 1983.
Bullock, Alan. *Ernest Bevin, Foreign Secretary.* London: 1983.
Churchill, Winston S. *The Gathering Storm.* London and Boston: 1948.
Gilbert, Bentley G. *Britain since 1918.* London: 1980.
Harrisson, Tom. *Living through the Blitz.* London: 1978.
Hathaway, Robert M. *Ambiguous Partnership: Britain and America 1944–1947.* New York: 1981.
Longmate, Norman. *How We Lived Then.* London: 1971.
Messer, Robert L. *The End of an Alliance.* Chapel Hill, North Carolina: 1982.
Nicholson, Nigel, ed. *Harold Nicholson: Diaries and Letters 1945–1962.* London: 1971.
Pelling, Henry. *A History of British Trade Unionism.* London: 1963.
Rothwell, Victor. *Britain and the Cold War, 1941–1947.* London: 1982.

Sissons, Michael, and Philip French, eds. *The Age of Austerity*. London: 1963.

Stewart, Michael. *Keynes and After*. London: 1967.

Thomson, David. *England in the Twentieth Century*. London: 1965.

The Soviet Union

Buhite, Russell D. *Soviet American Relations in Asia, 1945–1954*. Norman, Oklahoma: 1981.

Clark, Alan. *Barbarossa*. London: 1966.

Djilas, Milovan. *Conversations with Stalin*. Translated by Michael B. Petrovich. London: 1963.

McCagg, William O., Jr. *Stalin Embattled, 1943–1948*. Detroit: 1978.

Mastny, Vojtech. *Russia's Road to the Cold War*. New York: 1979.

Medvedev, Roy. *Let History Judge*. New York and London: 1971 and 1976.

Seaton, Albert. *Stalin as Warlord*. London: 1976.

Talbott, Strobe, ed. and trans. *Khrushchev Remembers*. London: 1971.

———. *Khrushchev Remembers: The Last Testament*. London: 1974.

Taubmann, William. *Stalin's American Policy*. New York: 1982.

Ulam, Adam B. *Stalin, the Man and His Era*. New York and London: 1973 and 1974.

Voznesensky, N. *The War Economy of the U.S.S.R.* Moscow: 1948.

Werth, Alexander. *Russia at War, 1941–1945*. New York and London: 1964.

The United States

Alperovitz, Gar. *Atomic Diplomacy: Hiroshima and Potsdam*. New York and London: 1965 and 1966.

Ambrose, Stephen E. *Rise to Globalism*. New York and London: 1983.

Anderson, Terry H. *The United States, Great Britain and the Cold War 1944–1947*. Columbia, Missouri: 1981.

Brinkley, Alan. *Voices of Protest*. New York: 1982.

Chaute, David. *The Great Fear*. London: 1978.

De Santis, Hugh. *The Diplomacy of Silence*. Chicago: 1979.

Donovan, Robert J. *Tumultuous Years*. New York and London: 1982 and 1984.

Haines, Gerald K., and J. Samuel Walker, eds. *American Foreign Relations: A Historiographical Review*. Westport, Connecticut: 1981.

Levering, Ralph B. *The Public and American Foreign Policy 1918–1978*. New York: 1978.

Parker, W. H. *The Super Powers: The United States and the Soviet Union Compared*. London: 1972.

Reeves, Thomas C. *The Life and Times of Joe McCarthy*. New York and London: 1982.

Sherry, Michael S. *Preparing for the Next War*. New Haven, Connecticut: 1977.

Williams, William Appleman. *The Tragedy of American Diplomacy*. New York: 1962.

East-West Diplomacy

Gimbel, John. *The Origins of the Marshall Plan*. Stanford, California: 1976.

Kuniholm, Bruce R. *The Origins of the Cold War in the Near East*. Princeton, New Jersey: 1980.

Levering, Ralph B. *The Cold War 1945–1972*. Arlington Heights, Illinois: 1982.

Lundestad, Geir. *America, Scandinavia, and the Cold War 1945–1949*. New York: 1980.

Paterson, Thomas G. *On Every Front: The Making of the Cold War*. New York and London: 1979 and 1980.

Vaizey, John. *The Squandered Peace*. London: 1983.

Articles

Boyle, Peter G. "The British Foreign Office View of Soviet-American Relations, 1945–46." *Diplomatic History* 3, no. 3 (Summer 1979): 307–320

Brogan, Hugh. "The Diplomacy of Cold War." *European Studies Review* 13, no. 3 (July 1983): 365–372.

Gerber, Larry G. "The Baruch Plan and the Origins of the Cold War." *Diplomatic History* 6, no. 1 (Winter 1982): 69–96.

Hilton, Stanley E. "The United States, Brazil and the Cold War, 1945–1960: The End of the Special Relationship." *The Journal of American History* 68, no. 3 (December 1981): 599–624.

Kaplan, Lawrence S. "Western Europe in 'The American Century.'" *Diplomatic History* 6, no. 2 (Spring 1982): 111–123.

Knight, Wayne. "Labourite Britain: America's 'Sure Friend'? The Anglo-Soviet Treaty Issue, 1947." *Diplomatic History* 7, no. 4 (Fall 1983): 267–282.

Lees, Lorraine M. "The American Decision to Assist Tito, 1948–1949." *Diplomatic History* 2, no. 4 (Fall 1978): 407–422.

Levine, Steven I. "A New Look at American Mediation in the Chinese Civil War: The Marshall Mission and Manchuria." *Diplomatic History* 3, no. 4 (Fall 1979): 349–375.

Ninkovich, Frank. "Ideology, the Open Door, and Foreign Policy." *Diplomatic History* 6, no. 2 (Spring 1982): 185–208.

O'Reilly, Kenneth. "The FBI and the Origins of McCarthyism." *The Historian* 45, no. 3 (May 1983): 372–393.

Pach, Chester J., Jr. "The Containment of U.S. Military Aid to Latin America, 1944–49." *Diplomatic History* 6, no. 3 (Summer 1982): 225–244.

Rabe, Stephen G. "The Elusive Conference: United States Economic Relations with Latin America, 1945–52." *Diplomatic History* 2, no. 3 (Summer 1978): 279–305.

Rosenberg, David Alan. "American Atomic Strategy and the Hydrogen Bomb Decision." *Journal of American History* 66, no. 1 (June 1979): 62–87.

Schaller, Michael. "Securing the Great Crescent: Occupied Japan and the Origins of Containment in Southeast Asia." *Journal of American History* 69, no. 2 (September 1982): 392–414.

Shai, Aron. "Britain, China and the End of Empire." *Journal of Contemporary History* 15, no. 2 (April 1980): 287–297.

Stoler, Mark A. "From Continentalism to Globalism: General Stanley D. Embrick, the Joint Strategic Survey Committee and the Military View of American National Policy during the Second World War." *Diplomatic History* 6, no. 3 (Summer 1982): 303–321.

Index

309